Prekarisierung und soziale Entkopplung – transdisziplinäre Studien

Series Editors
Rolf Hepp, Institut für Soziologie, FU Berlin, Berlin, Germany
Robert Riesinger, Journalismus und Public Relations (PR), FH Joanneum Gesellschaft mbH, Graz, Austria
David Kergel, HAWK Hildesheim, Hildesheim, Germany
Birte Heidkamp-Kergel, E-Learning Zentrum, Hochschule Rhein-Waal, Kamp-Lintfort, Germany

Die Zunahme sozialer Unsicherheit und kultureller Verunsicherung in postfordistischen Gesellschaften erzeugt einen Status Quo, in dem Prozesse der Prekarisierung und der „sozialen Entkopplung" (Robert Castel) verstärkt das Zentrum der Gesellschaft durchziehen. Der Verlust sozialer Garantien führt dabei zur Aushöhlung sozialstaatlicher Errungenschaften. Dadurch werden die Lebenskontexte und das Alltagsleben der Menschen stark verändert.

Das sozialwissenschaftliche Netzwerk S.U.P.I. beschäftigt sich auf europäischer Ebene seit Jahren mit den gegenwärtigen Formen von sozialer Unsicherheit, Prekarität und Ungleichheit. Die Reihe, herausgegeben von Mitgliedern des Netzwerks, präsentiert transdisziplinäre Forschungen zu den sozialen und kulturellen Transformationen in den sozialstaatlich geprägten Demokratien. Sie versteht sich als Forum für die Diskussion in nationalen, europäischen und auch globalen Kontexten. Ebenen einer kritischen Analyse aus multidisziplinären und feldorientierten Perspektiven werden dabei initiiert, aufgenommen und unterstützt. Überschreitung und Öffnung dienen programmatisch als Wegmarken für theoretisch-analytische Beiträge und empirisch-angewandte Forschung.

The increase of social insecurity in post-Fordist societies effect fundamental societal changes. As a consequence Precarity and Disaffiliation (Robert Castel) affecting increasingly the center of society. The loss of social guarantees leads to an erosion of the welfare state. As a result, living situations and everyday life are deeply changed.

The S.U.P.I.-Project (Social Uncertainty, Precarity, Inequality) is an European Research Group established by European and international scholars and experts. The network has been concerned with present forms of social insecurity, precariousness and inequality at European level for years. Edited by members of the network, the book series presents transdisciplinary research on aspects of social and cultural transformations in the democracies which are characterized by the welfare state. The book series opens a discursive space for discussions in national, European and global contexts. The contributions of the book series provide critical analyses from multidisciplinaryperspectives, theoretical-analytical reflections and empirical-applied research.

More information about this series at http://www.springer.com/series/15037

Tadeusz Rachwał · Rolf Hepp ·
David Kergel
Editors

Precarious Places

Social, Cultural and Economic
Aspects of Uncertainty and Anxiety
in Everyday Life

Editors
Tadeusz Rachwał
University of Social Sciences &
Humanities Chodakowska
Warszawa, Poland

Rolf Hepp
Institut für Soziologie, FU Berlin
Berlin, Germany

David Kergel
Carl von Ossietzky Universität
Oldenburg, Germany

ISSN 2509-3266   ISSN 2509-3274   (electronic)
Prekarisierung und soziale Entkopplung – transdisziplinäre Studien
ISBN 978-3-658-27310-1   ISBN 978-3-658-27311-8   (eBook)
https://doi.org/10.1007/978-3-658-27311-8

Springer VS
© Springer Fachmedien Wiesbaden GmbH, part of Springer Nature 2020
This work is subject to copyright. All rights are reserved by the Publisher, whether the whole
or part of the material is concerned, specifically the rights of translation, reprinting, reuse of
illustrations, recitation, broadcasting, reproduction on microfilms or in any other physical way,
and transmission or information storage and retrieval, electronic adaptation, computer software,
or by similar or dissimilar methodology now known or hereafter developed.
The use of general descriptive names, registered names, trademarks, service marks, etc. in this
publication does not imply, even in the absence of a specific statement, that such names are
exempt from the relevant protective laws and regulations and therefore free for general use.
The publisher, the authors and the editors are safe to assume that the advice and information in
this book are believed to be true and accurate at the date of publication. Neither the publisher
nor the authors or the editors give a warranty, expressed or implied, with respect to the material
contained herein or for any errors or omissions that may have been made. The publisher remains
neutral with regard to jurisdictional claims in published maps and institutional affiliations.

This Springer VS imprint is published by the registered company Springer Fachmedien
Wiesbaden GmbH part of Springer Nature.
The registered company address is: Abraham-Lincoln-Str. 46, 65189 Wiesbaden, Germany

Introduction

The book offers a cross-disciplinary perspective on the various aspects of precariousness in contemporary culture and society, concentrating on the topographical aspects of sources and causes of uncertainty and anxiety. Precariousness and precarity are themselves provisional and uncertain categories, though ones inviting to rethinking the scopes of precarity and precariousness from the perspective of locality and of places involved in their otherwise global range. The recent years have shown some ways in which precarity has changed its status and has become a strongly debated area not only in economic and political disputes, but also in philosophical debates and various fields of research related to cultural studies. The articles included in the volume address the spatial scope of anxieties and uncertainties involving numerous men and women affected by the several decades of the neoliberal insistence on various kinds of flexibility which, in turn, has put in motion numerous new mechanisms of exclusion and marginalization. Apart from this, a historical view on the making of precarious places is also offered in the pages of the book.

In his contribution *'A Banality of Evil: Precarity as the Offspring of Individualism'*, Ronald Arnett unfolds the thesis that precarity is a form of social inevitability in the West due to its love affair with individualism, which functions as a social myth'. Precarity, understood as an outgrowth of individualism. Individualism represents social ties and constraints, 'contrasted with selfishness that necessitates taking into account the social and commercial aspirations of others'. Arnetts 'essay contends that precarity is a natural outcome of individualism; addressing precarity requires acknowledgement of social assumptions and structures that go unexamined, giving rise to a banality of evil within the realm of corporate responsibility'.

António Duarte presents a literature review which aims to characterize artists' precarity in the context of their social integration, along with that precarity's consequences, the artists' reactions it provoques and possible ways to counteract it. For his review, Duarte uses an interdisciplinary approach: the review is based on specialized research literature from psychology, sociology and economy of art. One result of the literature review is that precarity is experienced in multiple ways and entails risky material and psychological consequences and also affects the artistic creative process.

Franz Schultheis presents in his article *'Socioanalysis beyond borders: fieldwork in a social world in crisis'* results of a research project, he carried out together with Nikos Panayoutopols (University of Athens) from 2012 to 2015. This research project is based on testimonies of Greek men and women talking about their daily life conditions under the impact of the economic crisis. One methodological aspect of the research project addressed the question, what does it mean to do interview centered fieldwork on social misery under these very specific conditions? This contribution tries to reflect these epistemological problems before offering some passages of an interview made by our Swiss research team.

Fernando Marhuenda-Fluixá and Mª Ángeles Molpeceres-Pastor address in the article *'Training for Work at the Margins of the Projective City'* the problem of transition programs for youth and adult people in Spain. The main thesis consits in the assumption that Precarity affects both the youth and adult themselves as the trainers and institutions trying to foster their employability. So both actors work at the margins of exclusion: 'Raising consciousness about these issues might allow those providing vocational training in the margins of the educational and training system to those in the margins of society to perform their work in alternative ways'.

Tadeusz Rachwał *(Placelessness and Precarity. Mobility of Labor in Quasi-Utopian Spaces)* discusses in his paper what Guy Standing calls a "mildly utopian agenda" of precariat's becoming a class-in-itself in the context of the idea no-place etymologically carried by the word "utopia". Referring to Thomas Moore's image of the ideal state and reading its topography as a space without outside, he reads the precarization of immigrants in the contemporary political reality as resulting from securitization of the inside as a similar kind of construct in which outside constitutes the surplus, or the residue, which can be always be translated into, and made political used a threat.

Piotr Sałustowicz's paper *(The Social and Political Implications of the Precariat. A Backlash or a Transformation of the Post-Fordism formation?)* addresses the alleged danger of the precariat and its formulation as a "new dangerous calss" in the light of the idea of the possiblity of transformation of social post-Fordism through the rise of the precariat a as social class. Crtically reading the idea of Unconditional Basic Income as too strongly dependent on the individual level of family income, exemplifying it with the Program 500 plus in Poland. He also claims that in the context of political disputes the idea of Basic Unconditional Income has become UBI is a subject of academic discourse of quasi-utopian disputes of academicians dreaming of a better society.

Piotr Skurowski (Warsaw: Precarious Spaces, Precarious Memories) looks in his paper at precariousness from the perspective of geopolitical realities of places. On the example of Warsaw he discusses the ascription of the sense of precariousness to city spaces, sometimes depending on their geographical location. In the process. This he associates with socially constructed meanings attached to urban spaces which, though elusive and evanescent, acquire new sets of spatial meanings and practices which, replacing the old ones, may well remain and carry the seemingly done away with senses of precariousness.

Jan Sowa's article (*On the Uses of Precarity. Knowledge, Innovation and Academic Labor in Precarious Times*), reads the urge to precarize as inscribed in the very logic of capitalist accumulation, critically looking at Guy Standing's idea of classification of the precariat as singular class as standing against the high diversification of the precarized. He also addresses the problem of the precariat's being prone to being captured by chauvinistic and nationalistic ideologies and their increasingly active presence. The prediction of the future uses of precarization and associated processes are themselves uncertain and precarious.

In his article *'Start Ups, Social Networking and Self-Tracking—The Neoliberal Freedom of the Entrepreneurial Self in the Digital Age'*, David Kergel analyses the transformation of freedom from a leftist concept into a neoliberal interpellation within the digital age. To unfold his thesis, David Kergel refers to the discourse about start ups, online based social networking and the practice of digital self-tracking. In his analysis Kergel reconstructs the concept of freedom as manifestation of a neoliberal ‚new spirit of capitalism' in the digital age.

In his article *'Revisiting Territories of Relegation: Class, Ethnicity and State in the Making of Advanced Marginality'* pursues Loïc Wacquant questions he discussed in his book 'Urban Outcasts (2008). Using a cross-continental sociology of "advanced marginality", he discusses in his article the trajectories of the black American ghetto and the European working-class peripheries in the era of neoliberal ascendancy. Via this strategy it is possible, to pint out the complex of the tangled nexus of symbolic, social and physical space in the polarizing metropolis at century's threshold in particular, and for bringing the core principles of Bourdieu's sociology to bear on comparative urban studies in general.

Contents

A Banality of Evil: Precarity as the Offspring of Individualism 1
Ronald C. Arnett

Artists' Precarity in the Context of Their Social Integration 19
António M. Duarte

**Socioanalysis Beyond Borders: Fieldwork in a Social
World in Crisis** 41
Franz Schultheis

Training for Work at the Margins of the Projective City 51
Fernando Marhuenda-Fluixá and Ángeles Molpeceres-Pastor

**Placelessness and Precarity. Mobility of Labor
in Quasi-Utopian Spaces** 73
Tadeusz Rachwał

**The Social and Political Implications of the Precariat.
A Backlash or a Transformation of the Post Fordism Formation?** 85
Piotr Sałustowicz

Warsaw: Precarious Spaces, Precarious Memories 109
Piotr Skurowski

**On the Uses of Precarity. Knowledge, Innovation and Academic
Labour in Precarious Times** 123
Jan Sowa

Start Ups, Social Networking and Self-Tracking—The Neoliberal Freedom of the Entrepreneurial Self in the Digital Age 139
David Kergel and Rolf Hepp

Revisiting Territories of Relegation: Class, Ethnicity and State in the Making of Advanced Marginality 149
Loïc Wacquant

Editors and Contributors

About the Editors

Tadeusz Rachwał, Prof., Ph.D. SWPS University of Social Sciences and Humanities, Warsaw
Research focus: critical theory, philosophy of language,
Web: https://www.swps.pl/
E-Mail: trachwal@swps.edu.pl
Address: SWPS University of Social Sciences and Humanities, Chodakowska 19/31, 03815 Warsaw, Poland.

Rolf Hepp, Dr. habil. Soziologisches Institut der Freien Universität Berlin
Research areas: Precarity Research, Social Inequality
E-Mail: kerghepp@gmx.de
Address: Garystr. 55, 14195 Berlin.

David Kergel, Ph.D. Habitussensitive Teaching and Learning, HAWK Hildesheim
Research focus: Research on Precarity, e-Education, Qualitative Research in Education and Learning
Web: www.learningcultures.me
E-Mail: davidkergel@gmail.com

Contributors

Ronald C. Arnett, Prof., Ph.D. Duquesne University, Pittsburgh, USA

António M. Duarte, Ph.D. University of Lisbon, Lisbon, Portugal

Rolf Hepp, Dr. habil. Soziologisches Institut der Freien Universität Berlin, Berlin, Germany

David Kergel, Ph.D. HAWK Hildesheim, Hildesheim, Germany

Fernando Marhuenda-Fluixá, Prof. Dr. Universitat de València, València, Spain

Ángeles Molpeceres-Pastor, Prof. Dr. Universitat de València, València, Spain

Tadeusz Rachwał, Ph.D. SWPS University of Social Sciences and Humanities, Warsaw, Poland

Piotr Sałustowicz, Prof. Dr. habil. SWPS University of Humanities and Social Sciences, Warsaw, Poland

Franz Schultheis, Prof. Dr. habil. University of St. Gallen, St. Gallen, Switzerland

Piotr Skurowski, Ph.D., Dr. habil. SWPS University of Humanities and Social Sciences, Warsaw, Poland

Jan Sowa, Dr. habil. Academy of Fine Arts, Warsaw, Poland

Loïc Wacquant, Prof. Dr. habil. University of California, Berkeley, USA

A Banality of Evil: Precarity as the Offspring of Individualism

Ronald C. Arnett

Abstract

Precarity is an acknowledged reality of the twenty-first century; the United Kingdom of Great Britain discerned the importance of this category of people in the 2013 Great British Class Survey, the largest class study in the UK, which unveiled the increasing presence of the precariat. The existence of precarity, those living in the margins of corporate success, consists of persons unattached to a single institution or career path and not fully employed, or underemployed, at best. This class has emerged to absorb corporate risk in the globalized world. Unlike the category of the proletariat, which includes wage earners outside the influence of salaried workers, the precariat may have salaries without security of their employment within a given institution. Insecurity of employment and temporary attachment to a corporate structure is not novel, but the intentional enactment of such insecurity generates social awareness and concern. The precariat represents a group of persons within an intentionally marginalized category set aside with one purpose—to lessen corporate risk with workers absorbing insecurity. Precarity is a defining feature of this historical moment. This essay contends that precarity is a form of social inevitability in the West due to its love affair with individualism, which functions as a social myth. Individualism resists social ties and constraints, contrasted with

---

The title of this essay draws upon Hannah Arendt's (1965) notion of the banality of evil.

R. C. Arnett (✉)
Duquesne University, Pittsburgh, USA
e-mail: arnett@duq.edu

© Springer Fachmedien Wiesbaden GmbH, part of Springer Nature 2020
T. Rachwał et al. (eds.), *Precarious Places*, Prekarisierung
und soziale Entkopplung – transdisziplinäre Studien,
https://doi.org/10.1007/978-3-658-27311-8_1

selfishness that necessitates taking into account the social and commercial aspirations of others. Selfishness recognizes prosperity and professional security as requiring attentiveness to others. Precarity, understood as an outgrowth of individualism, dwells within assumptions dismissive of consideration of the Other. Hannah Arendt (1965) defined banality of evil as extreme commonness that escapes social attentiveness due to its normative nature. A banality of evil consists of unreflective habitus (Bourdieu 1977) that gives rise to dangerous and hurtful unexamined consequences. Precarity is a corporate outcome of an individualistic culture. This essay contends that precarity is a natural outcome of individualism; addressing precarity requires acknowledgement of social assumptions and structures that go unexamined, giving rise to a banality of evil within the realm of corporate responsibility.

Keywords

Precarity · Banality of evil · Individualism · Judith Butler · Hannah Arendt

1 Introduction

The task of this essay is to link three major terms with precarity: individualism, banality of evil, and institutional marginalization. I assert that individualism makes precarity inevitable and that the banality of evil limits critical reflection on individualism. The contention of this essay is that precarity is an inevitable outcome of an unreflective endorsement of individualism in everyday communicative life.

This essay examines a contemporary conversation on precarity beginning with a review of the origins and roots of individualism from the Enlightenment onward in a section titled "Void of Social Connection." The next section explicates the communicative consequences of not knowing the how and why of social action. Individualism diminishes the power and importance of social connection, leading to numerous unrecognized and unacknowledged issues of separation.

Precarity is an exemplar of social destruction that emerges from acts of social dismissal of another. Taken-for-granted assumptions (Schutz 1967) remain masked and unattended to in an environment composed of normative routine that invites a social amnesia about the how and why of communicative behavior. Precarity is an expression of weakened social ties, resulting in inattentiveness to the insecurity of another. Precarity is an overt dismissive disregard for our collective connections with one another. Precarity tied to individualism and the banality of evil dwells within the Aristotelian (1980) adage of mistakes emerging from too much and too little, excess and deficiency. The rebellion against the individual invites a counter understanding of the sovereign with one's kingdom being one's own land of individualism. Rebellion against the excess of external authority, since 1776 and 1789, moved the West to another extreme of individualism that encompasses social life to such an extent that its enactments are difficult to discern, such as the malady of precarity. In the preface to his novel, *A Connecticut Yankee in King Arthur's Court* in 1889, Mark Twain reminds us that excess often fills the void of a previous excess. Twain's contention about the sixth century of England outlines a realistic conception about social change, as one moves from one excess to another. Twain (1889) writes, "One is quite justified in inferring that wherever one of these laws or customs was lacking in that remote time, its place was competently filled by a worse one" (p. ix). Recognizing the excess of the monarchy gives way to the surplus of individualism, which yields precarity. Aristotle was correct: grand errors dwell in excess and deficiency or, in this case, an excess then called a deficiency that invokes another excess in response, which suggests that individualism is an ongoing form of social deficiency.

Unlike enlightened self-interest, individualism propels the myth that one is above the ties of everyday experience in human existence. The self becomes a sovereign sitting upon a self-awarded throne, high above the people as one renders judgment upon them. The sovereign self reigns in the name of individualism with the performative character of self-preoccupation.

2   Void of Social Connection

Individualism is not a natural act; it is a myth that carries toxic consequences within the social domain. Alexis de Tocqueville in *Democracy in America* provides a sketch of this emerging experiment in the West, which he contended that the United States adopted in a wholesale manner. His book arose from observations of the United States in 1831; to place this in context, the President of the United States was Andrew Jackson, who then governed 24 states with a population of 12,860,720, compared to 326,474,013 today. The scope of Tocqueville's visit, along with his French colleague, Gustave de Beaumont, centered in Boston, Massachusetts; New York City; and Philadelphia, Pennsylvania, with limited time in New Orleans and Michigan. Beaumont and Tocqueville studied the prison system in the United States, a work that they collectively published in 1833. During that visit, Tocqueville also gathered research and insight for his major volume, *Democracy in America*, where he framed fundamental differences between individualism and selfishness, with the former a mythic social construction and the latter a natural act.

In an essay titled, "The Rhetorical Turn to Otherness: Otherwise than Humanism," Arnett et al. (2007) center on Tocqueville's critique of individualism. They explicate a historical fact: there were, at minimum, two major versions of the Enlightenment with one winning public acceptance embracing individualism, not communal activity. The Enlightenment folds into two quite different versions of human existence: moderate and radical Enlightenment conceptions. "In essence the difference between the moderate Enlightenment and the radical Enlightenment pivots on a small number of differing metaphors: individuals and freedom; individual possession and common concern; mechanism and organicism and finally, scientism and multiplicity of competing story-laden traditions" (Arnett et al. 2007, p. 116). The Radical Enlightenment embraces the individualism and possessive confidence in action. A central figure in the Radical Enlightenment was Johann Gottfried Herder (1744–1803). According to Watt (1996), Herder's works comprise of forty-five volumes, most unfinished. Herder worked under Immanuel Kant and Johann Georg Hamann at the University of Königsberg and became a teacher at the Cathedral School of Riga at the age of twenty. He left the Cathedral School to travel the seas, learning the importance to listen to signs as well as to grasp a more in-depth knowledge of Greek mythologies, as the Greeks were people of the sea. Herder worked from "empiricism and feeling" (Watt 1996, p. 185). His understanding of civic humanism called forth an emphasis on "an 'ethics of self-expression or self-realization, calling on nations and individuals to express the potentialities unique to them'" (Watt 1996, p. 116). The Radical Enlightenment embraced a dark side of social life that was individualistic and advocated methodological confidence that rejected multiplicity of authority.

The tyranny of the Church shifted to the tyranny of a disengaged "self-absorbed communicator" (Watt 1996, p. 118). When tradition lost its potency and influence, individualism of the Radical Enlightenment triumphed over concern for and about the common good. Tocqueville warned of individualism becoming the emerging tyranny of the eighteenth century, which is now a lynchpin of modernity. Tocqueville differentiated individualism and selfishness with the former abandoning social restraints and constraints and the latter being a natural act of self-protection ever aware of social fabric. Individualism is a social myth that invites an atomistic view propelled by a self-imbued ability to judge from afar, enacting a detached rendering of perspective on events and others. A disengaged self resists influence from others in the social arena, manifesting an unreflective lack of concern for the Other. This conception of individualism leads to social disconnection.

Individualism embraces a universal sense of rationality that yields a social communicative crisis ignited by a "mandate to stand above tradition, an increasing commitment to effectiveness and efficiency rebelling against the restrains of tradition, and the confidence of a communicative agent seeking autonomous implement of the above with ongoing contempt for the power of tradition" (Arnett et al. 2007, pp. 119–120). Classical and medieval life embraced the strength of tradition when situating one within a given social place. Tradition's influence continues in the Renaissance with a dialogic struggle between individual creativity and the person; tradition in the Renaissance dwells with a third alternative, a creative dialogic space. Modernity, on the other hand, begins a dismissive turn toward tradition; shifting from creative disagreement to a conception of tradition as ill-conceived. Disdain for tradition finds its rationale in the social myth of individualism that stands above the social arena and invites detached judgment unresponsive to persons and positions that existed prior to one's own entrance into the conversation. "Confidence in universal rationality wrested away the constraints of tradition" (Arnett et al. 2007, p. 120). Embeddedness of human existence within what Arendt (1977) understood as tradition gives way to a lofty observation point above the messiness of everyday looking, judgment, and life with others.

Individualism stands above the fray of social life and leads to misplaced confidence in one's own clarity of judgment and perspective. Misplaced judgment of individualism originates in an excessive effort to disrupt the expectation of blind allegiance to authority and tradition; however, when taken too far, undue confidence in one's own detached judgment invites yet another form of blind allegiance, individualism's embrace of the self as the new sovereign.

A positive perspective on the implications of this Radical Enlightenment's embrace of individualism continues with the vigorous defense of this perspective by Jonathan Israel (2002), a contemporary defender of the Radical Enlightenment. Israel's thesis is that the Radical Enlightenment was a dramatic break from all traditions. Israel grounds his argument in the insights of Spinoza; Israel contends that Spinoza was the lion of liberal radicalism, which sought to protect the present against the past and its traditions. Reason, not the narrative of faith, drives Spinoza's contribution. For this contention, Spinoza received excommunication from the Jewish faith (1656). Spinoza understood the world as one substance without requiring a God to create; he framed the notion that God dwells, not in the transcendent, but in nature. Spinoza's depiction undergirds the Radical Enlightenment's rejection of God that supported an old-order of view of tradition. Israel advocates this case, arguing for an individualism that eschews tradition and social constraints.

Israel's position finds opposition in particular from Samuel Moyn[1] (2010), who rejects the "package" that Israel presents on the Radical Enlightenment and our contemporary social order. Moyn disputes Israel's assertion that the Radical Enlightenment has all the answers. Moyn marshals evidence from a wide range of sources, as he counters Israel. Moyn's argument cites Dan Edelstein's[2] *The Terror of the Natural Right* where he agrees with Israel's argument that ideas matter and drive social action. Such is the reason Edelstein contends that Israel's version/ ideas are wrongheaded. Moyn states that "the most provocative argument in his [Edelstein's] books is that the ideas that made the revolution (French Revolution 1789) spiral out of control were the cult of nature and the belief in natural rights" (Moyn 2010, para. 33). Discussion centers on Edelstein's assertion that "natural law" lends itself to the identification and eventual destruction of nature's enemies (Moyn 2010, para. 32). The Terror of 1793–1794 has roots in an emerging "religion of nature" that permits the elimination of foes and those who cross one's own perspective (Moyn 2010, para. 37). Moyn's (2010) contention is that such a conception of the Enlightenment is not an answer that will assist the human community, particularly when grounded in a radical perspective that disdains social ties and traditions.

The contention of Moyn's essay is that the Radical Enlightenment gives the human too much credit to act responsibly in a crisis. Moyn (2010) ends with a critique of "George W. Bush's war against all enemies foreign and domestic" (para. 39). Decision-making tied to distance from social ties and rival traditions yields self-righteousness, which then justifies elimination of those not functioning as a natural part of a place or nation-state. Acts of self-righteous genocide find practical and theoretical support in the interplay of nature and natural rights. This social combination is akin to Herbert Spencer's (1864) uniting of Darwinian theory and social life. Spencer (1864) was a marketer of social progress with his

---

[1]Samuel Moyn is a Jeremiah Smith, Jr. Professor of Law and a Professor of History at Harvard University. He has written ten books covering topics such as European intellectual history and human rights history. He does work in international law, human rights, the law of war, and legal thought. He pays specific attention to twentieth-century European moral and political theory. He coedits the journal *Humanity* and has coedited the *Modern Intellectual History* journal, as well as serving on multiple editorial boards and book series.

[2]Dan Edelstein is a William H. Bonsall Professor in French and Professor of French and Italian History at Stanford University, where he is the Chair of Division of Literatures, Cultures, and Languages. His work focuses on literature, history, political theory, and digital humanities. He has published three books discussing the Enlightenment and the French Revolution, with two books in progress.

movement of "survival of the fittest" into the social realm. Spencer's work sought to combine science and philosophy; he promoted "social Darwinism," a conception of the world that he penned a little more than fifty years after the French Revolution, which he deemed a legitimate extension of the natural order of things discovered "scientifically" by Darwin. The danger of such a perspective resides within the self-righteous person unable to discern a dividing line between that which is natural and imposition of ideas for what one terms an alien or enemy.

We discover a contrasting position on the French Revolution in Tocqueville's assessment, which he wrote at a similar time as Spencer. Tocqueville's position was, however, in contrast. In *The Old Regime,* Tocqueville describes the French middle class of the late eighteenth century as divided into miniscule groups, sometimes as small as four people. Each petite group asserted their notability and privileges with each claiming themselves as more valued than the other groups. Tocqueville notes that "each of these small groups lived only for itself and, quite literally, minded its own business" (1856/1955, p. 96), inattentive to the needs of others. Tocqueville termed their action a form of individualism: "Each of the thousands of small groups of which the French nation was then composed took thought for itself alone; in fact, there was, so to speak, a group individualism which prepared men's minds for the thorough-paced individualism with which nowadays we are familiar" (1856/1955, p. 96). In his most famous work, *Democracy in America,* he coined the term individualism as another explication of aristocracy, constituted by a sovereign self. Individualism, for Tocqueville, included fleeing from "each other and to perpetuate in the heart of equality the hatreds to which inequality give birth" (Tocqueville 1835/1963, p. 485). Individualism was and is unnatural in that it attempts to deny our fundamental sociality. This conception contrasts with the natural social realities and constraints associated with selfishness.

Tocqueville's resistance to a world inattentive to that which came previously seeks to reclaim the importance and power of tradition. Tocqueville's counter narrative is directly and/or implicitly the center of critical indictments of Western individualism. Robert Bellah et al. (1985), Philip Rieff (1966), Alasdair MacIntyre (1981, 2016), and Hannah Arendt (1965) are key scholars who press the importance of dialogue between persons as a creative response to the horrific aftermath of the first and second World Wars. Scholars such as Martin Buber, Emmanuel Levinas, and Simone Weil sought alternatives to individualism irresponsive to social ties and traditions different from one's own. Disrespect for the tradition of another makes imperialism and totalitarianism possible; such is the warning of Arendt (1965). Just as the individual sees little reason for tradition, neither does a progressive mandate of progress inherent in such explicit utterances as "manifest destiny" (O'Sullivan 1845). Disregard for tradition invites dismissiveness of that which came before and roots, moving individuals to the "next" and the "new."

Tradition, for Arendt, unites past and present within a collective story that one meets and to which one responds in the pursuit of novel insight. The genuinely new must wrestle with the established (Arendt 1977). Arendt's position is akin to Kant's differentiation between imagination and fantasy. Imagination requires one to push off the real, as opposed to fantasy that responds to abstraction alone (Kant 2012). Using the language of Arendt and Kant *ensemble*, imagination necessitates knowledge of a tradition in order to yield innovative understanding (Arnett 2013, pp. 113–116). Yet another way to describe creativity emerging in response to tradition comes from Martin Buber (1965); he defined the "great character" as someone who knows the rules and regulations so well the person eventually earns the right to violate the learned norms. When tradition is no longer something one can respond to or push off of, one invites fantasy of individualism that rejects social traditions that offer restraint and constraint. Numerous books articulate the limits of individualism as an abstract social option (Lasch 1984; Watt 1996; Tocqueville 1835/1963; Taylor 1989). One of the most descriptive images of such social fantasy resides in Christopher Lasch's (1984) *The Minimal Self.*

Lasch's (1984) book is a classic depiction of a social world void of traditions in contention that require our attentiveness; the social abstraction of individualism invites a minimal self. The date of publication is interesting, 1984. Indeed, there is an echo of an Orwellian theme behind Lasch's depiction of the minimal self in action, which emerges when confidence in the traditions of the world before one is no longer. The minimal self is a defense against a meaningless void, a world without assurance of tradition that invites and demands creative response. Tradition is the carrier of a philosophical tradition that one must learn before offering a dismissive critique. Lasch (1984) contends that the minimal, "separate self" is a fiction (p. 253). The human being lives within a world in need of "practical reason" composed of common practices. According to Lasch, the sixteenth-century contributions of Machiavelli and Thomas More shifted the primary focus of the state from protection of persons to the protection of material goods. They invited "instrumental reason" that links means and ends in an external fashion. Practical reason of a classical age invited practices that enrich the internal self via attentiveness to externality, which connects the doing of practices with character-formation. When industrial societies lose sight of the importance of practices, their character-forming properties diminish.

There is a performative aspect to the development of character, which contrasts with a love of the image of "selfhood." Lasch (1984) cited Gregory

Bateson, calling selfhood "an obsolete idea" (p. 257). The key to a creative and healthy self is life lived within the social domain as one finds pull and influence from multiple directions and goods, which shapes a conscience capable of guilt as one struggles with the reality of a gulf between "human aspirations and human limitations" (Lasch 1984, p. 258). The uneasy relationship with the practices of the self is our best hope; the task of a Narcissus is to eliminate awareness of our divided nature composed of competing practices. Our social nature unites thankfulness with regret and forgiveness, and the notion of desire with unquenched passion for creativity and retaliation; the struggles between and among these conflicting tendencies is not our greatest enemy, but rather a pragmatic sense of hope. Contrary tensions generate the necessity for reflection, a natural act that reminds one that the social world calls forth thoughtful response.

Individualism divides us from the social Other and moves us into a world of abstraction. We then confuse the natural reality of curved lines within the social with the singularity of direction of individualism. The latter fails to affirm a conflicted heart, missing the existential importance of such division. When the disunions within the person no longer demand an inner dialogue of ongoing questioning, one loses natural social restraints of reflection about potential action and direction. One no longer engages an inner division; instead, one begins to divide oneself from others. The current commercial act of such detachment rests in the ongoing use of precarity, as institutions shift risk to those who labor for them.

In *Communication and Community: Implications of Martin Buber's Dialogue*, I stated that the principal communication problem of our era is "polarized communication" (Arnett 1986, p. 17). This essay explicates a contemporary path that exacerbates social life with blind reliance upon individualism. Precarity is a symptom of social division and frames economic difference as a normative reality in the manic desire to protect the economic health of an institution, which increasingly appears like a nation-state in the heyday of colonization and imperialism—protection for a few at the expense of the Other.

Precarity is a dismissive act toward another in defense of institutional security. Precarity banks on a background composed of individualistic assumptions dismissive toward the Other. This position is consistent with the comments of William James (2001): "No more fiendish punishment could be devised, were such a thing physically possible, than that one should be turned loose in society and remain absolutely unnoticed by all the members thereof" (p. 46). Precarity is a fiendish attack upon our public ties with one another. Note: from the standpoint of individualism, precarity necessitates counseling and leadership advancement rather than focusing on structural social change.

3 Precarity as Public Separation

Response to precarity and its structural dangers centers this essay on critical comments from a transatlantic virtual roundtable (Puar 2012). The contributors outline the social phenomenon of increasing disparity between full-time and part-time workers, with the former benefiting from institutional support and the latter unwillingly supporting the institution by bearing its risk. The conversation commenced in the summer of 2011 with five significant voices: Lauren Berlant, whose 2011 book, *Cruel Optimism*, addresses precarities in the United States and Europe; Judith Butler, an American critic of the nation-state; Bojana Cvejić, who examines the performative reality of precarity tied to practices understood through a musical and dramaturgic lens; Isabell Lorey, a political scientist attentive to community and issues of immunization; and Ana Vujanović, who is a freelance writer interested in the increasing presence of precarity in the performing arts. The contributors brought a diversity of perspectives on precarity, illuminated with an emphasis on performativity and precariousness.

The first question posed to this distinguished panel required defining precarity. Jasbir Puar turned to material from Butler's (2004) *Precarious Life*; she defined the term with "an acknowledgement of dependency, needs, exposure, and vulnerability" (Puar 2012, p. 163). Citing her other colleagues in the roundtable, Puar (2012) stressed precarity within the unrewarded labor of the middle class and the reality of biopolitical constructs within the population. Lorey stated that many committed to the arts necessarily must enact a livelihood of "self-precarization" (Puar 2012, p. 164). She contended that precarity within capitalism is, of course, not new; the reality of underpaid work, from a "woman's job" to migrant workers, has a long history (Puar 2012, p. 165). However, today precarity is a normative act of many corporations attempting to shore up their own insecurity.

Lauren Berlant then outlined precarity with five major coordinates. First, it is an "existential problem"; life is "contingent" (Puar 2012, p. 166). Second, it is a structured economic difficulty inherent within capitalism. Third, reproductive life finds limits due to an empirical fact—there is a limited amount of time in a given day. Fourth, privatization of wealth continues to suppress ingenuity within the public domain. Fifth, precarity is an expression of a basic financial reality that one has lost traction in the political and economic world and begins to slide backward into greater insecurity.

Berlant expressed ambivalence about the notion of precarity in that it lessens focus on economic disparity experienced by the proletariat. Instead of concentrating on class differences, precarity too quickly invites questions about good-life fantasies as people deal with debt bubbles, leaving behind the reality of transnational labor and the proletariat. Economic oppression then moves to the shadows with discussion of low wage labor/underemployment of the precariat at center stage. Berlant's primary interest in precarity pivots upon the question of marginality, which affects the economic and the emotional lives of people. She contends that precarity is a rallying cry for the recognition of our interdependence, calling for those within the public domain to assume responsibility for lessening spaces and lives governed by precarity.

Cvejić and Vujanović limited their comments to the arts, particularly the performing arts. Precarity finds destructive nourishment in a post-Fordism or a cognitive-capitalism environment where freelance workers embrace the myth of individualism without reflecting upon the fact that their lives find economic and social definition through precarity. Cheap-labor contracts and an increasing number of Ph.D. artists in the academy announce the precarity of being a performance artist in Europe; many are moving to academia, giving up autonomy for stability. This temporary shift toward security will eventuate in fewer academic positions, resulting in a larger precariat assemblage tied to part-time employment. Puar suggests that Butler disregards the assumption that a public sphere of security is possible within the academy. The existential fact of today is that "more and more laborers within the academy are subjected to new forms of precaritization" (Puar 2012, p. 167). Such workers feel increasingly disposable; universities contribute to this feeling, ever willing to replace a tenured faculty member with a non-tenure-track position.

As universities become more unaffordable, they also reify class ranks with the result of public "rage" about the cost of higher education (Puar 2012, p. 168). Puar contends that the hegemony of neoliberalism in higher education generates global protest. The performative gesture of occupying space in the public arena announces anger and reveals unintended consequences of university decisions centered on precarity. Such action frames precarity in the act of protest:

> Bodies on the street are precarious—they are exposed to police force, and sometimes endure physical suffering as a result. But those bodies are also obdurate and persisting, insisting on their continuing and collective "thereness" and, in these recent formations, organizing themselves without hierarchy, and so exemplifying the principles of equal treatment that they are demanding of public institutions. In this way, those bodies enact the message, performatively, even when they sleep in public, or when they organize collective methods for cleaning grounds they occupy, as happened in Tahrir and Wall Street. (Puar 2012, p. 168).

When people place themselves in the streets, we witness precarity and risk in performative action. Such movements reveal the importance of collective resistance, challenging the routines of those in control and power. The second major question in the roundtable centered on the emerging connection between the "political-economic usage" of the term "precarity" and the "ethical and psychoanalytic valances" of the term (Puar 2012, p. 169). The conversation among members of the roundtable gathered around imploding consequences from disenfranchising implications of precarity that alter relationships with one another, economically and institutionally. Puar (2012) cited Foucault and emphasized that precarity is not an identity, but a relation in terms of "bodies and populations" (p. 169). Butler then summarized comments from her colleagues, emphasizing the reality of social vulnerability that results from uneven forms of economic distribution and institutional participation.

One misses the implications of precarity when limiting its influence to a single event; precarity has unending influence on the gestalt of one's lifeworld. Precarity is a slow death that targets and marginalizes disenfranchised populations. Butler adds to the term "precaritization" with the notion of "the precarious"; she seeks to account for the feeling of insecurity in multiple dimensions of existence. Precaritization, for Butler, is a relational and emotional term that reflects affective change in a life propelled by political and economic marginalization. She connects the performative consequences of precariousness to the "bonds that support life" (Puar 2012, p. 169). The loss of connecting bonds between and among persons moves us to an imposed form of individualism with the consequence of disrupting social unions. Commitments to local and global interdependence requires struggle against the influence of precaritization, which marginalizes and lessens opportunity for authentic social connection. "Precarity exposes our sociality, the fragile and necessary dimensions of our interdependency" (Puar 2012, p. 170). Precarity assumes imposed individualism that lessens participation in the public domain of institutional influence.

Puar (2012) states that political life in modernity depends upon various forms and amounts of precarity. "Unequal distribution" of goods and security attempt to protect those with current privilege. "[U]nequal distribution of precarity ... depends upon dominant norms regarding whose life is grievable and worth protecting, and whose life is ungrievable" (Puar 2012, p. 170). Precarity is not merely an existential phenomenon; it has keen political implications. Social norms that abide by racism, classism, and separatism of equality of opportunity function as a warrant for the enactment of precarity. It is impossible to locate a space outside of precarity; however, it is necessary to resist efforts to institutionalize precarity through social-political life (Puar 2012, p. 170). The ongoing lament against precarity of the participants in the roundtable does not include a return to humanism; their answers dwell in the realms of politics and economic life.

A Banality of Evil: Precarity as the Offspring of Individualism

Puar (2012) then brought to the conversation a basic social question about exclusivity surrounding the term "precarity." She argued that marginalized people and activists of color have long understood precarity. Puar asks a probing question: Did acknowledgement of precarity begin with the disenfranchisement of "younger white populations" (Puar 2012, p. 170)? This question dominated the background of the ongoing conversation and went unanswered, but repeatedly re-entered the discussion. Butler then articulated importance of ethical obligation to the Other; she broadened the conversation to interspecies questions of vulnerability and interdependence. Butler's contribution pointed to language that leads to "commons-talk" (Puar 2012, p. 171) and issues of sustainability.

Berlant added conversation from her book, *Cruel Optimism*, that tracks life via acts of desperation and violence propelled by the fantasy of hopes tied to capitalism's mythology of the "good life" (Puar 2012, p. 171). When social democracy begins to fail, we discover neoliberal pressures capable of enhancing movement to privatize capital and its distribution. Such actions weaken the state and its ability to assure quasi-equal access to resources. Berlant suggested that we must discover, invent, and reinvent institutions, permitting us to enact a social imaginary of relational care and access to resources. Lorey states that we cannot return to a universal commons, if such an entity ever existed; we must reinvent the commons in a manner that protects difference and eludes the tempting protection of sameness. Such action requires active rejection of distribution of insecurity and precaritization for the non-same, the marginalized Other. To fail in such a political initiative invites a new danger, the normalization of precarity. Normalization of precarity is unacceptable. Lorey cites Bourdieu's contention that precarity immobilizes one with the fear of unemployment. She contends that it generates a "presentness" of fragmentation with a sense of continuity of time that invites a "paralysis of precaritization" (Puar 2012, p. 173). The marginalized is fast becoming a social norm.

Butler reminds us that precarity requires attentiveness to the human and the nonhuman; our environmental irresponsibility is another act of precarity. Puar (2012) contends that life is not simply about finding a place within it, but is rather about nourishing relationships that bind together the proximate and those afar with an interdependence and a care about the use and distribution of human and non-human elements of the human condition. Precarity, understood in post-humanistic language, attends to the physical, emotional, and material environments that shape persons and all of life and matter. Addressing precarity requires returning to discussion of performance within an information age; such an era makes it insufficient to engage a task alone. Precarity includes an implicit norm, demanding that one dance in a particular performative manner, accepting the normative modes of communication production with the gesture of a "managed smile" (Arnett 1992, p. 114). Such action calls for acceptance of software that accounts for each move in hope of keeping all in line with a distribution system that benefits the select.[3]

The above conversation about precarity offers coordinates that, when examined beyond economic insecurity, shift the discussion into multiple conceptions of social insecurity. The notion of relational insecurity invokes images of imposed separation from employment, others, authenticity of performance, and the environment. One of the major methods of enacting such separation is severing connections with and from the public domain. The more life becomes a performative expression of individualism, the greater the likelihood of precarity's march toward making insecurity a normative feature of social existence. Of course, insecurity is a given; life is existentially precarious. Life moves contrary to our hopes and expectations; however, this form of natural precarity contrasts with socially imposed separation from institutions, employment, and others. Denial of influence in the public domain requires the disadvantaged to bear the risk and insecurity of the privileged. In an effort to secure greater security for a smaller number, those on margins of public influence bear the weight of insecurity. My interest in the conversation of Puar and Butler dwells in their assertion that the diminishing inclusive reality of the public domain announced by precarity begins with relational separation.

Separation from influence in the public domain is not novel. This mode of behavior is a long-standing social game of exclusion. Arendt and others detail a wicked social game of separation tied to the performance of the parvenu, the person who desperately seeks social inclusion (Arendt 1957). This social disparity commences with a group in power informing the person who wants to join to enact particular acts; the person so charged, the parvenu, does so, only to discover that the actions are insufficient. Those in power, after saying no, encourage the person to continue with this process going on endlessly without acceptance as the final reward.

---

[3]One example of such software is Basecamp (which serves as a project management software that keeps communication focused on the project at hand.). The Basecamp website reads: "A Basecamp is a private, secure space online where people working together can organize and discuss everything they need to get a project done." "Basecamp's threads keep discussions on-topic and in-context so the whole story stays together in a way that's easy to follow and reference for the record later." See https://basecamp.com.

A Banality of Evil: Precarity as the Offspring of Individualism

I discuss the dangers of this social game that inflicts social pain upon the parvenu in *Communication Ethics in Dark Times: Hannah Arendt's Rhetoric of Warning and Hope* (Arnett 2013). In my judgment, precarity is the next step beyond social abuse of the parvenu with increased separation from the public domain. Precarity does not waste time on a ruse of social games; it links normative agreements within a society to acts of separation. Precarity justifies those in power in separating persons, lessening public access, and expecting them to absorb their risk and insecurity. The efforts of those with power work with an implicit message—precarity is a normative expectation undergirded by the myth of individualism.

The social game of exclusion tied to the parvenu is an extreme and cruel form of selfishness.[4] The goal is to separate persons. Precarity is yet another stage, dependent upon individualism. The intentional development of a society that asks the disadvantaged to bear risk and insecurity (precarity) depends upon something more than selfish human impulses; precarity necessitates a programmatic effort that includes the social myth of individualism in order to separate persons from social roots, economic opportunity, and emotional and active participation in influencing the public domain. While precarity depends upon estrangement from social ties and roots, selfishness is natural and part of the human condition. The wicked game of the parvenu depends upon social ties. Precarity, on the other hand, severs one from the connections of social ties via the background assumption of individualism. Precarity demands fragmentation of time and effort, discounting social ties that accompany collective interaction. One can suggest that movements such as the Tea Party,[5] Occupy Wall Street,[6] Third Way liberalism,[7] and Euro Mayday[8] provide persons with social connections. However, there are two major limitations. First, participation in such protest groups generally does not endure for long periods. Second, precarity separates persons from positions

---

[4]Individualism attempts to stand above all social restraints while selfishness recognizes the need for communal ties, even when used to achieve personal ends (Arnett 2013).

[5]The Tea Party movement emerged in 2009 as a conservative protest to the U.S. government. The movement protects and promotes traditional Judeo-Christian values. For more information, see http://www.teaparty.org.

[6]Occupy Wall Street began on September 17, 2011, as protestors occupied Zuccotti Park in New York City. Subsequent Occupy movements occurred worldwide as a protest to capitalist financial systems. For more information, see http://occupywallst.org.

[7]Third Way launched in 1998 as an effort to dismantles a political movement aimed toward rethinking right-wing and left-wing political binaries. It began in the U.K. with Tony Blair and soon spread to Germany and the United States (Leigh 2003, p. 10).

[8]Euro May Day began in 2004 as a "transnational demonstration of precarious and migrant people" aimed at ceasing migrant discrimination. The day finds celebration in over a dozen European cities. For more information, see http://www.euromayday.org/about.php.

of stability and influence, making it increasingly unlikely that one can influence the public domain. Selfishness depends on social interaction; precarity assumes a reality of increasing isolation and separation. Discussion of precarity begins with a basic assumption: disruption of the supportive power from the public domain.

Precarity is a symptom of a social disease housed within individualism. Individualism demands that one stand above social constraints and restraints. One of the consequences of such social separation is precarity. Precarity is a political and social issue gathering its energy from the Western fascination with a social experiment of individualism gone awry so badly that one laments for the return of selfishness as described by Tocqueville. Individualism denies our social connections, and precarity exploits this assumption, enacting a banality of evil.

References

Aristotle (1980). *The Nicomachean ethics.* Translated by David Ross. Oxford, UK: Oxford University Press.

Arendt, H. (1957). *Rahel Varnhagen: The life of a Jewess.* London, UK: East and West Library.

Arendt, H. (1965). *Eichmann in Jerusalem: A report on the banality of evil.* New York, NY: Viking Press.

Arendt, H. (1977). *Between past and future: Eight exercises in political thought.* New York, NY: Penguin Books. (Original work published 1961)

Arnett, R. C. (1986). *Communication and community: Implications of Martin Buber's dialogue.* Carbondale: Southern Illinois University Press.

Arnett, R. C. (1992). *Dialogic education: Conversation about ideas and between persons.* Carbondale: Southern Illinois University Press.

Arnett, R. C. (2013). *Communication ethics in dark times: Hannah Arendt's rhetoric of warning and hope.* Carbondale: Sothern Illinois University Press.

Arnett, R. C., Fritz, J. M. H., & Holba, A. (2007). The rhetorical turn to otherness: Otherwise than humanism. *Cosmos and History: The Journal of Natural and Social Philosophy, 3,* 115–133.

Beaumont, G. & Tocqueville, A. (1833). *On the penitentiary system of the United States and its Application in France.* Translated by Francis Lieber. Philadelphia, PA: Carey, Lea & Blanchard.

Bellah, R. N., Madsen, R., Sullivan, W. M., Swidler, A., & Tipton, S. M. (1985). Habits of the heart: Individualism and commitment in American life. Berkeley: University of California Press.

Bourdieu, P. (1977). *Outline of a theory of practice.* Cambridge, UK: Cambridge University Press.

Buber, M. (1965). *Between man and man.* New York, NY: Macmillan. (Original work published 1947).

Butler, J. (2004). *Precarious life: The power of mourning and violence.* New York, NY: Verso.

Israel, J. I. (2002). *Radical enlightenment: Philosophy and the making of modernity, 1650–1750.* Oxford, UK: Oxford University Press.

James, W. (2001). *Psychology: The briefer course.* Mineola, NY: Dover Publications. (Original work published 1892)

Kant, I. (2012). *Lectures on anthropology.* Cambridge, UK: Cambridge University Press. (Original work published 1798)

Lasch, C. (1984). The minimal self: Psychic survival in troubled times. New York, NY: W. W. Norton & Co.

Leigh, A. (2003). The Rise and Fall of the Third Way. *AQ: Australian Quarterly, 75*(2), 10–40.

MacIntyre, A. C. (1981). *After virtue: A study in moral theory.* Notre Dame, IN: University of Notre Dame Press.

MacIntyre, A. C. (2016). *Ethics in the conflicts of modernity: An essay on desire, practical reasoning, and narrative.* Cambridge, UK: Cambridge University Press.

Moyn, S. (2010, May 12). Mind the Enlightenment: Jonathan Israel's epic defense of "Radical Enlightenment" has the dogmatic ring of a profession of faith. *The Nation, 290*(21).

O'Sullivan, J. (1845). Annexation. In *The United States Magazine and Democratic Review, 17,* 5-10.

Puar, J. (2012). Precarity talk: A virtual roundtable with Lauren Berlant, Judith Butler, Bojana Cvejić, Isabell Lorey, Jasbir Puar, and Ana Vujanović. *The Drama Review, 56*(4), 163-177.

Rieff, P. (1966). *The triumph of the therapeutic: Uses of faith after Freud.* New York, NY: Harper and Row.

Savage, M., & Devine, F. (2015). BBC Great British Class Survey, 2011-2013. [Data collection]. UK Data Service. SN: 7616. doi: doi.org/10.5255/UKDA-SN-7616-1.

Schutz, A. (1967). *The phenomenology of the social world.* Evanston, IL: Northwestern University Press.

Spencer, H. (1864). *The principles of biology.* London, UK: Williams and Norgate.

Taylor, C. (1989). *Sources of the self: The making of the modern identity.* Cambridge, MA: Harvard University Press.

Tocqueville, A. (1955). *Democracy in America.* Translated by Stuart Gilbert. New York, NY: Doubleday. (Original work published 1856)

Tocqueville, A. (1963). *Democracy in America.* Translated by Harvey C. Mansfield & Delba Winthrop. New York, NY: Alfred Knopf. (Original works published 1835, Vol. 1; 1840, Vol. 2)

Twain, M. (1889). *A Connecticut Yankee in King Arthur's court.* New York, NY: Charles L. Webster and Company.

Watt, I. (1996). *Myths of modern individualism: Faust, Don Quixote, Don Juan, Robinson Crusoe.* Cambridge, UK: Cambridge University Press.

Artists' Precarity in the Context of Their Social Integration

António M. Duarte

> *(...) the world of art mirrors society at large.*
> Howard Becker (2008, p. 371).
> Why are artists poor?
> Hans Habbing (2002).

Abstract

The literature review here presented aims to characterize artists' precarity in the context of their social integration, along with that precarity's consequences, the artists' reactions it provoques and possible ways to counter act it. Using an interdisciplinary approach, the review is based on specialized research literature from psychology, sociology and economy of art. As the review shows, besides being specially affected by professional precarity, most artists are also exposed to ontological precarity, under the form of pressures on their creative work. Both forms of precarity stem from the nature of the artists' social integration, a critical process in attempting survivance, recognition and identity consolidation and which involves complex interactions with a variety of social players. Altought experienced in multiple ways, artists' precarity entails risky material and psychological consequences, also affecting the artistic creative process. Finally, artists' precarity can be counteracted through specific personal coping strategies, along with possible changes in the system.

A. M. Duarte (✉)
University of Lisbon, Lisbon, Portugal
e-mail: amduarte@psicologia.ulisboa.pt

© Springer Fachmedien Wiesbaden GmbH, part of Springer Nature 2020   19
T. Rachwał et al. (eds.), *Precarious Places*, Prekarisierung
und soziale Entkopplung – transdisziplinäre Studien,
https://doi.org/10.1007/978-3-658-27311-8_2

Keywords

Art · Artists · Ontological precarity · Precarity · Professional precarity · Social integration

As this text suggests, artists' precarity (considering artists that are or pretend to be professionalized) can be located at the professional level and at the ontological level, benefiting its analysis from a contextualization in the dynamics of artist's professional and cultural integration.

Due to its thematic, although attempting to focus mainly on the psychological aspects of artists' integration in the social context, the text grounds not only on psychology research, but also on literature on sociology and economy of art. This follows a perspective that defends the need of an interdisciplinary approach for the study of human development in context that integrates research in social sciences like economy, history, sociology and psychology (e.g., Diewald and Mayer 2008, as cited in Schoon and Silbereisen 2008).

1 Artists' Social Integration

As emphasized by a systems perspective on creativity (Csíkszentmihályi 1999), artists' inventiveness involves an interaction between the artist, his or her domain and the surrounding social environment, which eventually recognizes the created products, sooner or later, as "creative" (sometimes too late, as in the case of Van-Gogh that died in poverty). Correlatively, as Getzels and Csíkszentmihályi (1976) observed, in a study with young visual artists, the majority of them manifested a motivation to "show" their work and be social recognized, which reveals their awareness that beyond doing art, becoming (or performing the social role as) an artist requires social legitimization or symbolic approval by appropriate social institutions.

Besides, from a developmental psychology perspective, just graduated artists face the task of constructing a new form of social integration by finding an occupation that will satisfy both material and identity consolidation needs (Getzels and Csíkszentmihályi 1976). This implies experiencing a transitional change, which besides having general characteristics has a specificity for these artists.[1]

---

[1]Just graduated artists' social integration can be taken as a specific case of general human adaptation to transition, which accordingly to the model of Schlossberg (1981, p. 5), involves dealing with a *change*, in order to *adapt*, on the basis of *perception of the transition*, a *pretransition* and *posttransition environment* and a set of *individual characteristics*.

Artists' social integration (as individuals or as co-creative groups) involves their interactions with a variety of players that operate with different functions and in specific relations in what Dickie (1984) and Becker (2008) call *art world*, Di Maggio (1991) and Bourdieu (1996) adress as *art field*, Heinich (Heinich 1998a, b) sees as *aesthetic-actor network* or Luhmann (2000) as *art system*.[2]

Other artists or other workers involved in art making (e.g., technicians implicated in the making of a movie; music interpreters) play a role in collaborating and/or technically assisting artists' work, since art making might also imply a division of labour (Becker 2008). A diversity of social "provision" services (e.g., producing and suplying art materials) provide artists with a fundamental basis for work (Becker 2008). A variety of networks like art schools, art associations, "muses", impresarios, culture industries, patrons and Maecenas have a role in eventualy supporting and promoting artists (Aljena 2015; Becker 2008; van Maanen 2009). Art relevant urban centers (e.g. New York) potentially allow artists to contact with (and co-construct) trendy ideas and larger audiences (Getzels and Csíkszentmihályi 1976; van Maanen 2009). Political and civil institutions play a role in the art world by legislating on art and by selectively funding artists, determining their rights and programming art activities (Aljena 2015; Becker 2008; van Maanen 2009). Aestheticians develop philosophical systems that sugest criteria and aesthetic values which determine what is art and the value of it, thus influencing other behaviours in the artworld (e.g. apreciation, creation, support, *cf.* Becker 2008). Critics and the media play in the art world by opiniating and discoursing on art works and artists and therefore in creating meaning for them and also in indirectly influencing artists' status and work (Aljena 2015; Becker 2008; Getzels and Csíkszentmihályi 1976). Dealers buy and sell art (e.g., art galleries) and eventualy offer (a few) artists a contract (Aljena 2015; Becker 2008; Conde 2009; Getzels and Csíkszentmihályi 1976). Brokers arranje the buying/selling under comission, mediating between most artists and buyers or auction houses (Aljena 2015; Conde 2009). Art shows exhibit artists' works, from the low level sidewalk exhibitions or "chiken-wire" shows organized by neighborhood clubs or shoping centers to juried shows organized by major art associations and museums and to joint independent artists shows in art clubs or minor galeries (Getzels and Csíkszentmihályi 1976). Fairs and auctions have a function in comercialising reputated art works and artists (Aljena 2015; Becker 2008). Museums and their trustees, administrators and curators, as well as art editors of magazines and books select,

---

[2]Aljena (2015, Fig. 1., p. 140) also synthetizes the different players in the art world in a model labeled as "Ecosystem of contemporary fine art".

exhibite and ratify artists' works (Aljena 2015; Becker 2008; Getzels and Csíkszentmihályi 1976). Conservators and restaurers act in the art world by working on art maintanance and recover. Art buyers (individuals, companies, institutions) directly or indirectly buy to the artists (in artists' private spaces, like worshops and lofts, or mostly in galleries) for pleasure, exhibition or investment (Aljena 2015; Becker 2008; Getzels and Csíkszentmihályi 1976). Society (with its historical culture) and audiences (with their perceptions) play the role of apreciating art works and therefore making them "appeer" (Aljena 2015; Becker 2008). Besides, "art scientists" (e.g., biologists, psychologists, sociologists, historians and economists of art) play a role in the art world by describing and explaining art processes and also intervining on them. Art lawyers work on the legal processes related with art (e.g., copyright, authenticity, contracts). Moreover, as most artists split work into different kinds of activities not related to art (as further analysed), their social integration involves more peripherical professional relations with a diversity of social actors and organizations not specifically related with art.

The relations that artists' develop with these different players in (and out) the art world are diversified, including collaboration, support, tension and conflict due to pressure, dependency, employment, competition, reproval, hierarchy, etc. (Becker 2008; Bourdieu 1996; Conde 2009; Getzels and Csíkszentmihályi 1976). The necessity to interact with those players (for gaining status as an artist) also demand from the artist "marketing behaviors" (e.g., organization, publicity, salesmanship, social contact, economical judgment, Getzels and Csíkszentmihályi 1976). Problematicaly, these beviours unconfourtably contradict artist's typical basic personality and value system tendencies (i.e., introversion, social isolation, self-suficiency; low economic and social values), which are functional for a tolerance to the solitary and subjective conditions of art work (Getzels and Csíkszentmihályi 1976).

2 Artists' Professional Precarity

As for the general population nowadays, artists' professional integration consists in a normally problematic transition.[3] Moreover, in the case of the artists this integration detains particular specificities, focused here.

---

[3]Just graduated artists' professional integration is a specific case of the general phenomenon of school-to-work transition, which (along its psychosocial outcomes) can be problematic. This transition, exposed to a macroeconomic rising reduction of opportunities and of flexible employment, receives the influence of a variety of factors: institutional filtering; transition demands; economic, social and personal resources, like parental support, ability and motivation; and individual coping and adjustment (Schoon and Silbereisen 2008, p. 8).

Firstly, while many schools of skilled vocations (e.g., law, medicine and engineering) furnish certification that grant a professional status, this seldom happens with art schools (Getzels and Csíkszentmihályi 1976).

Secondly, comparatively to some other skilled vocations, the one in arts lacks the consistent support of formal institutions (i.e., professional schools, professional associations, trade schools, trade unions, licensing boards, employment agencies, political lobbies, etc.) that facilitate entry in occupations and that further protect peoples' interests after eventual entrance (Getzels and Csíkszentmihályi 1976). In the absence of this consistent formal support, a variety of informal systems perform an inconsistent support to the artist, as analyzed by Getzels and Csíkszentmihályi (1976) for the case of fine arts artists: the artist's loft, where finished or in progress sellable works are displayed and which communicates the message that one intends to become an artist.

Most importantly, although a few artists work autonomously under high incomes (Habbing 2002) and some are institutionalized (e.g. orchestras, museums, cultural industries, *cf.* Conde 2009), most artists' are vulnerable workers under professional contingencies of underemployment, intermittent and multiple jobs, freelance work, precarious contracts and low salaries (Becker 2008; Conde 2009; Frey 2011; Habbing 2002, 2011; Lazzarato 2011). Moreover, artists might volunteer for non-paid work in the area of the arts with the hope this will open them opportunities (Becker 2008), under a scenario where artists are actually subsidizing the arts (Withers 1985). Artists' professional vulnerability is partly understandable in the framework of a general professional precarity that characterizes the neo-liberal post-Fordist economy.[4] Not by chance, the decrease in the income and the increase in multi-employment of western artists was substantial especially in the second half of the twentieth century (Habbing 2011). Nevertheless, artists' work vulnerability might be also due to the specificity of the art world and seem more pronounced here than in other sectors. Effectively,

---

[4]General precarity at the work level has been defined (Brophy 2006; Waite 2009) as the experience of precariousness under material uncertainty and instability due to flexible employment arrangements. Precarious employment has also been defined as involving low wages and work intensification (Benach et al. 2014; Vosko 2006, as cited in Bain and McLean 2012) and lack of work rights, protection and recognition (Benach et al. 2014). According to Standing (2011) work precarity originated an heterogeneous "class-in-the making" of a precarious proletariat ("precariat"), below the working class, to which professional security is denied (i.e., absence of income-earning opportunities, stable wage, social security, non-arbitral dismissal, chances of developing skills and career and absence of a collective voice).

besides experiencing several forms of underemployment artists have higher rates of unemployment, self-employment and multi-employment (Menger 1999). In a study on European artists, for instance, Capiau and Wiesand (2006) found that above other workers, 18% of workers with a cultural employment had temporary jobs, 25% had part-time jobs, 9% had a second job and 29% were self-employed. The large majority of artists (especially the young artists) also gain very little (Habbing 2002, 2011), earn less than other professionals and workers of similar age, education and training and compared to these have greater income inequality and variability (Maranda 2009). For example, hourly income is lower than in other professions or even negative, novice artists face more uncertainty than the average beginning professionals, many artists have much difficulties in selling their work and many young art companies and small or fringe art institutions can't pay more than low salaries (Habbing 2002). Artists can be also exposed to the bargaining on the value of their work products, to a loss of a significant percentage of its selling (sometimes until 80%), and to payment delay (sometimes months or years), as it might happen with visual artists in a contract with a gallery (Getzels and Csíkszentmihályi 1976). In an interview, a Portuguese painter (Graça Morais) testimony characterizes some of these actual problems in the specific context of Portugal: "The great musicians do not have work; writers run the country to give conferences that are not paid [...] people in decision places of decision are very upstarts, having arrived there very quickly but without cultivating themselves. So it's using and throwing away." (Carita 2017, p. 57).

Having most artists a low income that originates from their artistic works, they compensate on the basis of extra money (i.e., family and partners support, savings, inheritances, social security and benefits, insurance payments), a frugal life style or, more often, a split of work into different kinds of activities (Becker 2008; Getzels and Csíkszentmihályi 1976; Habbing 2002; van Maanen 2009). As this analysis identifies, many artists have one autonomous art work, with which they identify and through which they attempt to express a personal style; and another work ("day job") with which they identify less or not at all and by which they *internally subsidy* the former. This "day job" can be in the that periphery of the arts (e.g., teaching art, creating commercial art products of lesser quality[5]; working as art support personnel; journal consultancy) or even not related with art (e.g., cleaning; waiting tables; modelling, acting in commercials, etc.).

---

[5]Subsidising artistic work with the production of commercial art works is prodigal in many photographers, as Edward Weston did with portraiture before "freeing" to Mexico (*cf.* Becker 2008).

Actually, it seems that most artists earn the biggest part of their income from secondary employment (Bain 2005). Eventually, when survival is guaranteed, an artist (special if he or she is a young artist) might reduce the later kind of work and invest more in the former at the cost of income while attempting to do what she or he likes and to gain a reputation that serves art (Habbing 2002). At such a stage, even selling might function more as a way of legitimization than of getting money (Habbing 2002). According to Habbing (2002), this is a reason why artist's income is relatively low. In fact, this pattern of work practice is not exclusive of young artists, being also possible in the case of already recognized artists. Due to necessity until middle age, when already recognized, composer Philip Glass maintained other jobs as a plumber and taxi driver parallel to the work as a composer, which he just quitted when his music (with his operas) started to be profitable (Glass 2015). One of his famous testimonies is illustrative: "I had gone to install a dishwasher in a loft in SoHo," he says. "While working, I suddenly heard a noise and looked up to find Robert Hughes, the art critic of Time magazine, staring at me in disbelief. 'But you're Philip Glass! What are you doing here?' It was obvious that I was installing his dishwasher and I told him I would soon be finished. 'But you are an artist,' he protested. I explained that I was an artist but that I was sometimes a plumber as well and that he should go away and let me finish." (Glass, cited in O'Mahony 2001, para. 28).[6]

As Conde (2009) stated, this all scenario brings artists on the ambivalent condition of being central and autonomous (to a society that recognizes creativity as fundamental) but also fragile and dependent (in a society where artists are precarious or poorly subsided). Several factors explain artists' professional precarity and vulnerability. One located factor, that blocks changes in artists' work conditions, is a social representation or idealization of the artistic work as a free-lance or self-organized activity based on competitive individual or subjective creative projects and of the artist as independent, idiosyncratic, rebel, exceptional, self-sufficient, adaptable and accustomed to risk (Christopherson 2008; Getzels and Csíkszentmihályi 1976; Osten 2011; Parker 2008; Ray 2011). Specifically, the generation in the art world of what is considered a new type of "institution"—the "project"—with no stable institutional structure, while allowing flexibility doesn't

---

[6]Although this text focus on artists' precarity it should be mention that, also due to the nature of the arts, that kind of precarity affects not only the artist but other key members of the art world. For instance, art support personnel (e.g., art executers or art technicians) often work under project-allocated contracts on a free-lance system, without a steady work and nothing more to protect their work than their reputation (Becker 2008).

counteract precarity (Nowotny 2011).[7] Moreover, in order to deal with the tension between "producing art" and "earning money", artists might develop a self-narration where division between working and private life dissipates (Kergel 2016). Bourdieu's (1987) analysis on the genesis of the modern representation of the artist as an autonomous unique singular individual (in contrast with being an artisan) suggests its origin in the Impressionist revolution led by Manet. In the same line (White and White 1993, as cited in Wuggenig 2011) point that this birth of artistic charismatic individualism was also supported by the emergence of art dealers as real entrepreneurs and the rising of art criticism.

Particularly artists' low income has been explained by the' difficulties many artists have in selling their works (Levine 1972, as cited in Becker 2008), which has to do with a variety of personal and contextual causes. Starting with personal reasons, a possible factor might be the rather slow development of a (eventual) social recognized artistic performance, which takes in average ten years (e.g. Oatley 2011). Testifying this, the writer Anthony Trollope alluded to the "(...) dogged perseverance [...] [of] ten years of unpaid unflagging labour (...)" which was necessary to build his reputation (Trollope 1947, as cited in Becker 2008, p. 24). It must also be considered that being most artists financially ignorant they often find themselves with contracts that alienate their benefits (Becker 2008)—for instance on the basis of such a contract a musician can have a gold record without making any money (Denisoff 1975, as cited in Becker 2008).

In parallel, considering the contextual causes of artists' low income, this can relate with the tendency of the market to valorise small differences and authenticity in the work of top artists, while being able to handle only a limited number of stars in an overcrowded supply of artists and art offers (Habbing 2002). Actually, artists' tendency of moving to urban centres overcrowds the art worlds in many Europeans and American cities (Getzels and Csíkszentmihályi 1976), where there is for instance an overplus of commercial galleries

---

[7]Not by chance, the 1970 s transformation of capitalism into neoliberalism—that trying to respond to global competition, technological advancement and a changing labour force produced a change of employment relationships and chronic work precarity (Merolli 2012, as cited in Blustein et al. 2016)—was inspired by the supposed attributes of artistic activity (assimilated therefore as the ones of the aimed new worker, Boltanski and Chiapello 2005, as cited in Lazzarato 2011; Osten 2011; Virno 2004, as cited in Lorey 2011). These are concepts related to "creativity", "flexibility", "mobility", "spontaneity", "autonomy", "self-motivation", "entrepreneurship", "self-responsibility" and "loft habitation".

(Habbing 2002). This over supply seems originated in the nineteenth century France's art world "overproduction crisis", which brought a precarious artistic "lumpenproletariat", used by artists like Manet as a catalyser of the Impressionist revolution against the standards of the French Academy (Bourdieu 1987). Wuggenig (2011) connects the same overproduction with the origin at that time of the view that an unrecognized artist can gain value in the long term, with new means that allow production of small pictures often painted in a quick time and the rise of a new potential market for art in the expanding middle class and more prosperous bourgeoisie. Presently, despite the tendency for low income in the arts, a large amount of individuals continue choosing to follow art studies and careers, possible because artists are more intrinsically motivated, more prone to take risks and usually uninformed about their professional future (Habbing 2002).

On the other side, being art business particularly sensitive to economic fluctuations many art dealers (e.g., gallerists) may have difficulties in paying to artists and even maintaining contracts they have with them (Becker 2008). The "artistic precariat" has also been explained (Bain and McLean 2012) on the basis of specific contextual factors, like the one of Canada, where a neo-liberal policymaking that aims to increase urban amenities that promise a good quality of life invests in ephemeral arts-led regeneration initiatives (e.g., arts festivals, music scenes) based on the low paid temporary work of culture workers.

Besides, the attempts of some (few) governments to reduce poverty in the arts trough subsidy programs instead of solving it maintain it by attracting more people to the arts professions (Habbing 2002), by encouraging an overuse of this system (Gurgand and Menger 1996) and by dissuading artists to orient their activities to the market (Aljena 2015). For instance, firms and artists use the "intermittency status" (i.e., state subsidy for artists employed for a certain time in the last months) by avoiding long-term employment commitments and by accepting short term ones (Benhamou 2011). Finally, it should not be neglected the fact that although low (compared with other professional areas), the present susceptibility of art jobs to computerisation is not null (Frey and Osborn 2013).[8] With the possible future developments of "computational creativity" (McCormack and d'Inverno 2012) and "computer art" (Lopes 2010) this vulnerability might increase and eventually also contribute in the future to unemployment and precarity in at least some art professions.

---

[8]Obliged to Peter Hermann for this reference.

3 Artists' Ontological Precarity

Artists are vulnerable workers not only due to their professional conditions (of professional precarity and insecurity) but also because, due to their status as "creative authors", they are particularly exposed to specific forms of symbolic power, competition with each other and with established or older artists (along cooperation), negotiation and gatekeeping in their attempt to be recognized ("ontological insecurity", Conde 2009). As a matter of fact artists are exposed to a variety of social pressures by other actors of the art world on their creative work that can happen through a variety of ways.

Social pressure on creative work acts most significantly through the social context's expectations and reactions regarding the work of the artist (Habbing 2002; Luhmann 2000), which can happen in a variety of forms. First, from the beginning of their training artists are pressured to work to solve problems set by their culture and historical time (i.e., to translate society's problems in artistic forms) and within a system of beliefs sanctioned by that context (DiMaggio 1991; Getzels and Csíkszentmihályi 1976). Actually, artists are constrained by the social accepted conventions in their art domain (e.g., scoring music in twelve music tones), specially to the fact that these exist in robust interdependent systems that prevent (based on habits, power interests, hierarchy, etc.) their change (Becker 2008; Bourdieu 1996). As Becker (2008) illustrates, Harry Partch composition of music in forty-two tones demanded invention of new instruments and learning to read a new notation; in the same line, many jazz musicians found the Beatles incompetent because they were not composing in the then usual eight-bar sections, disregarding the possibility they were creating mine-bar phrases by purpose. More sofisticatedly, social aesthetic standarts also "press" the artist trough his or her representation of them (Becker 2008). Moreover, an artist might be criticized if he or she doesn't conforms to a personal style to which he or she used an audience to, as it happened to the photographer Edward Weston when he deviated from his usual still life and landscapes to war pictures (Becker 2008). The same aplies when an artist becomes identified with an group and then experiences a social (limiting) expectation that his or her work conform to the style of the group (Getzels and Csíkszentmihályi 1976). In other cases an artist can be pressured by a client that orders his or her work and can even stipulate a contract that imposes specific characteristics of that work (e.g., although the era of the Renaissance contracts that would specify the colours of paintings is over, architects often find themselves constrained by clients' demands, Becker 2008). Alternatively, an artist might manage a contract with a patron (e.g., the state) or for instance a gallery. In this case, the artists might experience pressure on the

Artists' Precarity in the Context of Their Social Integration

form of demands and evaluations on the art product (e.g., style, content, media, size, quotas, deadlines); on timing impositions (e.g., dealers might want to hold a work in order to increase its value, while artists want to sell as soon as possible); and even on his public role (e.g., public appearances; acquaintances, Becker 2008; 1976). Particularly states can pressure artists to conform with political programs – for instance, in more authoritarian societies an artist can be pressured by the state to work as a propagandistic mean (Becker 2008). An illustrative case is the imposition of Pope Urban VIII on artists of representing his emblem and ocassionally bees (an element of that emblem) in a variety of commissioned works (Davis 1989). Moreover, against the erratic creative process, distributors tend to rationalize creative work (Hirsh 1972, as cited in Becker 2008). Eventualy a distributor like a galery can also pay in advance to an artist for his or her future work, possibly creating an uneasy feeling of work mortgaged (Getzels and Csíkszentmihályi 1976). Moreover, in order to achieve reputation, young artists might be tempted to compromise with opinions of critics who review their work but don't correspond to the principles that motivate their work (Getzels and Csíkszentmihályi 1976). It should be noted that the social pressures artists receive from these intermedieries between them and the market (e.g., art galleries; critics) frequently happen (with the exception of what occurs in more formal institutions) in small artistic spheres, where functionality is mixed with affection and power and relationships of the artist with others are structured on the basis of an ambiguous "gift/debt" dynamics (Conde 2009).

Paradoxically, pressure of the artist to conformity is simultaneous to social encouragement and even pressure for originality, independence, inovation and breaking of conventions (Becker 2008; Getzels and Csíkszentmihályi 1976). This connects with the fact that a source of "ontological vulnerability" for many artists relates with the contemporary loss of a stable set of symbols commonly meaningful and its correlative valorisation of change. Even if not all artists work uncomfortably in this context, this at least puts them with the program of reflecting through their art this scenario (and to be "original") and under the critique, by the broad society, of not corresponding or even destroying art (Getzels and Csíkszentmihályi 1976). These contadictions go along the fact that artists particularly face the Tocquevillean paradox in our culture: the contradiction between the social valorisation of equality and inner satisfaction (the assertion of fame and social recognition as irrelevant and corruptible) and the social valorisation of success and competition (Getzels and Csíkszentmihályi 1976). Besides pressures through cultural expectations and reactions, artists can also be constrained by non-artists that claim being annoyed or disturbed by their work's process or result (Becker 2008). As this author exemplifies, this might reflect in legal complains on film crews about neighbourhood disruption, on musicians about loud frequent sounds, on painters about smells or on any artist about "offensive" messages.

Constrains on artistic work can also take the form of limitations on needed material/human resources (e.g., some compositions of Charles Ives wrote in the 1900s could not be played by existing instruments), which can be less available in more monopolistic markets (Becker 2008). An artist might also feel constrained by the standards or interests of an executioner or technical auxiliary of his or her work. For instance, a technician might refuse to use a necessary technique that he or she considers as a sign of poor craftsmanship or for a work he or she doesn't value or finds bizarre, as it happened with the first visual poetry book "No thanks" of E. E. Cummings (*cf.* Becker 2008).

Artists' social systems also excert gatekeeping on artists (specially on female artists) and their art works by filtering their acceptance in existing art domains, being this filtering influenced by those systems' ideological openness and self-interest (often members of the system serve more themselves than the domain, Conde 2009; Csíkszentmihályi 1999). For instance, state, corporations or museums might under-support or reject works that do not conform to established values (e.g., the denial of political art by many American museums during the Vietnam War, *cf.* Becker 2008). An artist can also find him or herself pressured by a guild or academy that filters those who educates and that obstacles those that does not educate to practice (Pevsner 1940, as cited in Becker 2008). In a more extreme form, an artist can even be blocked to produce artistic works: artists that use or want to use a technology conventionally associated with a craft (e.g., art photographers at their begginings) can be socialy pressured to work as craftsmen (e.g., as commercial photographers) and so have their freedom to work as artists limited (Becker 2008). Besides, there is a prodigal history of political, religious and spontaneous acts of neglect, non-conservation, censorship, oppression (Becker 2008) exclusion (Heinich 1998a) vandalism and lately of terrorism against art works, artists and appreciators. Subtler is artist "self-censorship", on the basis of more private or interiorized social standards, like the hiding by Mark Twain of his pornographic writings (under his wife's pressure) or by Toulouse-Lautrec of his more clear brothel images, as exemplified by Becker (2008).

In opposition to gatekeeping, the social context might alienate the artists (especially dead artists) by exposing works he or she have deliberately withhold (Becker 2008). This author illustrates with the (fortunately) posthumous publication of Kafka's unpublished manuscripts (the majority of what he wrote, including *The trial* and *The castle*), by his friend Max Brod, against his orders that they should be burned. More intrusively, social pressure on artists' creative work can even demonstrate in a direct modification of the artist products by interpreters

Artists' Precarity in the Context of Their Social Integration

or persons that act as editors, as experienced by the poet Emily Dickinson who had her "illiterate" punctuation altered by professional editors (Johnson 1955, as cited in Becker 2008). Reversely, interpretors might feel preesured by artist's intructions, since as Becker (2008) remarcks they aspire to interpret them in order to maximize their advantages. Finnaly, being the end target of artists' work, audiences can naturally press artists by avoiding, giving up or not reacting positively to their works (e.g., going out in a long play, Becker 2008). In face of this variety of social pressures on their creative work, artists stand in a diversity of ways. Firstly, an artist might more or less consciously comply trough his or her work with social expectations in order to attempt to be successful and gain money (Habbing 2002). For instance, artists can react against potential censorship of their works by avoiding (or in the best-case hiding) dangerous topics (Becker 2008). This author exemplifies with the late sixteen-century English tomb sculpture that after the break with the Roman Church substituted the religious themes with symbols of the virtues of the departed. With time, social pressures can even fade out of the artist's consciousness, through interiorisation as a stronger influence on his or her work (Habbing 2002).

Alternatively, an artist might be primarily working based on an intrinsic motivation (which is higher in artists), deriving satisfaction mostly from the work itself and partly due to an internalization of the social representation of the artist as "selfless" (Habbing 2002). In this line, an artist can eventually react to social pressures to conform to accepted conventions or resource limitations by breaking with them and by creatively developing new artistic strategies or resources (e.g., as a reaction to such pressures Charles Ives wrote his then unfeasible fourth symphony for three orchestras and Harry Partch made his own musical instruments, Becker 2008). Nevertheless, although this increases the artist's freedom, it normally decreases the dissemination of his or her work (Becker 2008). Artists can also counteract to social reactions on their work—for example, artists can subtly change their product style to correct or neutralize "unwanted" social rewards perceived as undermining their reputation (Habbing 2002). Also preventively, some artists try to prevent eventual modifications of their works by other persons (e.g. interpreters) by using strategies (e.g., specifying directions) that limit those modifications (e.g., interpretative choices, Becker 2008). As example of these strategies, this author gives the example of the specification of directions and of the use of randomization procedures by contemporary composer John Cage, in order to create unfamiliar scores to his interpreters. More reactively, an artist might even react to social pressures by giving up publishing his or her work and keep it private, as it happen with Emily Dickinson that opted for not publishing through editors (Johnson 1955, as cited in Becker 2008)

Option for complying with social expectations or to go his or her own way depends partly on the *artistic conscience* or *habitus* the artist shares with artists of his or her background (Habbing 2002). For example, while fine art schools typically try to instil the value of being a "selfless" artists and of pursuing recognition (something affordable to students that usually come from above-average social milieus), applied arts schools tend to encourage commercial success. In addition, compliance with commercial pressure is higher in artists more interested in showing virtuosity than in expressing themselves (Becker 2008). Nevertheless, according to Habbing (2002), in most cases artists compromise by alternatively serving an intrinsic and an extrinsic motivation in a *motivational mix* that attempts to satisfy pleasure in art work and both recognition and survival through it. Moreover, social pressure on artists is complex since, based on a "sacralisation" of art, it exists a social representation that an artist should be selfless and non-commercial (Habbing 2002)—paradoxically an artist might comply with this social representation in order to gain monetary profit or recognition.

4 Consequences of Artist's Precarity

Involuntary precarity at the work level in general brings not only material but also psychological insecurity. As in the case of the insecurity related to unemployment, this has a deleterious effect on mental health and well-being (Blustein et al. 2016) at different levels. At the emotional level precarity tends to associate with a variety of problems: existential uncertainty and instability (Brophy 2006; Waite 2009); stress (Artazcoz et al. 2005)[9]; anxiety/fear (Benach et al. 2012, 2014; McRobbie 2011; Standing 2011; Kuster and Tsianos 2011); depression (Benach et al. 2012, 2014; McRobbie 2011); and anger (Standing 2011). At the cognitive level precarity tends to prevent workers' development of a sense of adult identity and purpose, of inclusion in social organizations (Blustein 2006; Benach et al. 2014) and of political awareness (McRobbie 2011). We can also hypothesize that precarity might hinder in individuals a "future time perspective" and therefore deregulating them, since as stated by Kergel and Hepp (2011, p. 126) it "potentially negate planning assumptions, future prospects and manageability of a regulated daily life for those who are affected.". Finally,

---

[9]Several studies also indicate a connection between work precarity and a number of physical health problems, like undesirable physiological indicators and cardiovascular risk factors (Benach and Muntaner 2007, as cited in Blustein et al. 2016).

at the behavioural level precarity might lead many workers to overwork and/or avoid taking needed time off, due to a continued uncertainty, based on a threat of job loss and a loss of control over the future (Clarke et al. 2007; Malenfant et al. 2007). Correlatively, Standing (2011) portraits the precariat as alienated and fighting with anomic, with a tendency to opportunistic behaviours and attitudes. Workers in precarity also tend to develop higher social isolation (Blustein 2006, 2011; Swanson 2012; Blustein et al. 2013; Flum 2015, as cited in Blustein et al. 2016), with fewer social connections and social support through work (Clarke et al. 2007; Evans and Gibb 2009 as cited in Blustein et al. 2016).

It seem to exist little research on the specific psychological consequences of precarity in artists. Foremost, the experience of precarity might affect artists in similar ways the ones described above for the general population. For instance, artists' troubles in selling their works, which signals them the difficulty in having it accepted, has been associated with despair, bitterness and avoidance (Levine 1972, as cited in Becker 2008). In addition, since one of the consequences of long-term poorness in general is the tendency for social isolation, artists might not be an exception to this (Habbing 2011). Moreover, in addition to the shame associated with poorness artists might feel the shame of "having failed as an artist" (Habbing 2011). It should also be considered that artists might intensify trough art the experience of their professional and ontological insecurity, as exemplified by the "born to write" perception found by Debora Ben-Shir (2008, as cited in Conde 2009) in the "identity-stories" of poets and writers (Conde 2009).

Furthermore, precarity can also have consequences in the artistic process. Actually, the split of work that many artists are obliged to (a work in the expressive arts and another in commercial arts or other area) might be lived with a sense of guilt and constrains artists' autonomy and freedom, which is a critical condition for the quality of artistic work (Habbing 2002). In fact, the widespread notion that artists' creativity demands an experience of suffering seems more a Western myth than a reality (Garcia 2004). Also, the precarious conditions of financially based free-lance systems, where artists are allocated temporally to specific art projects might make them leave these to be concluded projects and jump to a next one and loose the control of a work that ends up being changed. Becker (2008) exemplifies a situation with the movie "The Red Badge of Courage", not totally finished by John Huston, which had to move for the making of "The African Queen", and subsequently altered by MGM (Ross 1962, as cited in Becker 2008).

Nevertheless, despite this general panorama we should consider that artists' professional and ontological insecurity have different meanings for different artists depending on many factors (e.g., generation profile and career phase, labour markets, artistic specificities, Conde 2009). While for some artists insecurity is a sign of precariousness and/or impoverishment for others it might be perceived as a source of enrichment, valued eclecticism and empowerment (Conde 2009). Moreover, the experience and observation of precarity might even transform in artists on an artistic theme, as some art works seem to testify (e.g. the theme of the mountebank in early XX cent. art). This goes along with the known role of several "moderator factors" on the psychological results of precarity, like the worker's educational level (e.g., Artazcoz et al. 2005; Clarke et al. 2007) or the degree in which he or she chooses a temporary work (Benach and Muntaner 2007). Particularly regarding young art workers experience of precarity, in the context of their school to work transition and socio-professional integration, we hypothesize that precarity might affect well-being and identity construction under mediation of specific variables (Duarte 2016). Firstly, integration motives and strategies, secondly certain critical personal characteristics from which we can differentiate the personal perception of precarity, tolerance to uncertainty and contradictory demands, need of recognition, self-concept and self-efficacy, openness to compromise, coping style, ability and skills.

5 Conclusion

As analysed, artists' precarity manifests in two forms of vulnerability: professional or work insecurity; and ontological insecurity related to the nature of the creative work. These manifestations of precarity in artists are understandable on the context of the complex dynamics that characterizes artist's social integration, which involve a variety of social pressures on the artist and his or her work. As also addressed, artists stand in different ways toward these pressures and experience different consequences from them.

Although do not intending a deep analysis on the possible ways to counter act on artists' precarity, we would like to conclude with general notions regarding this issue. Concerning artists' ontological precarity, it seems that surviving and constructing an identity as an artist involves for most artists finding ways of compromising between their personal tendencies and values and the expectations of the social systems they are involved (Getzels and Csíkszentmihályi 1976; Habbing 2002). Nevertheless, some artists can cope with social pressures by financially self-supporting (e.g., through a second job) or by associating with other artists in distributing their works (e.g., the French "Salon des Refusés" in the 1860s), and therefore being independent of (and risking being taken as non-serious by) an external distributing system that would constrained them (Becker 2008).

Regarding artists' work precarity, an old strategy used by precarious artists, in order to guarantee the materials necessary for their work, was trading materials for their work or even stealing them: "Artists without money can steal; successful artists often admit, or brag, that they stole in their less successful days." (Becker 2008, p. 75). Alternatively, from a macroeconomic point of view, reduction of artists' work precarity has been typically tried through subsidy programs, but these have been counterproductive, since they attract more individuals to the arts and dissuade artists to relate with the market (Aljena 2015; Gurgand and Menger 1996; Habbing 2002). Independently of possible macro-economic changes that could be used in attempting to reduce artists' professional vulnerability (and precarity in general) different forms of action at the level of the artists themselves can be considered. Artists are in a privileged condition to articulate their precarity condition through their works. Moreover, in the line with the suggestions of Sieg (2011) regarding ways of helping workers to deal with precarity in general, artists could possibly benefit from psychosocial interventions directed to the development of self-analysis and of strategies to deal with their own precarity. In addition, development of awareness and cooperation among artists seem to configure significant "resisting" strategies. For instance, artists' organization in local collectivistic spaces where they can share resources, collaborate, build alternative community cultural economies have been observed (Osten 2011), and even suggested (Bain and McLean 2012). Furthermore, based on the suggestions of Blustein et al. (2016) regarding general precarity, we would advocate the development of research on artists' precarity (especially one that focus on artists' experiences) in order to give it a wider and deeper visibility.

Intervention in order to reduce or compensate for artists' precarity seems therefore to be possibly located both at the system's level (i.e., changes in the art world) and at the individual's level (i.e. changes in the artist). These two kinds of intervention might seem difficult to integrate, because they apparently follow different logics (changing the world *versus* changing the individual in order he or she "adapts" to the world). Nevertheless, a combination might be possible if those kinds of intervention are conceptualized in different times: changing the artist in the short term, for his or her surviving and changing the art world in the long term for a better living.[10]

---

[10]Obliged to Wolfgang Lind for inspiration on this idea, in one of many eight o'clock morning coffee talks.

References

Aljena, A. (2015). Why contemporary fine art artists are starving in Latvia? *Journal of Business Management* 10, 139–148. URL: http://www.academia.edu/19769193/WHY_CONTEMPORARY_FINE_ART_ARTISTS_ARE_STARVING_IN_LATVIA. Last accessed: 28 October 2018.

Artazcoz, L., Benach, J., Borrell, C., & Cortès, I. (2005). Social inequalities in the impact of flexible employment on different domains of psychosocial health. *Journal of Epidemiology and Community Health* 59, 761–767. doi:10.1136/jech.2004. 028704.

Bain, A., & McLean, H. (2012). The artistic precariat. *Cambridge Journal of Regions, Economy and Society, 6*(1), 93–111. doi:https://doi.org/10.1093/cjres/rss020.

Bain, A. (2005). Constructing an artistic identity. *Work, Employment, and Society, 19*, 25–46. doi:doi.org/10.1177/0950017005051280.

Becker, H. S. (2008) *Art Worlds,* 2nd ed.. Berkeley: University of California Press.

Benach, J. & Muntaner, C. (2007). Precarious employment and health: developing a research agenda. *Journal of Epidemiology and Community Health*, 61, 276–277.https://doi.org/10.1136/jech.2005.045237.

Benach, J., Puig-Barrachina,V., Vives, A., Tarafa, G. & Muntaner,C. (2012). The challenge of monitoring employment-related health inequalities. *Journal of Epidemiology and Community Health*, 66, 1085–1087.https://doi.org/10.1136/jech-2012-201103.

Benach, J., Vives, A., Amable, M., Vanroelen, C., Tarafa, G. & Muntaner, C. (2014). Precarious employment: understanding an emerging social determinant of health. *Annual Review of Public Health, 35,* 229–253. https://doi.org/10.1146/annurev-publhealth-032013-182500

Benhamou, F. (2011). Artists' labour markets. In R. Towse (Ed.) *A handbook of cultural economics*, 2nd. ed. (pp. 53–66). Cheltenham: Edward Elgar Publishing Limited

Blustein, D. L. (2006). The psychology of working: a new perspective for career development, counseling and public policy. NewYork, NY: Routledge.

Blustein, D. L. (2011). A relational theory of working. *Journal of Vocational Behaviour,* 79, 1–17. https://doi.org/10.1016/j.jvb.2010.10.004

Blustein, D. L., Kozan, S. & Connors-Kellgren, A. (2013). Unemployment and underemployment: a narrative analysis about loss. *Journal of Vocational Behaviour,* 82, 256–265. https://doi.org/10.1016/j.jvb.2013.02.005.

Blustein, D. L., Olle, C., Connors-Kellgren, A., Diamonti, A. J., Sartori, R., & Pouyaud, J. (2016). Decent work: a psychological perspective. *Frontiers In Psychology*, 7, 407. https://doi.org/10.3389/fpsyg.2016.00407.

Bourdieu, P. (1987). La révolution impressionniste, *Noroit*, 303, 3–18.

Bourdieu, P. (1996). The rules of art, genesis and structure of the literary field. Cornwall: Stanford University Press.

Brophy, E. (2006). System error: labour precarity and collective organizing at Microsoft. Canadian Journal of Communication, 31, 619–638. Doi:http://dx.doi.org/10.22230/cjc.2006 v31n3a1767.

Capiau, S. & Wiesand, A. J. (2006). *The status of artists in Europe*. Brussels: European Parliament & Ericarts.

Carita, A. (2017, February 18). Uma luta contínua chamada arte [A continuous struggle called art]. *E – A revista do Expresso*, pp. 52–57.

Christopherson, S. (2008). Beyond the self-expressive creative worker: an industry perspective on entertainment media. *Theory, Culture, and Society*, 25, 73–95. doi:http://dx.doi.org/10.1177/0263276408097797.

Clarke, M., Lewchuk, W., deWolff, A. & King, A. (2007).'This just isn't sustainable': precarious employment, stress and workers' health. *International Journal of Law and Psychiatry*, 30, 311–326. https://doi.org/10.1016/j.ijlp.2007.06.005

Conde, I. (May, 2009 11–14). Artists as vulnerable workers. Paper presented at the 3rd International Sociology Conference, Athens.

Csíkszentmihályi, M. (1999). Implications of a systems perspective for the study of creativity. In R. J. Sternberg (Ed.), *Handbook of human creativity* (pp. 313–338). New York: Cambridge University Press.

Davis, H. M. (1989). Bees on the tomb of Urban VIII. *Notes in the History of Art, 8/9*(4/1), 40–48. doi:http://dx.doi.org/10.1086/sou.8_9.4_1.23202696

DiMaggio, P. J. (1991). Constructing organizational fields as a professional project: U.S. art museums, 1920–1940. In W. Powell & P. J. DiMaggio (Eds.), *The new institutionalism in organizational analysis* (pp. 267–292). Chicago: University of Chicago Press.

Dickie, G. (1984). *The art circle: a theory of art*. New York: Haven.

Duarte, A. M. (2016, Abril 6–8). *Design of a research program on young adults' position regarding precarity*. Paper presented at the International Conference Precarious Places: Social, Cultural and Economic Aspects of Uncertainty and Anxiety in Everyday Life, Warsaw.

Frey, B. S. (2011). Public support. In R. Towse (Ed.) *A handbook of cultural economics*, 2nd. ed. (pp. 370–377). Cheltenham: Edward Elgar Publishing Limited.

Frey, C. B. & Osborne, M. (2013). *The future of employment: how susceptible are jobs to computerisation?* Oxford: University of Oxford - Oxford Martin Programme on Technology and Employment.

Garcia, E. E. (2004). Rachmaninoff and Scriabin: Creativity and suffering in talent and genius. *Psychoanalytic Review, 91*(3), 433–442. https://doi.org/10.1521/prev.91.3.423.38305.

Getzels, J. W. & Csíkszentmihályi, M. (1976). The creative vision: a longitudinal study of problem finding in art. New York: Wiley.

Glass, P. (2015). *Words without music – A memoir*. New York: Liveright Publishing Company.

Gurgand, M. & Menger, P. M. (1996). Work and compensated unemployment in the performing arts. Exogenous and endogenous uncertainty in artistic labour markets. In V. Ginsburgh & P.M. Menger (Eds.), *Economics of the Arts* (pp. 347–81). Amsterdam: Elsevier.

Haabing, H. (2002). *Why are artists poor? The exceptional economy of the arts*. Amsterdam: Amsterdam University Press.

Haabing, H. (2011). Poverty and support for artists. In R. Towse (Ed.) *A handbook of cultural economics*, 2nd. ed. (pp. 344–349). Cheltenham: Edward Elgar Publishing Limited.

Heinich, N. (1998a). *Le triple jeu de l'art contemporain*. Paris: Minuit.

Heinich, N. (1998b). The sociology of contemporary art: questions of method. In J. Schaeffer (Ed.). *Think art. Theory and Practice in the art of today* (pp. 65–76). Rotterdam: Witte de With.

Kergel, S. & Hepp, R. D. (2011). Ways of precarisation. In P. Herrmann & S. Kalaycioglu (Eds.), *Precarity – more than a challenge of social security or: cynicism of EU's concept of economic freedom* (pp. 112–127). Bremen: EHV.

Kergel, S. (2016, April 6–8). *Precarisation of creative work*. Paper presented at the International Conference Precarious Places: Social, Cultural and Economic Aspects of Uncertainty and Anxiety in Everyday Life, Warsaw.

Kuster, B. & Tsianos, V. (2011). Experiences without me, or, the uncanny grin of precarity. In G. Raunig, G. Ray & U. Wuggenig (Eds.), *Critique of Creativity: Precarity, Subjectivity and Resistance in the 'Creative Industries'* (pp. 91–99). London: MayFlyBooks.

Lazzarato, M. (2011). The misfortunes of the 'artistic critique' and of cultural employment. In G. Raunig, G. Ray & U. Wuggenig (Eds.), *Critique of Creativity: Precarity, Subjectivity and Resistance in the 'Creative Industries'* (pp. 9–21). London: MayFlyBooks.

Lorey, I. (2011). Virtuosos of freedom: on the implosion of political virtuosity and productive labour. In G. Raunig, G. Ray & U. Wuggenig (Eds.), *Critique of Creativity: Precarity, Subjectivity and Resistance in the 'Creative Industries'* (pp. 79–90). London: MayFlyBooks.

Lopes, D. M. (2010). *A philosophy of computer art*. Oxon: Routtledge.

Luhmann, N. (2000). *Art as a social system*. Stanford: Stanford University Press.

Malenfant, R., LaRue, A. & Vézina, M. (2007). Intermittent work and well-being one foot in the door: one foo tout. *Current Sociology* 55, 814–835. https://doi.org/10.1177/0011392107081987.

Maranda, M. (2009). Waging culture: a report on the socio-economic status of canadian visual artists. Toronto: The Art Gallery of York University.

McCormack, J. & d'Inverno, M. (Eds.) (2012). *Computers and Creativity*. Berlin: Springer.

McRobbie, A. (2011). Rethinking creative economies as radical social enterprise. *Variant* 41, 32–33. URL: http://www.variant.org.uk/41texts/amcrobbie41.html, last accessed: 28. October 2018.

Menger, P.-M. (1999). Artistic labor markets and careers. *Annual Review of Sociology, 25*, 541–574. doi:doi:http://dx.doi.org/10.1146/annurev.soc.25.1.541.

Nowotny, S. (2011). Immanent effects: notes on cre-activity. In G. Raunig, G. Ray & U. Wuggenig (Eds.), *Critique of Creativity: Precarity, Subjectivity and Resistance in the 'Creative Industries'* (pp. 9–21). London: MayFlyBooks.

Oatley, K. (2011). *Such stuff as dreams – The psychology of fiction*. West Sussex: Wiley-Blackwell.

O'Mahony, J. (2001, November 24). When less means more. *The Guardian*. Retrieved from https://www.theguardian.com.

Osten, M.-v. (2011). Unpredictable outcomes/ unpredictable outcasts: on recent debates over creativity and the creative industries. In G. Raunig, G. Ray & U. Wuggenig (Eds.), *Critique of Creativity: Precarity, Subjectivity and Resistance in the 'Creative Industries'* (pp. 133–145). London: MayFlyBooks.

Parker, B. (2008). Beyond the class act: gender and race in the 'creative city' discourse. *Research in Urban Sociology* 9, 201–232. doi:https://doi.org/10.1353/fmt.2011.0018.

Ray, G. (2011). Culture Industry and the administration of terror. In G. Raunig, G. Ray & U. Wuggenig (Eds.), *Critique of Creativity: Precarity, Subjectivity and Resistance in the 'Creative Industries'* (pp. 167–180). London: MayFlyBooks.

Schlossberg (1981). A model for analyzing human adaptation to transition. The *Counseling Psychologist* 9(2), 2–18. https://doi.org/10.1177/001100008100900202.

Schoon, I. & Silbereisen, R. K. (2008). Conceptualising school-to-work transitions in context. In I. Schoon & R. K. Silbereisen (Eds.). *Transitions from school to work – Globalization, individualization, and patterns of diversity* (pp. 3–29). Cambridge: Cambridge University Press.

Sieg, A. (2011). Theorethical thoughts for psychosocial interventions in precarious working and living conditions. In P. Herrmann & S. Kalaycioglu (Eds.), *Precarity – more than a challenge of social security or: cynicism of EU's concept of economic freedom* (pp. 100 – 111). Bremen: Ehv.

Standing, G. (2011). *The Precariat: The New Dangerous Class*. Huntingdon: Bloomsbury Publishing.

Swanson, J. L. (2012). Work and psychological health, In N. A. Fouad, J. A. Carter & L. M. Subich (Eds.), *APA Handbook of counseling psychology* (pp. 3–27). Washington, D.C: American Psychological Association.

van Maanen, H. (2009). How to study art worlds. On the societal functioning of aesthetic values. Amsterdam: Amsterdam University Press.

Waite, L. (2009). A place and space for a critical geography of precarity. *Geography Compass* 3, 412–433. doi:http://dx.doi.org/10.1111/j.1749-8198.2008.00184.x.

Withers G. (1985). Artists' subsidy of the arts, *Australian Economic Papers*, 24, 290–95. doi:http://dx.doi.org/10.1111/j.1467-8454.1985.tb00117.x.

Wuggenig, U. (2011).'Creativity and innovation' in the nineteenth century: Harrison C. White and the impressionist revolution reconsidered. In G. Raunig, G. Ray & U. Wuggenig (Eds.), *Critique of Creativity: Precarity, Subjectivity and Resistance in the 'Creative Industries'* (pp. 57–75). London: MayFlyBooks.

Socioanalysis Beyond Borders: Fieldwork in a Social World in Crisis

Franz Schultheis

Abstract

During the last years, it has become an evidence that nations like Greece, Portugal or Spain, but also Italy and France, are not only deeply destabilized by the financial crisis and its consequences, but still more deeply and preoccupying by an extremely important rate of unemployment in general, and jobless young people particularly. The countries of the northern Mediterranean share this dramatic social question with their southern neighbours like Tunisia, Algeria or Egypt, where we find actually a level of economically and socially excluded young people, especially those having a high level of school and university diploma, of more than 50%. Concerning the Mediterranean region as a whole, it seems appropriate to speak of a profound crisis of social reproduction with radical long term economic and political consequences not only for this region in itself, but more and more also for the rest of the world. Together with Nikos Panayotopoulos (University of Athens) we have let from 2012 to 2015 a research project based on testimonies of Greek men and women talking about their daily life conditions under the impact of the economic crisis. One methodological question was, what does it mean to do this kind of fieldwork on social misery under these very specific conditions? This contribution tries to reflect these epistemological problems before offering some passages of an interview made by our Swiss research team.

F. Schultheis (✉)
University of St. Gallen, St. Gallen, Switzerland
e-mail: franz.schultheis@me.com

© Springer Fachmedien Wiesbaden GmbH, part of Springer Nature 2020
T. Rachwał et al. (eds.), *Precarious Places*, Prekarisierung
und soziale Entkopplung – transdisziplinäre Studien,
https://doi.org/10.1007/978-3-658-27311-8_3

> **Keywords**
> Crises sciences · Fieldwork on social misery · Interpretative method of
> sociology · Social crises of the mediterranean region · Interview study

1   Introduction

During the last years, it has become an evidence that nations like Greece, Portugal or Spain, but also Italy and France, are not only deeply destabilized by the financial crisis and its consequences, but still more deeply and preoccupying by an extremely important rate of unemployment in general, and jobless young people particularly. The countries of the northern Mediterranean share this dramatic social question with their southern neighbours like Tunisia, Algeria or Egypt, where we find actually a level of economically and socially excluded young people, especially those having a high level of school and university diploma, of more than 50%. Concerning the Mediterannean region as a whole, it seems appropriate to speak of a profound crisis of social reproduction with radical long term economic and political consequences not only for this region in itself, but more and more also for the rest of the world. The recent events called "Arabian spring" have been a rather clear demonstration of the explosive political effects of what we can call a "sacrificed generation" and it seems more than urgent to take into account seriously this dramatic crisis of large geopolitical scale, to try to reach a scientifically grounded understanding of its sociohistorical origins and determining causes.

Together with Nikos Panayoutopols (University of Athens) we have let from 2012 to 2015 a research project based on testimonies of Greek men and women talking about their daily life conditions under the impact of the economic crisis. Some of those interviews have been undertaken by scholars from a Swiss University, coming to Greece from their very privileged home country and confronting in the interview situations the problem of intercultural communication in a very specific way. What does it mean to do this kind of fieldwork on social misery under these very specific conditions. This contribution tries to reflect these epistemological problems before offering some passages of an interview made by our Swiss research team.

2 Sociology as "Crisis Sciences" (Krisenwissenschaft)

If sociology is understood essentially as a "crisis science", this is not only due to the fact that one gladly falls back on it in times of crisis as a repair workshop in order to cushion the social impact of dysfunctions of the economic system or of mistaken political decisions and their consequences.

It is rather the case that central sociological concepts such as "habitus", i.e. "the ensemble of social structures internalized or incorporated by the individual" are never as empirically clear and comprehensible as in times of crisis. Discontinuities and contradictions arise between the durable dispositions of "habitualized practices" which reflect social normality and have proved their worth before the occurrence of the crisis and the often abrupt emergence of new relationships and their requirements.

The consequent discrepancy between routinized mental, moral and behavioural dispositions and the unfamiliar new conditions is accompanied by a loss of orientation in time and space and also in regard to personal identity and role, and is frequently a source of manifold suffering.

Such a crisis penetrating the entire social context, or as one used to say "the social body", can accordingly be truly called a "collective disorientation", to borrow a term from the anamnesis of psychic pathologies. It can also be traced back to the distinctly sociological concept of "anomie" which, since Durkheim's pathbreaking study of suicide, is understood as the loss of reliable normative coordinates for orientation in the social world.

Since Durkheim we know that rapid social change, for example in the form of a radical economic upheaval in both a downward and an upward direction, regardless of whether prosperity and welfare suddenly decline or increase, is accompanied by such disorienting consequences for the individuals concerned, and the related pathological symptoms of suffering from loss of orientation take on in extreme cases the form of "anomic suicide". But, according to Durkheim, they can also occur in the shape of a radical decline in the birth rate, as could be observed in exemplary fashion among the inhabitants of the former GDR after the fall of the Berlin Wall.

In view of a profound and multiform crisis of society on a global scale, sociology is at present more and more called upon to fulfil its role as a crisis science and to make the central hot spots of the crisis, whether they are located at home or abroad, the terrain of sociological research and diagnosis. After all, the handwork of sociology in the sense of a "public sociology" consists not in waiting in the ivory tower until the burning issues of the time come to it or land on its desk for solution, but in undertaking a socioanalysis of social upheavals and their after-effects in confrontation with objective empirical circumstances, and also specifically with their subjective representations and interpretations by the individuals involved and acting within them.

While the processes of the so-called globalization, for example in the field of financial capital, are progressing at a furious speed and are reflected not least in the symptoms of crisis thematized above, social scientific research on these crises continues to be largely restricted to the national contexts and their sociologies in each case, even though the illusion is indulged in at big international conferences or in scientific collections of essays that a simple stringing together of contributions to a social issue from various national contexts opens up the path for cross-border scientific perspectives and "transnational" diagnoses.

In order to arrive at the long overdue international opening up of social scientific research and socio-critical analysis the sociologist himself must first approach the relevant scenes of the events no matter how difficult the empirical work may turn out to be in view of his "foreignness" and not least of the often not inconsiderable problems of communication. This might at first appear to be an unnecessary handicap and tempt one to follow the good advice to "stick to one's trade" and be concerned with the home-made social issues of one's own country instead of wishing to play the uninvited prophet in foreign lands. But a weighty heuristic opportunity lies concealed behind the factor of "foreignness": it is accompanied by "distance" to the apparently self-evident givens of the every-day life-world of another society. As a result of the lack of personal involvement in the social relationships to be dealt with, being foreign provides the opportunity for a participant but nonetheless critically distanced objective approach. It offers a chance for a consciously displayed "naïve curiosity" in the face of an unknown and even seemingly "alienating" reality.

One might be tempted to consider this kind of socio-analytical ethnography or ethnographic socioanalysis and the epistemic stance necessary for it in the attempt to re-enact interpretatively "foreign" subjective experiences and interpretations as a special methodological path clearly distinct from traditional sociological procedures. But this would be a fallacy and would underestimate the manifold analogies involved in the problem of understanding what is foreign beyond class borders, distances between generations, gender differences or sub-cultural particularities in the relationship between the researcher and the researched.

The interpretative method of sociology always brings with it the danger of ethnocentric perspectivity and the accompanying misunderstandings and

Socioanalysis Beyond Borders ...

misinterpretations, but we are then dealing precisely with specific variants such as class or gender ethnocentrism.

But what are the epistemological interests of social science in dealing with subjective witnesses to the experience and handling of crises in a foreign country? How far does such an analysis remain rooted in the genre of the ethnography of a singular case? How far can it claim to make an exemplary contribution to the sociology of social crises and the diagnosis of social suffering? Here one can call to mind classical predecessors and models such as Friedrich Engels: In the meantime, however, the established fact of wretched conditions in *England* will impel us to establish also the fact of wretched conditions in *Germany*", Engels wrote in the year (1845) in his preface to "The Condition of the Working Class in England", a work in which he "wanted more than a mere *abstract* knowledge of my subject; I wanted to see you in your homes, to observe you in your every-day life, to chat with you on your condition and grievances" (Engels 1845/2010, p. 33).[1]

Emphasizing that in his depiction of the everyday life of the English workers he observed and wished to observe them not as "members of a single isolated nation" but as men, as "human beings in the most emphatical meaning of the word", Engels presented a relentlessly candid analysis and critique of society in early industrial England.[2] Although it had the status of a well-informed and well-documented "country study" it aimed essentially at an empirical analysis and theoretical penetration of the "social question" of the industrial age and the corresponding forms of human suffering in the social world which went beyond the constraints of the national framework and the ethnographic character of the subject under study. In view of the general intention and relevance of Engels' study, which consciously took a concrete exemplary case as its starting point and then passed beyond it, scarcely any reader in this country would make the mistake of considering it primarily with the curious but distanced and uninvolved gaze of the "tourist" as an English "special case". No matter how much the meticulously collected detailed knowledge of English institutions (from factory laws to the school system) and the everyday world (from family life to the popular culture of the public houses) may often "disconcert" the German reader, the sensitively

---

[1]Engels, Friedrich (1845/2010). Condition of the Working Class in England. URL: https://www.marxists.org/archive/marx/works/download/pdf/condition-working-class-England.pdf. Last accessed: 24 April 2018.

[2]Marx, Karl u. Engels, Friedrich: Werke, Bd. 2, Berlin 1976, p. 225–507, hier p. 231. English translation: The Condition of the Working Class in England with an introduction by Eric Hobsbawm, Panther Books, St. Albans 1969, at pp. 19, 323–324.

depicted conditions of human life and human fates, the social contradictions and constraints disclosed in the work are nonetheless empathetically comprehensible to him "just as they are", and beyond all superficial exoticism they have the character of intercultural variations on a familiar shared basic theme.

In regard to the social question in Europe today it can be said that the state of crisis experienced in Greece and mediated through this experience is not expressed in a fundamentally different way in many neighbouring countries and that instead of being treated as a special case it ought to be taken as a kind of model case. From such a sociological point of view Greece presents a huge sociological laboratory in which all conceivable contradictions and states of tension, all the dislocations and breaks in our contemporary late capitalist society are concentrated through a burning glass, and a sociological analysis of the conditions there can provide the foundation for a more comprehensive transnational diagnosis of society and our times. This sociological laboratory includes above and first of all the members of society affected by the crisis and their subjective mental states, their changing relationships to themselves and their life projects in the time of crisis, their coping strategies and their resistance. It also includes the emerging symptoms of social and subjective disorientation and the accompanying forms of hurt and suffering. These can certainly be understood empathetically by contemporaries in the materially privileged north of Europe and can thus contribute to the prevention of shallow moralization and sweeping assignments of guilt.

The research-ethical demand formulated by Bourdieu et al., following Spinoza, in the pathbreaking study "The Weight of the World" (La Misère du Monde): "Do not deplore, do not laugh, do not hate, understand" (Polity Press 1999, p. 19), acquires even greater validity when using interpretive interviews in a foreign social context, as in the encounter between two cultural contexts or national affiliations structures of symbolic rule or hierarchical international relationships consciously or unconsciously assert themselves.

3 Excerpt of an Interview

The following text passage is an excerpt of an interview which took place in Athens, 27/06/2012. The Interviewees were Eleni (27), Theo (30) and Markos (38), unemployed university graduates and Syriza members.

I   […] perhaps you can start with the situation, the global situation, what's going on in your country? How would you say what's going on?

ELENI	I think that too many things have happened in Greece in too little time. And in two years it was like "the wave" that came to Greece.
I	A tsunami.
ELENI	Yes, a tsunami. You can see that in all areas: in education, in health, security, health insurance, in work, in our everyday life when we walk in the streets and we see *too* many people that live in the pavements and don't have a house to stay, a lot of people with drug addiction problems that are just living on the streets because there are no places to go. [...]
I	What people in Greece are the most touched by this: young people, old people, families, single people, well instructed or poor instructed; what would you say? Everybody is...?
ELENI	I think everybody... Everybody, everybody. Some people more. Ok. Some people that had loans in the banks are in very big trouble because their salary is decreased but they have to give most of their salaries to the bank, so, they have sometimes only 50 Euro to stay for the month. I think, me, myself, I am lucky because I have a family that can support me in a way. My mother has a job, my father is a..., in pension. We are okay. But the saddest thing is that we feel – and also my environment and my friends feel – that there's no way out; there's no hope, there's nothing you can do... Every day is worse and worse...; and you get really depressed and you have to fight with depression every day and find a way to survive and, also, to *change* the situation. Because young people *want* to do something. [...]
I	What about the elections? In Switzerland, the media were writing "yeah, well, but it's better for Syriza to be in the opposition because they can fight for their program better there". Is it...?
THEO	It's better for Syriza to be in the opposition; it's not better for the people. Yes, of course. [ELENI: Hm!] But I think that elections would have..., can change a thing. It's a matter of Greek

construction of power. It's not about who is Prime Minister, it's a thing that… Corrupting goes…

ELENI Yes. But I think if Syriza was in the government and the people were together on this, you know, supporting the government and working together… It's not Syriza that could change everything. It's the feeling that Syriza could, you know, grow in people that we have to fight all together, we have to work… our way out the crisis. And, ok, a government cannot change anything, a Prime Minister and a person cannot change this; it's a problem that has grass roots, you know, in the society. […]

I You've just talked about your strategies. Among these strategies you've just… you have to "do your way" and even if by… informal ways.

MARKOS Yeah, it's an informal way. Ok. In Greece there is this situation, I think, from the beginning of the State, during the nineteenth century. I don't know these things very well, it's mainly for historical reasons, how the Greek state was constructed from the beginning, on one hand; on the other hand, I think it's a typical cultural element which has to do with orthodoxy, orthodox cultural element of people. Because our relationships cannot be like the worst in Europeans, you know, typical with the states. "Non-…", I don't know if it's the correct word, non-personalized. For example, we'll go to a doctor who is not corrupted. And we say: "I come to you and this guy sent me to you"; every social relationship in Greece… And the left people often don't realize it, except if they are sociologists or something. But we do this kind of relationships. For me this has to do, also, with the corruption of course, on the one…, on one hand, but, on the other, it's a very deep cultural element which is completely different from the other… from the people from northern Europe. Completely. And, for me, that explains why we cannot have such a state as the German and Swedish people. For me it's the most basic public discussion that never has started in Greece and it's…, it has to start *now*! Now it's the time to start this discussion: "what kind of state we want and we are able to have in Greece".
[…]

I	You think you have been stigmatized by the European community? Do you feel ... the stigmatization from the other countries?
THEO	Very much. Very much. I travelled and everyone was asking me be about Greece like it's Iraq or something.
ELENI	Yeah. *[laughs a bit]* "Do you have electricity?" Yes, and in Paris. I went to a photo exhibition and they heard that I was speaking Greek and they said: "Are you Greek? Yes". And the security guy said: "Ah, I don't have a Euro to give you". And everyone was laughing. [...]
I	Does the crisis change the relationships between children and their parents? I mean, you told us something very interesting. You feel like children by still living with their parents. Does this transform the relationship? How do you manage the family relationship because of the crisis?
MARKOS	I think it's worse, first of all, because dependency is always bad. And you can't get creative and things like that, the things that, you know, when you first look at this situation... But there's also another kind of crisis that hits the young people. Because I think Greek working ages like from 18 to 65 are separated by this line, the line of crisis, the line of 2010, maybe. So maybe they have the less salary but they still have their house... they have their children, their family, they're married. From an age and downwards you get nothing of this. I mean you can't plan your life. You just wait. [...] No. But if you ask about the family relationships or something... For me, the big problems were before the crisis; the structure of the Greek family. On one hand, it replaced the lack of social state, of course... It was a very good thing. On the other hand, this...
ELENI	...was problematic.
MARKOS	Yeah..., created some problems, between the parents and ..., yeah, you know very well, I suppose. But probably the crisis..., these problems that pre-existed, they raised up or something. [...] The problem is in the symbolic aspect. All the symbolic systems have collapsed. That' why for me there is no hope. Not for me. *[laughs a*

bit] But, eh, that's why…, because all the symbolic systems are… it's not economical. […] Maybe in Greece that happened during the last two decades; from the early 90s. Ok. It didn't happen in December' 08. It was about 20 years. The Olympic Games… the stock market… the new lifestyle, ok, with, you know, luxury cars… big houses…

ELENI   …big loans…, from the bank… fake money…

MARKOS   Ok, the changing of ethical values in Greek society. All this led to the "December' 08". For me

Training for Work at the Margins of the Projective City

Fernando Marhuenda-Fluixá and Ángeles Molpeceres-Pastor

Abstract

Drawing upon the work by Boltanski and Chiapello and Boltanski and Thévenot, the training provision that is offered in Spain both to vulnerable youth and to socially excluded adults is analyzed here. It is too often the case that trainers in those programs work under temporary contracts. The reason for this is that the institutions they work for, often Non Governmental Organizations but also municipalities or trade unions, work under the so called *projective city*—i.e., a connectionist rationale. This fact has an impact upon the notion of work that these trainers portray to trainees attending their vocational training schemes, on-the-job training as well as guidance support. It is also the case that multiple and competing demands placed upon such institutions and trainers result in a fragile balance that seriously threatens their effectiveness. If transition programs and processes from education into work for vulnerable people are settled upon precarious conditions, they may be questioned for attempting control rather than transformative or emancipatory practices. The role of work as an axis for integration policies and for social inclusion is therefore under scrutiny, particularly when the trainees occupy the lowest levels of qualification and their employability will hardly compete with that of people that have not undergone processes of social exclusion. Precarity affects both the youth

F. Marhuenda-Fluixá (✉) · Á. Molpeceres-Pastor
Universitat de València, València, Spain
e-mail: marhuend@uv.es

Á. Molpeceres-Pastor
e-mail: molpecer@uv.es

© Springer Fachmedien Wiesbaden GmbH, part of Springer Nature 2020
T. Rachwał et al. (eds.), *Precarious Places*, Prekarisierung und soziale Entkopplung – transdisziplinäre Studien,
https://doi.org/10.1007/978-3-658-27311-8_4

and adult themselves as the trainers and institutions trying to foster their employability. Raising consciousness about these issues might allow those providing vocational training in the margins of the educational and training system to those in the margins of society to perform their work in alternative ways.

Keywords

Connectionist rationale · Vocational education · Employability · Transition programs · Teachers and trainers working conditions · Teachers and trainers' vocational identities · Third sector organizations

1 Introduction

This paper reflects upon research results of three different strands of research upon transition programs for youth and adult people in Spain (SEC2000-081,[1] SEJ2007-62145/EDUC,[2] EDU2013-45919-R[3]). These reflections constitute current debates we hold in our research group, formed by scholars from different disciplines: social and developmental psychology, sociology and curriculum studies and educational policy studies. It is a debate over issues we have been studying over the past 15 years: Precariousness as the horizon for young people and adults attending training provision; vulnerability as the condition upon which these people have this chance and not others; public institutions as well as non-profit organisations that become training providers with the aim to help improve the living and working and learning conditions of these people; trainers who work and manage these institutions as well as the trainees they try to educate and that have been disregarded by the education system as well as the ordinary labor market. This debate is one on professional traning, on the provision of social services, training included, but also on identities: Those of the institutions (Jacinto 1999) as well as those of trainers and trainees that are shaped and trying to be shaped. There is a clear interface among those issues.

---

[1]The formation of occupational identities in Social Guarantee Schemes. The incidence of transformations of education in vocational education and training processes.

[2]Occupational intermediation practices and the fostering of employability. Managing integration itineraries with vulnerable populations.

[3]This is a current research project funded by the Spanish Government: Training, accompanying, qualification and personal development in Work Integration Enterprises: Innovation in social inclusion through employment (EDU2013-45919-R).

Education is a field of practice, and vocational education and traning a particular arena that can serve as an adequate observatory for changes in social relations due to its location whithin the system but with the focus upon successfully leaving it and entering adult life. In the past, vocational education was the space for career initiation and development; from there it turned into the field for skill formation; while nowadays it has also shifted into a combination of positions that are occupied and the expectations upon the positions that people are going to occupy afterwards (Gil 2006; Abiétar et al. 2017). And vocational education and traning for people in the margins has become an arena where it is posible to study transitions, not only from youth into adulthood, but also from exclusion into inclusion, from education into work (or into unemployment), an space where people can redefine their own lives.

What we try to understand in these training programs, what is at the core of the debate, is whether we understand this provision as something netly mandated, as something rather undefined and even risky; whether VET provision is something useful for living on the edge or is it far more attractive and helps people surfing the wave and taking free enlightened career choices. Along the past three decades, we have seen how VET has shifted from education for employment into education instead of employment, where employment has been replaced once more, this time by employability (Llinares et al. 2016) and even by entrepreneurship. We have seen how the labor market works differently to educational processes. We have seen how the meaning of work, of decent work, of a good work, has changed. We have seen how the role and weight of training and education for work has been replaced by the role of assessment and accreditation (Chisvert et al. 2015). One question that we need to revisit is what sort of guarantee constitutes VET any longer. It is to this that we will try to find an answer in this chapter.

2 Contexts of Research

In this section we want to give a brief overview on the three aspects that help us contextualize our research: The theoretical approaches we have used in our work along the past decade, the legal reforms affecting the context of education, work and their relations along the past 40 years, those of the Democratic Spain after a long period of isolationism; the socio-historical context of those particular VET practices that provide the empirical basis for our research work; and the changes that education and training regimes have undergone in the last two decades regarding the notion and the value of education and work themselves.

2.1 The Legal Context in Historical Perspective

Spain has suffered seven overall education reforms since 1970. Every time there was a significant change in the government, a new education law was passed, as education has remained one of the main confrontation arenas between the two main political parties, conservative and social-democrats, and it has been one of the few areas where ideology still makes a difference, mainly due to the weight of the role of the Catholic Church in the provision of education: More than one third of the students of primary and secondary education are enrolled in church controlled institutions even if most of them are publicly funded. We have studied the effects of these reforms in Martínez et al. (2015), where there have been changes in the trends from an initial decentralization process into a consistent recentralization move, inspired by a combination of neo-liberal and neo-conservative trends that has shaped policy reforms in the past three decades in other Western countries.

Along this period of time, there have been more than thirty reforms in the labor market, started by the approval of the Statute of Workers as early as 1980: All other reforms ever since have meant a decrease in workers' rights and they have meant a deterioration in terms of hiring and firing policies, regulations about working conditions and allowances related to the dole. The de-regulation of the labor market has been extreme but yet the recent financial crisis of 2008 has provoked demands that last to nowadays, where international bodies like the International Monetary Fund or the World Bank still demand for more flexibility on the side of the working class and more facilities for the capital to allow, so they say, for an increase in the generation of employment.

All of the previous, both education and employment reforms, needs to be seen in the light of the poor and weak development of the Welfare State in Spain, which could have happened between 1981 and 2015, and where the increase of the public provision has been slow while the role of the third and voluntary sectors has been encouraged (Martínez et al. 2015), hence encouraging the charities to be involved in the provision of social services to an extent that there are a few nation-wide institutions that are as relevant providers as the municipalities: Caritas, the Red Cross, the National Organization of Blind People (ONCE) as well as the General Secretariat of the Roma People (Fundación Secretariado General Gitano). These developments have been characterized by relying a large part of the social services upon private donations on the one side, and some saving banks institutions acting as main sources of funding that might even replace the regulative role of the public system due to its lack of sustainability, particularly after the application of austerity measures in the past decade.

2.2 Vocational Education and Training as the Field for Empirical Research

Wage society, as the main embodiment of a civic-industrial compromise described by Boltanski and Thévenot (2006), had to cope from its very beginning with the problem posed by unemployable people—the invalids, the physically or mentally disabled, the deviants. These people challenged the compatibility of two quite different grounds for social inclusion—on the one hand, an industrial criterion whereby full membership in society would only be accomplished through productive contribution and, on the other, a civic criterion whereby full membership would be grounded on a potentially universal and inalienable legal statute of citizenship. Civic-industrial wage society tried to skip this issue by establishing sort of a 'dual citizenship'—an alternative system to guarantee and recognize the civil rights of the unemployable was set up, that of social assistance; while employment was still the essential device of social integration for those who were potentially employable, by means of social insurance (Castel 2002).

However, the crisis of full employment would result in a new category of unproductive people who were not unemployable in principle, although they were actually unemployed. The category dichotomy between valid and invalid would fall apart, challenging the existing dual system. While social misfits—able-bodied, but socially unproductive people—had long created tension and doubts as to which of both systems they belonged to, massive unemployment suddenly increased the volume as well as the awareness of an 'intermediate class' between both traditional categories (Castel 2002).

The most significant consequence of this phenomenon might be the shift from the clear boundaries of a dichotomous model of valid/invalid, insurance/assistance, labor market/social aid, towards a new model of quantifiable and graduated deficit, whereby the distance that sets each individual apart from full productive contribution was regarded as a deficiency that must be compensated and overcome.

Such a 'personal deficit perspective', that started to be massively applied to unemployed people during the 80s and 90s, resulted in the emergence of the 'insertion system'—a new kind of intermediate social space between the wage-productive space of the integrated and the aid-unproductive space of the unemployable. This system, although initially operating as an aid system, strived to bring unemployed people into a wage statute of full productive contribution and thus full citizenship. The development of differential policies aiming to 'normalize' aptitudes and opportunities of lacking social groups became key in an evolving assimilation rationale that made of insertion policies and integration policies two complementary arms in the pursuit of a common goal. It is in this perspective that our empirical contexts of research have to be regarded (Chisvert et al. 2018; Marhuenda 2018; Martínez and Molpeceres 2010).

Most of our research has focused upon educational provision 'in the margins', this expression having two different meanings. On the one hand, by 'the margins' we refer to educational offers that take place away from the educational system, hardly recognized by it and out of the control of schools, beyond the legal responsibility of teachers. It is the education happening in the borders of the system. In the other hand, this educational field is also 'in the margins' because it is addressed to people that are already out of the system, that are at risk of being excluded or that have been already excluded. These may be young people that have dropped out of the education system with no qualifications, sometimes referred to as NEETs (Marhuenda 2016; Simmons et al. 2014), or adult people that have undergone severe exclusion processes: either in prison, with addictions of different kinds, prostitution, homelessness, etc.

From an institutional and policy perspective, this VET provision—key to social insertion policies for at least three decades—finds itself at the intersection between vocational education, adult education and social education; at the crossroads between these forms of education, social services but also the social economy, mobilized by the Third Sector. VET provided in these contexts has the expectation that it will be able to contribute to social inclusion, that it will be a relevant means to facilitate integration into adult and social life and to develop the conditions necessary to achieve full citizenship while restoring one's personal life. Let us examine with more detail the features of this varied VET offer in the Spanish national context.

2.2.1 Basic Vocational Education and Training

The first one is known nowadays as Basic Vocational Education, even if it has changed name (and some features too) along the past twenty-four years: Social Guarantee Schemes, Initial Basic Qualification Programs, nowadays Basic Vocational Programs.

Basic VET has a threefold purpose: Guaranteeing the right to education, this implying retention within the system even if sometimes through an external provider of education; initiation into an occupation, through the provision of a basic acknowledged qualification for low achievers; and all of these while safeguarding transition into adulthood, through a particular effort to foster personal and social development, to help people become adults, to support maturational processes.

This threefold purpose has been understood differently by each of the training providers. The training providers are secondary schools, NGOs (small locally based civic promoted institutions working for specific people or for a particular territory or neighborhood, as well as large NGOs that act and play as global actors), municipalities and trade unions as well as some employer federations. They provide a qualification at level 1, they try to move between rejection and retention, segregating while equipping the people they serve with something else, they try to provide affective and effective learning environments, they try to facilitate exploration as well as preparation in a certain occupation or occupational domain.

The staff engaged in these programs and hired by these institutions are on one side educators, teachers, people with a focus upon academic education, personal and social development; and on the other hand trainers, with their focus upon the technical competencies to be achieved, and the personal and social features they should embed, but often lacking a rigorous educational background and fairly relying upon their own experience and expertise as workers within their occupational domain.

2.2.2 Work Integration Social Enterprises

The second VET offer that we have studied since 2007 is that of Work Integration Social Enterprises, WISEs. These are entrepreneurial institutions ruled by law which are devised as transition companies, where people are hired in order to get further training and work experience, to develop working habits, to improve their professional as well as personal and social skills in order to facilitate their access into jobs within the ordinary labor market.

The purpose of WISEs is namely to achieve social inclusion for people that have been excluded from the labor market and to do so precisely through work.

Institutions promoting WISEs are of different kinds, mainly NGOs and non-profit organizations, social service providers, sometimes of a religious inspiration, often of civic nature, and to a lesser extent public institutions such as municipalities or local councils. Most of them provide social services of different nature (housing, legal advice, health support, financial aid, training provision, educational support, intermediation services with the labor market) and they have experienced how hard it is for their audience to reenter work not because of the lack of competencies but due to social prejudice, and here is where WISEs play their role, hiring these people up to three years; a time considered long enough to equip the people they hire not only with the technical skills but also with the personal, social and working competences and habits that will help them compete with other jobseekers in the ordinary labor market.

WISEs are part of the social economy and they consider themselves as social entrepreneurs. They provide staff development, they are grouped in two employer confederations (AERESS[4] and FAEDEI[5]). They should provide expansive learning environments, as they declare that their main interest is to take care of their employees.

There are around 200 such companies in Spain, employing approximately 6000 people. WISEs give people out of the system a contract lasting up to 3 years, as a transition into the ordinary labor market, while conceding good enough working conditions.

Three types of staff are employed in WISEs: We have production workers, those with the technical abilities; integration workers, under their processes of social inclusion; and accompanying workers, so defined by law, whose mission is to foster personal and social development of integration workers. In WISEs, we have trainers and apprentices that have a contract, that are subject to employment legislation. It is training provision within employment, where stability is provided. Education is the aim of these companies, and production is a means to support it.

2.2.3 Subjects of Research: Trainers and Trainees in Basic VET and WISEs

Trainees attending these two kinds of programs are young people, NEETs, early school leavers, people starting their adulthood in very complex processes (i.e. gender violence, illiterate adults, migration origins, social exclusion, long term unemployed). All of them have suffered precarious or erratic transitions: Since they left education, they have not been able to achieve what they wanted, they had to reject or lower their expectations. At some stage of their lives, they have even abjured of their own expectations, some of them have been dehumanized.

WISEs are hiring people that have been rejected by ordinary companies even if they have the skills and the accreditation. These are people willing to sign a contract for the first time in years. WISEs have to cope with people who have been out of the market for years and who lack the habits that the labor market expects, or that have alternative habits useful for their survival elsewhere.

Trainers constitute a heterogeneous group, people with many different backgrounds, not a professional group but a mix of workers with very different

---

[4]http://www.aeress.org, last accessed: 12 January 2019.
[5]http://www.faedei.org/es/, last accessed: 12 January 2019.

careers until they entered the field of non-formal VET, either under the form of basic VET or as WISEs workers. Most of them good-willed people, in search of professional development, a record of work experience in the occupational area of the training provision they are in charge of, but with a lack of career prospect as trainers, as their contracts often depend from short-term funding mechanisms and external sources (local and European administration, saving banks, donations, ...).

2.3 The Emergence of a Connectionist Rationale in Education and Training Regimes

In an effort to rend different national VET systems comparable, Eric Verdier (2011, 2016) has described five different Education and Training Regimes (ERTs), regarding a *regime* as a combination of political principles, actors' logics and technical instruments that shape and are shaped by a certain conception of knowledge, a set of rules for selection and guidance of individuals, a system to access initial education and training, the funding of the VET system, etc.

Among what he labels as 'de-commodified' ETRs, Verdier distinguishes among a *corporatist* regime grounded on vocation and aiming at overall mastery of an occupation; an *academic* regime grounded on school-based selection and aiming at the provision of academic competencies and certifications of a hierarchical nature; and a *universal* regime grounded on an imperative of social cohesion and aiming at compensation for initial inequalities in both basic knowledge and practical skills. Besides, two *market* regimes are described that are grounded on utilitarian principles and regard education and training as a commodity, aiming at the development of human capital.

Armed with such schema of ideal-type ETRs, Verdier approaches the task of comparing and describing the evolution of different European national VET systems and even life-long learning policies. Among the trainers that we have come along our research, many of them are social entrepreneurs, they are proud members of this projective city, of this new way of understanding life, being connected, their agenda is their most valuable property. They are ready to start a new business, to change institutions, to go after the funding mechanisms available for them and matching their own expertise. But they also suffer multiple tensions: Lack of funding sources, lack of specific professional training, their diverse duties (mediators, counselors, trainers, workers, networkers), and very often they also have to do commercial work to find places for their trainees for their work placements but also for their own survival. They are a group of people working under precarious conditions, and they have to train people to cope with these while they face them at the same time. Both trainers and trainees, as well as Basic VET and WISEs as a certain form of educational provision, are suitable for the projective city, and they are all committed to the promotion of individuals, of their skills, of their wellbeing and living conditions, while at the same time they are committed to social transformation and to the defense of their own rights as adults and as workers, devolving them the status of citizens, one that is often neglected to people under vulnerable conditions.

3 Competing Demands, Precarious Balances

A variety of different and competing demands are expected from institutions that manage Basic VET programs, as well as WISEs: vocational qualification, social accompaniment, personal development. Promotion of technical skills, promotion of core skills, promotion of basic skills. Further literacy and technical knowledge. Fostering specialization while allowing room for flexibility. Serving learners' demands and supplying the needs of the local labour markets. Disciplining people and promoting critical thinking. Promoting autonomous work and cooperation skills. Under such plurality of demands and requirements, institutions and trainers are often caught in the crossfire of a range of disparate rationales that are not easy to reconcile—in a space of convergence and interaction between different rationales that may be promising and fertile, but it is also vulnerable to many risks.

A field of practice where different justification rationales converge has got a significant potential for self-correction and innovation. Co-existence of disparate ways to understand 'what is right' is an essential requirement of critique, because action undertaken within a certain value rationale can only be challenged from a different value rationale (Boltanski and Thévenot 2006). But such plurality also involves a degree of strain and friction that may pose a threat to goal attainment or even to the very survival of institutions operating in the field.

Conciliation of different interests and action rationales among stakeholders is an imperative requirement of joint action. But the need to overcome or ignore tensions for the sake of consensus may lead institutions and trainers to establish *compromises* between conflicting rationales. A *compromise* appears when two or more actors who differ about 'what really matters' agree to put aside their discrepancies in order to work cooperatively—they act as if there were a higher-order principle able to reconcile their dissonant assessment criteria (Boltanski 2000). For instance, take the case of WISEs, where pedagogical concepts and goals lie somewhere in-between a domestic principle of 'knowing how to behave' and the technical 'know-how' of industrial tradition. Both rationales subscribe to very different models of evaluation—domestic rationale seeking to avoid typically industrial tests focused on differences of realization and favoring a global and subjective evaluation proposal. A compromise is reached when different learning goals are assigned to different types of workers (accompanying workers and production workers). Such a compromise makes it possible for actors with different assessment rationales to coordinate and act together. However, it is inherently fragile because it avoids a showdown that might settle the dispute and, therefore, it remains open to criticism from any of the conflicting principles. Such is the case with production and accompanying roles, that are well differentiated in the handbook on educational processes in WISEs (FAEDEI/AERESS 2014); but then very often this is an ideal pattern that finds no correspondence in everyday practice in WISEs. Their practice proves to be far more complex and not always as educational or productive as one might expect.

Accompanying practices are sometimes resisted and even rejected in some cases, as adult people do not perceive the need to be reeducated, thinking of WISEs as ordinary employment, where they are producers, sometimes confusing educational practices with psychological therapies that they do not always want to do. This has been more the case in men than in women, as the latter are willing to improve their self-esteem and their ability to cope with past situations of gender violence; and the more the accompanying role is embodied by someone away of the production tasks, the harder this result. However, when such accompanying practices are embedded in production tasks, these are often welcomed.

In some of the companies, accompanying workers retreat themselves to a second line, in order for integration workers to make their own decisions, to take control over their tasks, their production goals as well as their own personal development. In these cases, there is no curriculum to be followed, at least not one prescribed by the educators within the company, hence giving space to informal learning to happen, where most training and learning happens embedded in everyday work and relational practices.

Moreover, most accompanying workers are under strong pressure due to the manifold tasks that they are responsible of: Beyond their duties as accompanying workers in the WISEs, where their workload is very variable, they are also involved in other educational and administrative tasks in the institutions promoting WISEs, often Trusts or Civic Associations. They are often responsible for managing training plans, preparing memorandums and reports, representing their institutions in different networks (social economy, alternative funding sources), intermediation practices and job-seeking in the ordinary labor market; and some of them are also responsible to follow-up integration workers in more than just one WISE. All of these result in their educational encounters happening with a frequency lower than the one expressed as desirable. Taken this fact in relation to the rejection and resistance that we have mentioned above, the combination results in a situation where almost everyone finds comfortable, yet the actual accomplishment of WISEs manifold goals might be questioned. To this we must add the lack of support that accompanying workers express in some cases on the side of the managers of the WISEs, who tend to perceive their work as a loss in productivity, with some exceptions.

On the other hand, employment in WISEs imply a stability (up to three-year contracts) and standardization of life that most integration workers have lacked in their past, and these result in confidence and commitment that fosters their employability, understood in both internal or personal dimensions as well as in contextual terms. However, such an increase in their employability is often not enough in terms of competition with other job-seekers within the ordinary labor market. Nevertheless, the fact that integration workers experience labor as a positive feature in their lives, and not a sign of exploitation, is also a very valuable component to take into account when assessing the role WISEs play in terms of labor relations.

The feedback and support that are provided by both accompanying workers (often in the long run and around personal issues) and production workers (usually in the short term and focused upon specific production tasks, of technical and social nature) contribute to develop a sense of personal, social and occupational ability that increases self-esteem and confidence, that allows integration workers to set their own goals and rhythm of progress in their transition, and to appreciate the educational added value of supervision, rather than considering it a form of external control attempted to punish them. However, this positive sense of belonging among the staff that many WISEs manage to develop by relaxing production goals in favor of a more family-like interaction often becomes, towards the end of the contract, an obstacle in getting out of the WISE in order to search for a job in the ordinary labor market.

In summary, at least four different intertwined logics can be identified in everyday educational and work practice of those institutions that manage educational provisions aimed at socially vulnerable people. A domestic logic that entails caring for those considered part of my own group, family or tribe, and particularly 'the small' among them, fostering a sense in them that there is a group to which I belong. An industrial logic, based upon efficacy criteria, the competencies that one has developed, the productive contribution that one is able to provide. A civic logic, to which everyone is entitled, regardless of productive competences—people are entitled to a citizenship statute, this is not something that you deserve or

Training for Work at the Margins of the Projective City   63

not. And a market logic, often absent in Basic VET provision but clearly present in WISEs, due to their productive nature and their aspiration to generate economic benefits. The convergence of such disparate rationales in everyday practice is what allows WISEs and entities providing Basic VET to progress toward the accomplishment of their ambitious—if often loosely defined—goals of social inclusion through occupational training. But it is also responsible for the tensions that both trainers and trainees face on the way, something that not only has an impact upon the training they provide to their trainees but also on the very working and living conditions, sense of belonging, occupational relations and identities of the staff working in these institutions.

4 Changing Conceptions of Education and Work

Boltanski and Thévenot (2006) described six traditional 'economies of worth' or value rationales that help guide and evaluate social action in different contexts, fields and/or historical periods. However, Derouet (1989, 2005) found that only three of those rationales provide a satisfactory ground upon which to articulate educational establishments and educational practice—the *domestic* city, modeled upon the family, that inspires small *educational communities* characterized by inherent hierarchy and an imperative of protection; the *industrial* city, modeled upon the factory, that inspires *corporate training* driven by efficiency; and the *civic* city, modeled upon modern States, that inspires a *public school system* characterized by universality, egalitarianism and impersonality in the provision of services. Not surprisingly, these three rationales and/or a combination of them are prominent in the way trainers conceive their educational work. Our research for over a decade (Molpeceres 2004; Bernad and Molpeceres 2010; Bernad 2007; Martínez and Molpeceres 2010; Bernad et al. 2013) has allowed us to identify two fundamental representations that trainers and institutions in the realm of social insertion have of their job. The first of them is mainly domestic, the second one stems from the civic-industrial compromise that founds wage society.

The first conception regards work as a moral axis that fosters a sense of belonging in the community and aims at re-socializing and socially integrating people at risk of exclusion through the acquisition of fundamental work habits. Work is regarded here as an element allowing for personal development and integration rather than as a productive contribution to society. The mere fact of engaging in some sort of labor helps shape our time, organize and give sense to life spaces, place a person in a framework of obligations and responsibilities, shape and strengthen personal will—that is, labor triggers a personal and social dynamics that fosters human development. From this perspective, working is a need for people at risk of social exclusion—it requires an effort that makes them step out of their idle inertia and brings them back into a network of reciprocal commitments that constitute the very essence of sociality. In this kind of discourse, basic work attitudes such as effort and responsibility are key, and a strong emphasis is placed both on the acquisition of relevant habits such as daily attendance, punctuality, neatness and order and the development of basic social skills such as discipline, obedience and cooperation. Training for work is thus regarded as a sort of 'occupational therapy' whose ultimate goal is personal re-construction.

The second conception regards the productive dimension of work, which provides a sense of efficacy which sustains the development of both wellbeing and self-esteem, which are aims of the work with vulnerable people. By being productive people incorporate to the ordinary dynamics of modern society, and this may imply assuming the dominant values that have made them vulnerable. But the civic component of this compromise also stresses the relevance of being critical against the harming mechanisms of industrialism and the need to keep a vindicating ability to pressure institutions.

Some trainers consider work as a call (a mix of inspiration logic and domestic one), you are what you want to become, the call comes prior to the training. Then, there are people who see work as a trade or an occupation (industrial logic and justification). A third view is that of work as employment, as a position I occupy, useful to earn my living even if this is only part of my life, where there are other spheres in which I can develop my identity. This turns out into an exchange (market logic). Finally, there are those trainers who understand work as a right, a constitutional right, where inclusion comes through a job, a legal contract (civic logic); otherwise you run the risk to be stigmatized.

All of these views converge in the connectionist logic in terms of personal achievement. Change is a feature of this logic, and trainers have to be ready to change, and so they are, be it their call, their competencies, their training, their position, their rights! Trainers have become used to be flexible, adaptable and mobile. Therefore, work ends up becoming a personal achievement, an individual responsibility.

4.1 Compromising with a Connectionist Rationale in Educational Work

The logics described above are mixed and embedded in NGOs, municipalities, trade unions, employer confederations and even VET schools. And they are all

Training for Work at the Margins of the Projective City

happening at a time where the dominant logic is that of connectionism, of being networked, where one's value depends upon one's agenda and one's contacts...

We have mainly found three differentiated institutional discourses among Basic VET providers, all of them compatible with the hegemonic ruling logic described by the projective city.

First, institutions that hold both industrial and domestic logics. Institutions have to be productive, but they also have to be human, for they deliver VET provision for people in the margins. There is a compromise that we have named the 'humanitarian professional', where trainers have to do their work properly but they have to care for people, part of acting professionally is taking care for people. The aim of Basic VET for these institutions is the productivity of the character. This results in a profit for the connectionist logic, it ends up producing raising people to be productive, that is what is embedded in this combination. There is a second discourse, composed by the combination of the civic logic and the service provision, the civic and the industrial rationales. The civic criticizes the industrial for it is demobilizing people by making them productive and focusing upon the individual development of competencies. The industrial criticizes the civic for politicizing everything, not allowing people to be productive: society needs competent people, properly trained people, particularly those at risk; hence institutions have to empower them in productive and not only political ways. You have to make people competent, to train them, train them for work, for labor and for social rights. So, they come to the compromise of an 'apolitical citizenship', social rights within a productive domain. This being almost an oxymoron in itself, apolitical citizenship, turns out to be useful again for the projective city, as it is reinforcing service competition. Institutions provide services for these people, but they are trained to compete, therefore the service is not a right, people need to deserve it.

There is third discourse which is a combination of the civic and the domestic logic, the universal rights and the individual needs. Institutions cannot focus only on those that are close to them, even if the domestic logic says that they are good at dealing with people that are of the kind they are used to serve. We find here a de-standardization of the service and the training provision, while the civic logic is in favor of standardization of rights and conditions. The compromise they achieve is that of 'positive discrimination', institutions are serving the needs of diversity, which once again becomes a good means for exploitation within the projective city.

We have finally found several discourses upon educational practice, by those who train and educate. Education as pastoral care, as accompaniment work, as taking care of other persons. If you train someone who has been living in the margin, suffering, your main duty is to provide training for a person, to take care of the person, to make this person progress in personal and social terms. This is a very domestic approach, a way to moralize and discipline people, to tell and indicate them how they have to be, while you tell them that you are caring for them, so they have to behave. This discourse is somewhere between correction and protection.

A second discourse is defined by the master-trainee relation, and it lies behind the industrial logic: Working habits proper of a trade are relevant, including the socialization in the trade and the occupation, through the collective traditions of the occupation and the professional bodies. Practice is relevant not only in terms of professional life but also of adult life, there are acceptable ways to behave, one has to conduct his/her life in the socially agreed terms, be they related to shifts, sleep or rest patterns. That is the work order, the social order, that is the order of adult life. A third discourse is an empowering one, consisting of socializing people so they are conscious of their own possibilities and the conditions surrounding them. Training implies raising civic consciousness in people, so they decide whether they want to be included or to remain in the margins and to find their ways to survive out there.

In terms of the projective city, there is also the discourse of intermediation. Me, as a trainer, accompanying worker, as your job-coach or life-coach or mentor, I am here ready to activate yourself, to increase your employability, to open before you my toolbox to provide you with some contacts, and this will be a different relation, not an empowering one, not a disciplining one, not a training one.

5 Reflecting upon VET Practices Within the Projective City

As we have reached the final section of this chapter, we attempt to reflect upon our research results and come to terms with what are the complexities and the uses of VET practices, both in training provision as well as on-the-job, in dealing with precarity as a condition embedded in the life of trainers, in the sustainability of institutions, and in the vulnerability of the trainees and apprentices to whom the training on and off the job is provided. Is precarity here a condition of alienation, or do these practices, as they are conducted by trainers and institutions, an element not taken for granted but handled in a way that takes into account the situation with the focus upon the individual, with the aim to facilitate authentic social inclusion? Are these training practices helping people out of precarity? Is it possible in such practices to reach a compromise between adapting to precarity and coping with it? We have for instance women who come to work as care workers, they enter the country illegally, some institutions prepare them and make them competent in that professional domain, even through accreditation. Trainers are focusing on the individual even if institutions introduce differences between the individuals, as some succeed and some do not. Once a person reaches the status of legal, she/he gets better chances, to raise hers/his expectations, to can bring their families into the country, like their teenagers, that might end up attending a similar sort of Basic VET provision to those of their mothers.

Among the circumstances with an impact upon successful results, we have identified several. the occupation offered by the training institution or company is the first one: Gardening and cooking demand a higher qualification, like laundry services or domestic care; while others do not. A good amount of such institutions provide employment and training within the recycling domain, also with the attempt to become part of an alternative economy (including, among other practices, the development of a social balance, the contribution of the company to the society). But success also depends on the institution that you are attending: A municipality, a union, an NGO … Sometimes you do not find civic logic where you expect to find it, all of them have adapted to the context of the projective city. However, we have seen in our work that different institutions prove to be valuable for different sort of people or, to put it on other words, that different institutions play a better role according to the moment along their transition that people join them to get training. This matching process becomes therefore relevant, even if too often selection processes are either random or within a limited number of trainees.

Success is also dependent upon the trainers, that may have changed not the trade but perhaps the institution. That is the case in Basic VET, not really in WISEs. The values that trainers hold are not always shared within the institution. Depending on who is working in which institution, there are relevant matching processes, it is not everything up to training provision and competence development, but also to the selection processes. Whom is the audience that this institution serves best? And by the audience, we are now in the condition to say that this is not only an audience of trainees, but also an audience of trainers. The composition of the working teams is very relevant in order to plan a training device capable of doing a good job. We come therefore to the conclusion that different stakeholders may play a good role even despite their role, depending upon appropriate processes of matching. This implies a change in how we consider the role and value of institutions and their recruiting as well as training policies, where a series of strategies have an impact upon the success of their educational practices, from the formation of skilled labor to the education of properly mannered people, the assessment of sills, the accreditation of qualifications, the relations to the jobs that the labor market offers, or the demands set by both the public administrations and the funding sources, be they public or private.

We still have many doubts: Whether VET is at all proactive in fostering citizenship, a constitutional element, in our view, of social inclusion. Whether cooperation and political consciousness can be raised among individuals. We are clear that class consciousness was developed more than a century ago, a collective notion of work and a sense of belonging to a class was developed within vocational education policies. Yet, nowadays, can we consider VET as a subaltern offer or can it be regarded as an education provision of its own? What is the case when it comes to the education of people left aside by societal institutions? Perhaps people are learning precariousness, which is the opposed to what is desired. If you attend a training provision addressed that does not guarantee access to an accreditation, that is stigmatized insofar you learn a trade that leads you to low qualified employment, bad working conditions, low paid employment, then the answer is clear. Yet, that very same training provision happens in an institution and within educational practices where not only qualification count, but also other dimensions such as personal development, self-esteem and self-control, social and relational skills, … If we consider such training provision as part of a transition program, is this what the United Nations Office for Education, back in the 1960s once declared as permanent education, later renamed as continuing education, and most recently by the European Union authorities as lifelong learning. Is there authentic educational value within them or is such training provision rather a never-ending process and therefore tiring, exhausting, one provoking anxieties and subjecting people to precarious conditions? All of these doubts we find at a time when vocationalism, the vocationalization of education, does not suffice the end of achieving a job position, while social bonds do not depend on employment the way they used to fifty years ago.

We end up, therefore, trying to be aware of the extent to which the training provision that we have examined here contributes to a collective or to an individualizing project. Whether it is the autonomy of people that is fostered or rather a disciplining aim that tries to standardize the population in the margins. Vocational training as we have seen is a form of social engagement that can be part of resistance practices, and institutional solidarity can be developed while also fostering individual agency. The management of transitions that these training programs provide is not only a personal matter, but an institutional orientation well aware of the economic conditions and the harshness to achieve social inclusion through low qualified work nowadays. Citizenship is a right but at the same time, as we have seen in the Basic VET and WISEs examples, a condition that people can gain through education and training, where skilled work can also be part of citizenship development (Arnanz and Barba 2015; Peña-López et al. 2013; Subirats 2010). Even if we have to be aware of liberating and empathetic pedagogies (Orteu 2012), these training measures have shown capable of addressing social inclusion (Pérez 2005) beyond preparing apprentices for a subaltern workforce, not being simply practices of social control (Sales 2014), where the apprentice and the trainee is seen by the trainers and institutions as an ally not an enemy to be submitted. Employability in these institutions not always reflects the dominant view, but it may be part of vocational education for social inclusion, fostering critical views on the labor market and one's possibilities within it, trying to raise consciousness on social and political issues. These training practices do so by addressing work as a content in educational terms, co-reading the world of work and reconsidering notions of work, vocation, identity and socialization, moving away from the individual subject into a historical one.

References

Abiétar, M., Navas, A., Marhuenda, F., & Salvà F. (2017). La construcción de subjetividades en itinerarios de fracaso escolar. Itinerarios de inserción sociolaboral para adolescentes en riesgo. *Psychosocial Intervention – Intervención Psicosocial* 26 (1) 39–45.

Arnanz, E., & Barba, C. (2015). Ciudadanía y calidad democrática. Recuperar la dignidad de la política. Barcelona: Esplai.

Bernad, J. C. (2007). Noves configuracions identitàries al capitalisme flexible. València: Uveg.

Bernad J. C, Martínez I., Molpeceres M. A. (2013) Les lògiques de funcionament de la formació a les perifèries del sistema educatiu. El cas particular dels Programes de Garantia Social al País Valencià. Germanía: Alzira.

Bernad, J.C., & Molpeceres, M. A. (2010). Discursos emergentes sobre la educación en los márgenes del sistema educativo. *Revista de Educación* 341, 149–169.

Boltanski, L. and Thévenot, L. (2006). On Justification. Economies of Worth. Princeton, NJ: Princeton University Press.

Boltanski, L. (2000). El amor y la justicia como competencias: tres ensayos de sociología de la acción. Buenos Aires: Amorrortu.

Castel, R. (2002). La metamorfosis de la cuestión social. Barcelona: Paidós.

Chisvert-Tarazona, M. J., Ros-Garrido, A., Córdoba-Iñesta, A., & Marhuenda-Fluixà, F. (2015). Mapa de cualificaciones profesionales acreditables en las empresas de inserción. Certiuni Journal 1(1), 36–50.

Chisvert-Tarazona, M. J., Palomares-Montero, D., Hernáiz-Agreda, N., Salinas, M. (2018). Learning trajectories in informal settings. The case of three insertion companies. *Ciriec*, 94.

Derouet, J. L. (1989). L'établissement scolaire comme entreprise composite. Programme pour une sociologie des établissements scolaries. In L. Boltanski & L. Thévenot (eds). *Justesse et justice dans le travail*. Paris: PUF.

Derouet, J. L. (2005). Repenser la justice en education. *Education et sociétés*, 2/16, 29–40.

FAEDEI/AERESS (2014). El acompañamiento en las empresas de inserción. Madrid, Faedei-Aeress.

Gil, G. (2006). Trabajo precario... futuro incierto. Valencia, AREA.

Jacinto, C. (1999). ¿Qué es la calidad en la formación para el trabajo de jóvenes en situación de pobreza? *Por una segunda oportunidad. La formación para el trabajo de jóvenes vulnerables, Montevideo, Cinterfor-RET*, 311–341

Llinares, L., Zacarés, J. J., & Córdoba, A. (2016). Discussing employability. *Employee Relations* 38(6), 961–974.

Marhuenda, F. (2016). Becoming precarious? *Pedagogy, Culture and Society* 25(2), 309–313.

Marhuenda, F. (2018). Educadores militantes. Educar para la vida mediante el trabajo en empresas de inserción. *Educatio Siglo XXI*, 36.

Martínez, I., & Molpeceres, M. A. (2010). Lógicas de justificación en el sector asociativo. *RETS* 14, 17–40.

Martínez, I., Bernad, J. C., Molpeceres, M. A., Abiétar, M., Navas, A., Marhuenda, F., & Giménez, E. (2015). Comprehensive education boundaries and remedies on the edges of the Spanish educational system. *European educational research journal 14* (3–4) 293–311.

Molpeceres, M. A. (Ed.) (2004). Identidades y formación para el trabajo en los márgenes del Sistema educativo. Montevideo: Oit-Cinterfor.

Orteu, X. (2012). *Trabajo y vínculo social*. Barcelona: Uoc.

Peña-López, I., Zubero, I., Giménez, C., & Arnanz, E. (2013). *Ciudadanía y ONG. El nuevo papel del Tercer Sector ante el cambio de época*. Barcelona, Esplai.

Pérez, B. (Ed.) (2005). Políticas de activación y rentas mínimas. Madrid: Foessa.

Sales, A. (2014). El delito de ser pobre. Una gestión neoliberal de la marginalidad. Barcelona: Icaria.

Simmons, R., Thompson, R. and Russel, L. (2014). Education, work and social change: Young people and marginalization in post-industrial Britain. Croydon: Palgrave McMillan.

Subirats, J. (Eds.) (2010). Ciudadanía e inclusión social. El Tercer Sector y las políticas públicas de acción social. Barcelona: Esplai.

Verdier, E. (2011). Insertion professionnelle. Les 100 mots de l'éducation, Patrick Rayou & Agnès Van Zanten, Paris: PUF, 96–97. (Que sais-je?).

Verdier, E. (2016). The social conventions of guidance as a major component of Lifelong learning systems. A French-Danish-British comparison. In E. Berner & P. Gonon (eds.) *History of Vocational Education and Training in Europe: Cases, Concepts and Challenges*, Bern: Peter Lang Verlag, 29–44.

Weiterführende Literatur

Bernad, J. C., Martínez, I., Molpeceres, M. A. (2011). Trabajo, precariedad y ciudadanía. Las políticas sociolaborales en el contexto del desmantelamiento de la sociedad salarial. In A. Córdoba & I. Martínez (Eds.), *Trabajo, empleabilidad y vulnerabilidad social* (pp. 34–46). Valencia: Uveg.

Bernad, J.C., Martínez I., Molpeceres M. A., & Marhuenda, F. (2015). La transformación de las políticas educativas desde la gobernamentalidad neoliberal: El caso español como ejemplo. En Políticas Educacionais, Gestão Democrática e Movimentos Sociais: Argentina, Brasil, Espanha e Portugal. *Sao Paulo, Cultura Acadêmica*, 149–172.

Llinares, L., Córdoba, A., & Zacarés, J. J. (2011). La medida de la empleabilidad desde las empresas de inserción social. In A. Córdoba & I. Martínez (Eds.), Trabajo, empleabilidad y vulnerabilidad social (pp. 46–78). Valencia: Uveg.

Marhuenda-Fluixá, F. (2015). Dimensions educatives al voltant de les dinàmiques entre formación i treball amb persones adultes *Quaderns d'Educació Contínua* 32, 23–32.

Marhuenda-Fluixá, F. (2015). Vocational Education Abused: Precarisation Disguised as Dual System In A. Heikinnen & L. Lassnig (Eds.) *Myths and Brands in Vocational Education* (pp. 59–77). Newcastle upon Tyne: Cambridge.

Marhuenda, F.; Salvà, F.; Navas, A. and Abiétar, M. (2015). Twenty Years of Basic Vocational Education Provision in Spain: Changes and Trends.*International Journal for Research in Vocational Education and Training* 2(2), 137–151.

Placelessness and Precarity. Mobility of Labor in Quasi-Utopian Spaces

Tadeusz Rachwał

Abstract

The paper offers a reading of Guy Standing's idea of politics of paradise along with its offer of a mildly utopian agenda in the context of Thomas More's vision of an ideal world described in his *Utopia*. Standing's quasi-utopian vision of a world without uncertainties and inconveniences ascribed to the notion of the precariat seems to be a world following various strategies of securitization and seems to be following the principle of sovereignty which offers an appearance of oneness both of the state and the individual, thus regulating and "ban-optically" controlling the multiplicity and diversity of the everyday.

Keywords

Precarity · Utopia · Panopticon · Ban-opticon · Non-places

1 Introduction

Answering the question of where the precariat is taking us, Guy Standing suggests in his *The Precariat. The New Dangerous Class* that "unless the precariat is understood, its emergence could lead society towards a politics of inferno. This is not a prediction. It is a disturbing possibility. It will only be avoided if the precariat can become a class-for-itself, with effective agency, and a force for forg-

---

T. Rachwał (✉)
SWPS University of Social Sciences and Humanities, Warsaw, Poland
e-mail: trachwal@swps.edu.pl

© Springer Fachmedien Wiesbaden GmbH, part of Springer Nature 2020   73
T. Rachwał et al. (eds.), *Precarious Places*, Prekarisierung
und soziale Entkopplung – transdisziplinäre Studien,
https://doi.org/10.1007/978-3-658-27311-8_5

ing a new 'politics of paradise', a mildly utopian agenda and strategy to be taken up by politicians and by what is euphemistically called 'civil society'" (Standing 2011, p. viii). The precariat, which is "just a lot of us" (ibid., p. 183), must classify itself, become a clearly recognizable and identifiable unit of the social structure and thus begin to occupy a place within it. The threat of the politics of inferno, which Standing associates with neo-liberalism and the Darwinian principle of the survival of the fittest, anathematizes losers and "has a disquieting tendency to turn strugglers into misfits and villains, to be penalised, locked up or locked out" (ibid., p. 132). The crucial aspect of this kind of politics is the necessity of panoptical surveillance through which the state claims to grant security to its citizens, a crucial aspect of the Benthamite watchword of the greatest happiness of the greatest number in which the smaller numbers do not really count, and may be reduced by various means of exclusion. Standing's "mildly utopian agenda" of establishing the precariat as a class-for-itself seems to be posited against Bentham's fear of organized plotting, the fear of collective agency which may "jeopardize the panopticon project" (ibid., p. 133). Since the precariat itself can be broadly understood as rooted in insecurity of one's professional and social position, it is the notion, and feeling, of security which links it with state politics. The inclusion of the precariat as a self-organized class into the body politic of the state may weaken the threat of some of the precariat joining the populist choir more and more loudly singing in Europe, but it will simultaneously strengthen the global processes and ideologies of securitization along with their uses of measures and frequently extraordinary means so as to exclude those who, perhaps paradoxically, threaten the precariat with an increase of its number and of thus making their insecurity even more insecure. This seems to be the case of the problems with the control of immigration and the ideologies which treat immigrants as invaders and attackers of the otherwise peaceful order of things. What is associated with this way of thinking is the idea of place, of a secure and stable territory which, in the case of globalized economies and politics, is, as it seems, quite an anachronic notion.

If Thomas More's Utopia was literally a no-place, its milder version could be seen as a non-place (non-lieux), something which Marc Augé sees a space which allows us to look at ourselves not through the genealogy of where we come from, but through distancing ourselves from the misleading fixities of places which "exist only through the words that evoke them, and in this sense they are non-places, or rather, imaginary places: banal utopias, clichés" (Augé 1995, p. 95). Though we live in what is called the world, the broadness of the range of the word "world" is all too inclusive to be an easily identifiable place, and what is called globalization is applicable to more or less everything, perhaps also including the Moon and its vicinities which have already become at least potential object of tourist industry. More's Utopia, written quite a long time ago, was an attempt at constructing a place away from the world, a distinct place where there was no room for anxieties concerning work and employment. It also fact foresaw the necessity of control of the state's outsiders thus granting both economic and territorial security to its citizens. This was achieved not only by the lack of private property in the state, but also by control and surveillance of its citizens, though not exactly by means of the system of panoptic observation which Standing discusses in the chapter titled "A Politics of Inferno" (Standing 2011, p. 132 ff.). One point which he raises there is the necessity of making right choices, with the wrong ones trigger various mechanisms of exclusion:

> The key point for Bentham was that the prisoner was given an appearance of choice. But if he did not make the *right* choice, which was to labour hard, he would be left to 'languish on bad bread and drink his water, without a soul to speak to'. And prisoners were to be isolated, to prevent them forming 'a concert of minds'. He realised, just as neo-liberals were to realise, that collective agency would jeopardise the panopticon project. (Standing 2011, p. 133)

Choices within the panopticon project are purely individual, and it is this individuation that seems to directly observed from the central tower of power constructed in such a way, that the observed are never certain whether they are actually observed or not. More's Utopia seems to be a space constructed on a slightly different basis which is enabled by the architectural project. This project might be called a loggia-portico principle which blurs the distinction between inside and outside. This blurring seems to be a borrowing from the changes in Italian Renaissance architecture, an example of which can be the improvements of a few churches carried out by Alberti who tried to reflect the correspondence between inside and outside through the use of the same decorations both on facades and on inner walls (*cf.* Wittkower 1940, p. 17). More's architecture in Utopia seems to be a repetition of this scheme on a somehow larger scale:

> The streets are twenty feet broad; there lie gardens behind all their houses. These are large, but enclosed with buildings, that on all hands face the streets, so that every house has both a door to the street and a back door to the garden. Their doors have all two leaves, which, as they are easily opened, so they shut of their own accord; and, there being no property among them, every man may freely enter into any house whatsoever. (More 1997, p. 31)

No citizen of Utopia is, or can be, and outsider, and it seems to be this broadly understood sharing of space that defines one's belonging to the society. Though the establishment of the state was clearly colonial, its design seems to have been left to the common wisdom of the inhabitants. Utopus, the establisher, realized that singular authorship of perfection was unthinkable: "they say the whole scheme of the town was designed at first by Utopus, but he left all that belonged to the ornament and improvement of it to be added by those that should come after him, that being too much for one man to bring to perfection" (More 1997, p. 32). This say, masonic vison of a community of builders, dwellers, and thinkers may be read as a vison of togethereness based on systemic participation in which any negligence of it is, and must be, noticed by others.

Unlike the prisoners inside the cells of the Benthamite prison, the citizens of Utopia are constantly aware of being seen and it is this shared certainty of being visible that translates them into one people. If the dwellers of panopticon may take the risk of transgression, assuming they are at some moment invisible to the eye of the state, such putative moments are unthinkable in Utopia which, in this respect, may be compared to one body capable of fully controlling any movement of its parts. Thanks to what Travis DeCook calls "the society's obliteration of private space" (DeCook 2008, p. 11), the whole state itself lives in a singularity without exception, a unity in which particular families constitute the family of the people of Utopia. More clearly declares in the text that "indeed the whole island is, as it were, one family" (More 1997, p. 42), though the bond which holds this family together is the obligation to believe in one god whose name is Mithras "which is the common name by which they all express the Divine Essence, whatsoever otherwise they think it to be" (ibid., p. 79). Utopian landscape constitutes a horizontal space, or surface, of visibility upon which the Utopians can see and control the whole system of what might be called modest living, a system in which there is no possibility of having too much. This imposed modesty reverberates in Standing's mildly utopian project which implants modesty within the rather immodest system of the capitalist free market. The core of Standing's proposal is, as he puts it,

> that every legal resident of a country or community, children as well as adults, should be provided with a modest monthly payment. Each individual would have a cash card entitling them to draw a monthly amount for basic needs, to spend as they see fi t, with add-ons for special needs, such as disability. (Standing 2011, p. 171)

This "basic income" is to be shared by all legal residents, without restraining larger sums of money earned by labor, "with a waiting period for migrants, for pragmatic reasons" (Standing 2011, p 172). These "pragmatic reasons" might be various, but one of them is certainly population, the number of all legal residents within the state. The pragmatic reasons may also stand for reserve, and the waiting period as a temporary exclusion, a time of non-belonging, a purgatorial kind of precarious living before entering the projected economic paradise. Interestingly, there is no politics of purgatory in Standing's proposal, though a politics of inferno and a politics of paradise are presented in two subsequent chapters of his book. The waiting period for migrants seems to be a method of keeping balance within the state, a balance which, in the case of Great Britain's colonial past, brings in the problem of the outside of the state, of the space which as it were feeds the place of the state if need be. Standing definitely places Great Britain in the center of his considerations, and, very much like Thomas More, matches the new system against the present one. More's Utopia also follows some paths of colonial ideology though, importantly, not of colonial expansion. Colonies in Utopia stand in reserve as an invisible outside which, however, may at any time be made use of in order to secure the proportional organization of the island. The mobility of the people living in the island also mainly serves the purpose of saving its proportionality and of granting sustenance to its people.

> [L]est any city should become either too great, or by any accident be dispeopled, provision is made that none of their cities may contain above six thousand families, besides those of the country around it. ... If an accident has so lessened the number of the inhabitants of any of their towns that it cannot be made up from the other towns of the island without diminishing them too much (which is said to have fallen out but twice since they were first a people, when great numbers were carried off by the plague), the loss is then supplied by recalling as many as are wanted from their colonies, for they will abandon these rather than suffer the towns in the island to sink too low. (More 1997, p. 37)

Before they are recalled, those living in the colonies wait for admission which is based on purely pragmatic reasons. Those who live outside the island have a seemingly equal status as the inhabitants of the Island, though they simultaneously constitute a populational surplus which is sent to the "neighbouring continent" where they "fix a colony" only if the aboriginal inhabitants have "more soil than they can well cultivate" (ibid., p. 37). The colonizers simultaneously either accept those aboriginals who are willing to live with them as a part of their society, or wage war against those who do not find them attractive in the name prevention of waste: "they account it a very just cause of war for a nation to hinder others from possessing a part of that soil of which they make no use, but which is suffered to lie idle and uncultivated, since every man has, by the law of nature, a right to such a waste portion of the earth as is necessary for his subsistence" (ibid., p. 37). Utopian colonization is thus not exactly a drive to possess land, but rather a drive to possess waste land and regain it for cultivation and culture. The reserve thus produced grants security to the state Utopia, its absolute stability which is reflected in the stability of the basic unit of the state which is family. The size of the family is clearly determined by the law of the city, and any exceeding growth or diminishment of that size is brought back to the state of balance through the possibility of removing some of its members and placing them somewhere else:

> No family may have less than ten and more than sixteen persons in it, but there can be no determined number for the children under age; this rule is easily observed by removing some of the children of a more fruitful couple to any other family that does not abound so much in them. (ibid., p. 37)

Utopia stands on the visibility of proportion which grants the unity of the state, its oneness along with the oneness of its citizens. Eva Eylers writes that this formal standardisation of the island not only reflects the concept of equality, "but also finds its origins in Plato's thoughts about the adherence to the right state size for adherence to inner unity" (Eylers 2015, p. 7). Equality is also a geometry-related term, and in More it applies only to the citizens of the island, or those who, when needed to keep and maintain the proportions of the system, agree to conform to Utopia's rules.

Proportion and balance as a method of life offer a kind of living in constant measure and measuring, one of whose tools is observation. Utopia is a state of mutual observation rather than the state of surveillance. It is state in which the panoptic surveillance—which needs the center, or some headquarters of power—has already been replaced by self-discipline of one who both observes and is observed. Observation, unlike surveillance, also demands adherence, a loyalty of sorts, which, in the case of Utopia, makes one visible to himself or herself only in comparison with others, a comparison whose measure is a contiguity which grants continuity, and adhesion which translates plurality into oneness. It is this oneness which is to be protected with all possible security measures. In Utopia, this oneness is based on the equality of non-possession, on the lack of private property which regulates the even distribution of the means of sustenance. Standing's milder version of the utopian project inserts the possibility of inequality of the equal in which the precariat, offered some minimal means of survival, will not threaten the unity of the state for the sake of the security thus granted. Simultaneously, as a class for itself, it will find a secure place within the system and will do everything to protect it rather than undermine it. The problem is thus removed to the outside, to the purgatory of the waiting migrants who stand almost exactly as in More's *Utopia* as the surplus or the residue which can be made use of if there is such a need. Standing does not say where the migrants are supposed to be waiting, and this unmentioned purgatory is a place of exclusion which may well be located outside the state, or within it, though as a place beyond the state's system of securitization.

In contemporary neoliberal labor market, securitization fuels the precarity of migrants—the phenomenon which Veronica Nagy analyses on the example of Roma migrants to the United Kingdom. Securitization of migration is strictly connected with protection of citizens. In the case of EU, immigration to any of its member states may constitute a threat to other countries, a threat which was clearly expressed in the media discourse before Brexit. Additionally, the transnational mobility within the EU has created an additional outside for the individual state, an internal outside within the EU itself. This, in obvious ways, has complicated the idea of state as singular place, the issue which, implicitly, stands behind numerous nationalist and populist discourses which read it as a deprival of sovereignty. Such discourses place EU as an outside, simultaneously trying to reduce immigration to EU as a threat to both. Brexit seems to be an effect of the fear of the two outsides which make, in this case British, welfare state not their own. Interestingly, Veronica Nagy's paper brings in the question of migrants who are stereotypically seen as placeless, as a residue of nomadic nonbelonging, though, equally interestingly, she limits the scope of her paper to Roma newcomers to England from Central and Eastern Europe (Nagy 2018, p. 33), where they are frequently seen, and attacked for the same reasons. Simultaneously, however, other Central and East European migrants are frequently seen in a similar way as opportunist and welfare dependent. This threat of immigration is an important aspect of securitization and its construction by various kids of media posit this threat as existential:

> Issues that become securitised do not necessarily represent problems that are essential to the objective survival of a state, or its citizens, but rather represent situations where someone (usually a political agent) was successful in constructing an issue into an existential threat to the host society. (ibid., p. 33)

The making of the precariat into a class-for-itself inserts it within the body of the state and thus makes it a part of the securitization system of the welfare state to the exclusion of those who, like migrants, precariously live outside it and may become, however paradoxically, a threat to the precariat itself. Hence the limbo of uncertainty and the waiting period offered by Standing to those migrants who do not become embodied within the state. The embodiment of the precariat within the state may of course empower it and allow for its becoming "the agency of a politics of paradise" (Standing 2011, p. 3), though this politics, if it is confined within a state's limits, is bound to create some measures to control this paradise to come, and thus to securitize it. Standing's precariat is a new dangerous class not because it may endanger the system, but because, without organizing itself, it may follow a wrong path of intolerance and fall prey to the growing populist tendencies.

> A group that sees no future of security or identity will feel fear and frustration that could lead to it lashing out at identifiable or imagined causes of its lot. And detachment from the mainstream of economic affluence and progress is conducive to intolerance. [...] Many will be attracted by populist politicians and neo-fascist messages, a development already clearly visible across Europe, the United States and elsewhere. This is why the precariat is the dangerous class and why a 'politics of paradise' is needed that responds to its fears, insecurities and aspirations. (ibid., p. 25)

The issues of security and identity are crucial here, and fascist ideology also held up the watchword of security and pure identity. What Hitler granted the Germans in the labor conscription decree of the Office of Four-Year Plan (1938) was that "a worker could not be fired by his employer without the consent of the government employment office. He had job security, something he had rarely known during the Republic" (Shirer not dated, p. 234). More's Utopians also had job security and lived a generally secure kind of life. Standing's precariat, as it seems, should follow a different road to security and identity, a road of an organized participation in which it is the collectivity of the endeavor which brings the precarians together. The passive voice used in the demand for a politics of paradise ("is needed") does not quite explicitly define the subject and problematizes the question of the "who" who needs it. In the above formulation, at least one task of the politics of paradise is to securitize the precariat as a safe element of the capitalist system, the "who" possibly referring either to politicians and labor providers, or to the united precariat which will carry out the work of change and perform a milder kind of revolution than that of the proletariat.

Nagy notes in her article that in is not only the availability of paid and stable work that constitutes one of the sources of precarity, but also exclusion from certain kinds of labor which she sees as culturally acknowledged. This new division of labor is structurally embedded in global capitalism, and though employment outside of conventional work arrangements may go unnoticed by local authorities, the mechanisms of that kind employment "lead to social exclusion of those who are not engaged with formal employment schemes" (Nagy 2018, p. 129). This sphere of labor seems to be constituting a waiting zone within the system. This zone is posited between unemployment and the paradise of secure employment, it is an "employment niche" (ibid., p. 133) "away from bureaucratic surveillance mechanisms" (ibid., p. 133).

A niche is also a kind of non-place, a hollow or a cavity, a place within a place which may go unnoticed only as long as those who hide in it are not too numerous. A niche is also an inside which hides the outside. Gerald Rauning looks at the precariat from the perspective of Marx's idea of the lumpen proletariat which has become heterogenized and may include nearly anybody who feels, however figuratively, excluded:

> The figure of the precarious indicates dispersion, fragility, multitude. The precariat does not represent a unified, homogeneous or even ontological formation, but is instead distributed and dispersed among many hot spots, not only because of weakness or incapacity, but also as a discontinuity of geography and production, as distribution in space. (Rauning 2010, pp. 104 f.)

It is in this sense, it seems, that the precariat is already "an image of the outside permeating society" (ibid., p. 103), a space of various uncertainties which, though ascribed to an excluded minority, threatens and questions the very idea of the immutable core of society. The precariat is a fluid category and, as Rauning claims, it "cannot stand for an empirically determined problem nor for a future mode of salvation" (ibid., p. 104). The precarious multitude stands between inferno and paradise, exactly in the perhaps "limbal" space of waiting, of the not-yet of a finality which always may turn out to be only a promise. The precariat, for Rauning, is not a something, a defined class or a closed group, but rather "a constant becoming, questioning, struggling" (ibid., p. 104), a mobile non-entity for which precariousness constitutes a mode of existence. "If the precariat *is* anything at all, then it is precarious" (ibid., p. 105). It seems to be no coincidence that the idea of precarity became expressible during the complex processes of European unification. Precarity is, of course, not confinable to Europe or EU members, but it owes its appearance to the amalgamation of economic, social, political and ethical challenges which the idea of unification carries as its burden. European Union is a precarious place, a place which in a sense evades singularization, and, as I have noted earlier, is a non-place, a singularly-plural space of the work of mutuality and solidarity. This does not mean that this space can be void of precariousness, of various uncertainties and anxieties, but one in which there is no need for securitization policies which are always imaginary constructions of a utopian kind of safety which, as we have seen, is rooted in control of balance through the organized control of stability of places. Europe, as Zygmunt Bauman wrote, is an unfinished adventure, and as an adventure—with all the senses implied and connoted by that word—it is necessarily "pregnant with danger or threat of loss" (Bauman 2004, p. 2). It seems to be in this sense that the EU, as Hans Kundnani phrases it, "is a paradox: an anti-utopian utopian project" (Kundnani 2014, not paginated). The precariat stands as a kind of visible evidence of the non-ideal reality, a kind of reality without mythologies of paradises or golden ages in which all of us live and dwell, the reality which is utopian only because we, fore some reason, refuse to see and live in, organizing various means of keeping the utopia of security secure. One of those means is *ban-opticon* which, unlike Bentham's panopticon, locates those who should be excluded from the protection of the state, and sited in the state of waiting for a paradise, or a Godot, who might never come. The ban, writes Didier Bigo who has coined the term, "attempts to show how the role of routines and acceptance of everyday life protects some over others, or how the protection of these others against themselves is the profound structure which explains the 'moment' of the declaration of exception" (Bigo 2006, p. 47). Ban-opticon is a system which controls places and protects them from becoming non-places, the latter being to be eliminated at the cost of saving the sovereignty of the place, be it the place of the subject, or that of the state. Perhaps the precariat, with all the uncertainties and inconveniences to which it is exposed, is the sign of time which points to the possibility that the capital itself has no place, and the strategies securitization it disseminates throughout the space of the world are in fact the strategies of the rule of the sovereign about which the precariat does not really care, caring and resisting this rule of seeming oneness with multiplicity and diversity of the everyday. Utopias are, anyway, imaginary no-places. Those places, however, need not be blurred by making their visions milder. They are in fact here, around us and with us, in what we are doing rather than in what we should do. The problem is, of course, that of seeing no-places in the non-places which we keep building.

References

Augé, M. (1995). Non-places. An Introduction to the Anthropology of Hipermodrnity, transl. John Howe, London: Verso.

Bauman, Z. (2004). *Europe. An Unfinished Adventure*. London: Polity Press.

Bigo, D. (2006). Security, Exception, Ban and Surveillance. In David Lyon (Ed), *Theorizing Surveillance. The Panopticon and Beyond* (pp. 46–68). Routledge: Wilan.

DeCook, Travis (2008). Utopian Communication. *Studies in English Literature, 1500-1900*, Vol. 48, No. 1, 1–22.

Eylers, Eva (2015). "Thomas More's Utopia: Amaurotum and the vision of a public life." Paper presented at the international conference on "The Ideal City: between myth and reality. Representations, policies, contradictions and challenges for tomorrow's urban life." Urbino, Italy. URL: https://www.rc21.org/en/wp-content/uploads/2014/12/B2_Eylers.pdfs. Last accessed: 28. November 2018.

Kundnani, H. (2014). *Europe as Utopia*. URL: https://hanskundnani.com/2014/03/23/europe-as-utopia/. Last accessed: 28. November 2018.

More, T. (1997). *Utopia*. Dover Publications: New York.

Nagy, V. (2018). The Janus Face of Precarity – Securitisation of Roma Mobility in the UK. *Local Economy* 33(2), 127–146.

Rauning, G. (2010). A Thousand Machines. A Concise Philosophy of the Machine as Social Movement. Los Angeles: Semiotext(e).

Shirer, W. L. (not dated). The Rise and Fall of the Third Reich. A History of Nazi Germany. URL: http://www.tronest.cn/user/tronest/ebook/The+Rise+And+Fall+Of+The+Third+Reich.pdf. Last accessed: 28. November 2018

Standing, Guy (2011). *The Precariat. The New Dangerous Class*. London: Bloomsbury Academic.

Wittkower, Rudolf (1940). Alberti's Approach to Antiquity in Architecture Author(s). *Journal of the Warburg and Courtauld Institutes*, Vol. 4, No. 1, 1–18.

The Social and Political Implications of the Precariat. A Backlash or a Transformation of the Post Fordism Formation?

Piotr Sałustowicz

Abstract

The paper consists of three parts. The question, what precarity could mean, is discussed in the first part. It contains a short characteristic of the meanings of "precarity" referring to a) the human body; b) political issues; c) culture, and d) the economic situation. The main question regards insecurity resulting from employment and work relations in the Post-Fordism era. The debate on the precariat is the subject of the second part. The core of this debate is whether the precariat is a "new dangerous class" whose "historical mission" is a transformation of Post-Fordism society. Different answers are given by several experts. The last part concerns the question of the possible reaction on precarity and on the precariat. It presents a short outline of the discourse about project "Social Europe" and "unconditional basic income" regarding the precariat.

Keywords

Precarity · The precariat · Social europe · Unconditional basic income

P. Sałustowicz (✉)
SWPS University of Humanities and Social Sciences, Warsaw, Poland
e-mail: author@noreply.com

© Springer Fachmedien Wiesbaden GmbH, part of Springer Nature 2020
T. Rachwał et al. (eds.), *Precarious Places*, Prekarisierung
und soziale Entkopplung – transdisziplinäre Studien,
https://doi.org/10.1007/978-3-658-27311-8_6

1   Introduction

There is not any doubt that postmodern capitalism faces new and serious social and political challenges and different social groups try to transform agenda-based politics. Poland seems to offer an example of transformative politics nowadays— a politics of "a good change". Beside of growing skepticism: how much does this have to do with a really good change and what does this transformative politics mean socially, culturally and politically not only for Poland and those who seem to be the main supporters and beneficiaries of this politics, we could not deny that the world has been in a process of growing polarization between North and South, Rich and Poor, Included and Excluded, Educated and Uneducated, Working and Unemployed, Secured and Insecure and teeters on the brink of disaster. The Utopia of the End of History as a Victory of Democracy and the Market seems to lose its attraction for most people. The coming of Post-Fordism was a result of the economic crisis in the 70s and the neo-liberal policy of many governments in the 80s and 90s as well. But, we should not ignore such factors as globalization and technological, to some extent, revolutionary development in many spheres of life. Do we have cause for concern? Are the possible social and political implications of all these changes that have taken place in the time of Post-Fordism dangerous? If yes, for whom or for what? Do we have to expect a backlash that will aims at a return to Neo-Fordism and Neo-Keynesian policies or we have to expect a new political and social project that aims at a transformation of Post-Fordism in a new direction? What the kind of strategies could be successful: "bottom up" or "top down"?

In the fact, the end of Fordism-era means a growing of diverse kind of insecurities in the life of individuals. One of these is caused by the flexibility of the labor market. Steven P. Vallas (1999) formulates several critical reservations addressed to flexibility theory. One of them regards the question of inevitability of replacement Fordism by a new flexibility concept. He points out "that this reasoning overlooks the manifold ways through which flexibility can be achieved, several of which need involve only minor shifts in the organizational logic of Fordist institutions". (Vallas 1999, p. 75). Another critical point concerns neglecting the new dualism by Post-Fordist theory, that should "fasten on stably employed manufacturing workers who enjoy the benefits of standard work arrangements" (Vallas 1999, p. 76). It overlooks the possibilities of hiring externalized or contingent labor from other firms or the environment. These possibilities seem to be an important source of the emergence of the precariat. Another important aspect of the emerging of the precariat concerns the refashioning of the structure of work, labor markets and the employment relation itself

(Vallas 1999, p. 91). Vallas points out, that this refashioning leads to the redrawing of the boundaries that distinguish different groups of employees from one another. Especially critical is the sharp boundary that firms begin to draw between "core" and "peripheral" employees. Those in the former group perform functions that are deemed essential to the firm, while the work of the latter group is deemed dispensable (Vallas 1999, p. 91; also Buttler 2013, p. 34).

We can say, that so-called Post-Fordism time is primarily conflated with precarity and with the emergence of the precariat, for many experts a new category among working people. Precarity seems to be a substantial feature of the present situation not only of individuals but also at the macro-level (nations or international organizations such as the European Union). Precarity raises a question, how much uncertainty and insecurity is tolerable in society? In order to give an answer, it seems necessary to clarify what precarity concerns This will be the first part of my paper. Another important aspect concerning my questions refers to the debate on the precariat. In comparison to the situation of working class in the time of Fordism—era many experts notice the growing of insecurity—Standing (Standing 2013b, p. 4) numbers seven of them—on labour market that embrace a large number of people. One part of the precariat, the so called "cognitariat" seems to be able to develop a new project, or a new utopia, another part of the precariat are those, who possess low cultural and educational capital, or work places that are high uncertain/insecure, low waged, unhealthy, without any social protection. They seem to be able to carry out diverse protest actions (wild strikes or demonstrations). Observing these changes Standing (2014a, p. 8) comes to the conclusion that in the case of the precariat, we are faced with a process of the emerging of a "new dangerous class" whose "historical mission" is a transformation of Post-Fordism society. There are experts, who are rather critical to the possibilities of transformative politics carried on by the precariat. This will be subject of my second part. My last part will concern the question of the possible reaction on precarity and on the precariat. I will present a short outline of the discourse about project "Social Europe" and "unconditional basic income" regarding the precariat.

2 Precarity

Precarity means "uncertainty", "insecurity" and can concern different aspects of life. Precarity can refer to a) the human body; b) political issues; c) culture, and d) the economic situation. The question of precarity in the case of human body regards illness and death. Although there is no doubt that everybody will pass away, we are often completely uncertain about when and how. This is a cardinal feature of human life. The medical sciences try to improve this state by development of better diagnostic processes. The philosophy and religion reflect this *human condition* in order to help us manage our uncertainty. Regarding politics, in recent times we have been confronted with a growing uncertainty and insecurity. We are talking about precarity of politics in terms: a) of visible international conflicts with a realistic threat of military confrontation; b) the instability of liberal democracy (democracy fatique) due to populistic movements and political parties that receive more and more support in elections; c) of the crisis of the European Union and the worst projection of possible collapse. We are looking at Brexit with a very uncertain feeling about the future of Europe. Precarity of politics has a great impact on citizens' feelings of security.

The so-called time of postmodernism is characterized the pluralism of values and norms that creates precarity of decision making or choices regarding the "right" way of life. The responsibility of finding the right solution or choice of the "right way of life" relies on each individual, who cannot count on traditional value communities (family or class) as a deliverer of commonly accepted cultural patterns ("risk society"—Ulrich Beck). Coping with this kind of precarity requires a high level of tolerance or means an escape to religious cults or fundamentalist movements. The classical case of cultural precarity is represented "the marginal men" by Robert Ezra Park and Everett Stonequist. Of course, special attention is paid to precarity in the economy. The state of the capitalistic economy on the macro-level is precarious in terms of stability and crises. I am not going to elaborate this issue, instated, I would like to pay attention to precarity regarding employment and work relations.

The International Labour Organization defines it as 'uncertainty as to the duration of employment, multiple possible employers or a disguised or ambiguous employment relationship, a lack of access to social protection and benefits usually associated with employment, low pay, and substantial legal and practical obstacles to joining a trade union and bargaining collectively' (ILO 2012, 27 quoted Näsströma and Kalm 2015, p. 8).

Bourdieu points out that precarity is a generalized state of insecurity produced by neoliberal economic reforms (quoted Näsströma and Kalm 2015, p. 7). Judith Buttler emphasizes the question of dispensabilty and substitutability, as a source of precarity for the vast majority of people. She adds:

> I think that we can certainly say that „neo-liberalism" is responsible for this increasing precaritization of the population, but so, too, are security regimes, and new forms of state racism. (Buttler 2013, p. 33)

Schultheis (2008) shares a similar view. He refers to opinion that the present social diagnosis indicates the vulnerability of social security systems. It means that threats to existence of those, who are not able to manage a self-directed life based on material security. All those, who have only their labour to offer the market, concerns precarity und vulnerability (Schultheis 2008, p. 27). For Seymour (2012) precarity is primarily connected with mass unemployment and depends on different institutional factors existing in different countries:

> Those societies which did best had an institutionalised commitment to maintaining low unemployment that was not gainsayed by any other agenda, and which enabled them to ride out the deep recessions of the 1970s and 1980s. Those societies which saw mass unemployment tended to be those which adopted harsh austerity measures, reflecting institutional commitments to low inflation and 'sound money'. In the UK, this was partially linked to the prioritisation of the City. This is far from exhaustive, but the point is that precarity in this sense is an ensemble of concrete effects arising from consciously chosen class strategies within each capitalist formation. (Seymour 2012, para 35)

Jasiewicz (2013) defines precarity as:

> a form of exploitation, an advanced form and state of casualisation, a state of work devoid of rights, but the class is the same, the position is the same. It's just that the nature and form of exploitation has changed, intensified, capital is stronger; the relationship between capital and worker has become one of increased domination by capital. (2013, p. 157)

Ahmad (2008) points out that precarity means the loss of control of one's time:

> the right to plan one's future with a minimum of security and job certainty; the right to the minimum degree of 'predictability' that is necessary 'to build social relations and feelings of affection'. (2008, p. 303)

Such precarity is specially typical for illegal migrant workers. The level of precarity can vary depending on the categories of workers and of economy sectors as well. A high level of precarity is associated with the service sector in the new economy:

> Firstly, it illuminates the prevalence, across sectors of the creative industries, of precarity, that is, of financial, social, and existential insecurity exacerbated by the flexibilisation of labour under post-Fordism, a process exemplified by freelancing, shortterm contracts, internships, solo self-employment, and other unstable work arrangements that are familiar in creative industries. A second general observation

about the research on labour in creative industries is that greater attention has tended to be given to manifestations of precarity as compared to collective efforts to confront precarious conditions of labour and life. (de Peuter 2014, p. 266)

Jerzy Szarfenberg (2016) points out that there is an array of indicators measuring precarity. He mentions such indicators: job stability, income risk, job insecurity, job quality. The last concept is used by OECD (2016) and consists of three objective and measurable dimensions of job quality:

- Earnings quality refers to the extent to which the earnings received by workers in their jobs contribute to their well-being. While the level of earnings provides a key benchmark for assessing their contribution to material living standards, the way earnings are distributed across the workforce also matters for well-being. Therefore, the OECD measures earnings quality by an index that accounts for both the level of earnings and their distribution across the workforce.
- Labour market security captures those aspects of economic security that are related to the probability of job loss and its economic cost for workers. This is measured by the risk of unemployment which encompasses both the risk of becoming unemployed and the expected duration of unemployment. It is measured by the degree of public unemployment insurance, which takes into account both the coverage of the benefits and their generosity.
- Quality of the working environment captures non-economic aspects of job quality and includes factors that relate to the nature and content of work performed, working-time arrangements and workplace relationships. Jobs that are characterised by a high level of job demands such as time pressure or physical health risk factors, combined with insufficient job resources to accomplish the required job duties, such as work autonomy and social support at work, constitute a major health risk factor for workers. Therefore, the quality of the working environment is measured by the incidence of job strain, which is a combination of high job demands and limited job resources.

If we look at the results of the measurement of job quality, we realize that there are significant difference among countries. For example, in Portugal "earnings quality stagnated and labour market security fell considerably because of the upsurge in unemployment that is still far from being reabsorbed, while quality of the working environment improved for those people still employed. Conversely, in Sweden earnings quality improved but labour market security decreased and the quality of the working environment worsened (albeit from a relatively high level, (OECD 2016, p. 5).

3 The Precariat

Standing (2014b) points out that there are two ways of defining, what the term precariat means. The first is based on a distinctive socio-economic status—Max Weber. The second is a combination of the adjective "precarious" and the noun "proletariat" (Standing 2014b, p. 37). In this case we can claim *that the precariat is a class—in—the—making, if not yet a class—for—itself, in the Marxian sense of that term.* (Standing 2013b, p. 1). The current social class structure is characterized by fragmentation and regarding the working class or the proletariat we can observe the disappearance of the classical characteristics—of industrial workers from the time of Marx. Standing makes clear that this does not mean, that we have to do with a classless society. Quite the opposite, the class structure remains but it consists of many different groups—Standing differentiates seven: 1) elite; 2) salariat: "still in stable full—time employment, some hoping to move into the elite, the majority just enjoying the trappings of their kind, with their pensions, paid holidays and enterprise benefits, often subsidised by the state. The salariat is concentrated in large corporations, government agencies and public administration, including the civil service"(Standing 2013b, p. 1); 3) proficians—combination of "professional" and "technician"–*"covers those with bundles of skills that they can market earning high incomes on contract, as consultants or independent own—account workers";* 4) old "working class"; 5) precariat; 6) army of unemployment; 7) lumpenproletariat—people living on the margin of society (Standing 2013b, p. 1 f.; also 2014b, p. 37).

Who is the precariat? According to Standing (2013b) the precariat has the class characteristics:

> It consists of people who have minimal trust relationships with capital or the state, making it quite unlike the salariat. And it has none of the social contract relationships of the proletariat, whereby labour securities were provided in exchange for subordination and contingent loyalty, the unwritten deal underpinning welfare states. Without a bargain of trust or security in exchange for subordination, the precariat is distinctive in class terms. (Standing 2013b, p. 2)

But the precariat can be described regarding the status—it means "person's position in the labour process" (Standing 2013b, p. 2). The status of the precariat seems to be new, different from the status professional or middle-status craft occupations. Standing calls it "truncated status". He gives an example of the situation of Japanese students—He points that "higher status positions in Japanese society entail a set of rewards providing socio—economic security that is worth far more than can be measured by monetary incomes alone" (Standing 2013b, p. 3).

The lack of all those rewards is typical for the precariat and results in the understatement of income inequality. Standing (2014a) proposes various delimitation of the precariat. The main criterion is lack of labour security.

> Essentially, their labour is insecure and unstable, so that it is associated with casualisation, informalisation, agency labour, part-time labour, phoney self-employment and the new mass phenomenon of crowd-labour discussed elsewhere. (Standing 2014a, p. 3)

The precariat is suffering from a lack of the seven forms of labour-related security:

> Labour market security: Adequate income–earning opportunities; at the macro–level, this is epitomised by a government commitment to "full employment".
> Employment security: Protection against arbitrary dismissal, regulations on hiring and firing, imposition of costs on employers for failing to adhere to rules and so on.
> Job security: Ability and opportunity to retain a niche in employment, plus barriers to skill dilution, and opportunities for "upward" mobility in terms of status and income.
> Work security: Protection against accidents and illness at work, though, for example, safety and health regulations, limits on working time, unsociable hours, night work for women, as well as compensation for mishaps.
> Skill reproduction security: Opportunity to gain skills, through apprenticeships, employment training and so on, as well as opportunity to make use of competencies.
> Income security: Assurance of an adequate stable income, protected through, for example, minimum wage machinery, wage indexation, comprehensive social security, progressive taxation to reduce inequality and to supplement low incomes.
> Representation security: Possessing a collective voice in the labour market, though, for example, independent trade unions, with a right to strike. (Standing 2013b, p. 4 also 2014a, p. 41)

Other features that characterize the precariat, are—according to Standing (2014a)—a) distinctive relations to distribution; b) distinctive relations to the state; c) its class consciousness. In the first case, the precariat experiences its dependency on money wages usually experiencing fluctuations and never having income security. Again unlike the twentieth century proletariat, which experienced labour insecurity that could be covered by social insurance, the precariat is exposed to chronic uncertainty, facing a life of 'unknown unknowns' (Standing 2014a, p. 4). Standing (2014a) says that the concept of "social income" makes it possible to work out the difference between the precariat and all other groups.

A feature of the precariat is not the level of money wages or income earned at any particular moment but the lack of community support in times of need, the lack of assured enterprise or state benefits, and the lack of private benefits to supplement money earnings (Standing 2013bb, p. 5)

In the second case, the precariat experiences fewer rights than most others. He asserts that more and more people, not just migrants, are being converted into denizens, with a more limited range and depth of civil, cultural, social, political and economic rights. (Standing 2014a, p. 4).

The final distinctive feature is its class consciousness, which is a powerful sense of status frustration and relative deprivation. This has negative connotations, but it also has a radical transformative aspect, placing it between 'capital' and 'labour'. It is less likely to suffer from false consciousness while performing jobs that come its way, partly because there is no sense of loyalty or commitment in either direction. For the precariat, jobs are instrumental, not life defining. The alienation from labour is taken for granted. (Standing 2014a, p. 4).

In order to gain class consciousness, or the consciousness to be member community, the precariat would have felt itself to be a part of a labour community with solidarity but they know that they are bound in very short term relationships.

Taking these characteristics into consideration, can we treat the precariat as a new class? Standing seems to answer "yes". Many scholars are quite skeptical whether the precariat can be considered a new class "as a class−in−the−making" (Seymour 2012; Bauman 2013; Wright 2016). I do not believe that this debate at the present stage of development could give us a clear answer. How far are the differences between the precariat and other parts of working class an insurmountable obstacle? To what degree do these differences reflect more the specific "class position" of the precariat than its "class determination"? (Poulantzas quoted by Seymour 2012).

As a new phenomenon in social structure and in labour relationships the precariat could be a subject of concern from two perspectives: We can see it as a sort of social problem that is a challenge for social policy or as a new radical political potential that could be mobilised by different political parties,interest groups or social movements or it strives to be organised as an autonomous agent. To what extent these concerns should be taken seriously, results from the dynamic. Is the precariat really a quantitative growing phenomenon? If "yes", it would be meant the growing social weight of the precariat, but if "no"—then what? The answer to this question is not easy and depends on decision, who should be considered as belonging to the precariat in terms of who really suffers insecurity and uncertainty in labour relationships. In order to observe the dynamic of the precariat, we need to describe all the groups that we want to count among the precariat. The dynamic of the different parts of the precariat could result from many diverse factors. According to Standing (2014b) the precariat consists of the following groups or categories: 1) from the demographic perspective there are men and women and young and old; 2) from the "wellbeing" perspective there are "satisfied-smiling" and "unsatisfied – complaining" categories. This differentiation regards every category—we have satisfied and unsatisfied young people, the smiling aged or the complaining aged and so on Standing (2014b) also mentions ethnic minorities, the disabled, prisoners. We miss such categories as migrants/ especially undocumented (Ahmad 2008), or the academic precariat. Seymour also embraces categories that Standing refers for instance to the salariat. Seymour (2012) points out that precarity concerns *public sector workers, from the bin men to the civil servants, from contract cleaners to health professionals.*

> In the debate about the categorisation of the precariat we can differentiate (in addition to Post- Fordism) the diverse approaches as: "Cognitive Capitalism" (Fumagalli and Lucarelli 2014; Ratajczak 2015) or "the New Economy" or "Creative Economy". The New Economy and creative industry as "producing" the precariat (Ratajczak 2015, p. 66). This kind of precariat that emerges from the "creative economy, consists of artists, designers, writers, and performers, who are perfectly adapted to the freelancing profile favoured by advocates of liberalization […] Cultural word was nominated as the new face of neoliberal entrepreneurship, and its practitioners were cited as the hit-making models for the IP (intellectual property – ps) jackpot economy" (Rose 2009, p. 16).

One category, which is strongly related to "cognitive capitalism" are college-educated workers. The steadily quantitative growing number of this category of workers has an impact on the wage level of this group and on the proper adaption between qualifications and the requirements of labour market.

> For instance, in the United States 'between 2000 and 2012, the real (inflation-adjusted) wages of young high school graduates declined 12.7 percent, and the real wages of young college graduates declined 8.5 percent'. This reflects, of course, that many skilled college and university graduates are stuck in jobs that do not require advanced skills or a degree. According to the OECD, Canada has the highest over-qualification rate of advanced nations at 27 percent for all of its workers. (Means 2014, p. 8 f.)

Whether the main response to this problem lays in the educational system raises some serious doubts, when nothing radical happens in order to change the labour conditions. If we agree with the statement that educational system "needs to become more closely aligned with emergent human capital imperatives in order to produce the highly skilled, flexible and entrepreneurial workers said to be required to fill and invent the job of the future" (Means 2014, p. 2), we accept the rules of game. The college-workers are often so-called "peripherial workers", who are "outsourced or subcontracted to smaller, satellite firms (shifting work into the secondary labor market), or contracted out to temporary help firms (expanding the contingent economy)" (Vallas 1999, p. 91). In the case of their employment on the payroll base they are disadvantaged to core employees regarding access to internal labor markets, job security, and autonomy in their work (Vallas 1999, p. 91). I would like to give one example, how job applications for high qualified college workers were handled by Polish employers.[1] My example is based on the paper by Desperak (2013): [UN]Grateful slave gender dimension of the "dangerous classs"of precariat. She starts with the presentation of one of her interviewees:

> She was 28 years old, she was a graduate with three university degrees in different specializations, living together with her parents, having only some temporary or volunteer jobs and unpaid trainings. In her education she combined acquiring full teaching qualifications with art studies and a specialization in art education. Moreover, she started a new course of fashion design, to it to the profile of Lodz – a city with textile industry traditions aspiring to become the new centre of fashion. She spent years studying, and was still a student. She tried to work in her field, but apart from a training period succeeded only in getting a short substitute teaching job. To pay for her next studies, she had to take any job. She was completely depending on her parents, living with them and spending all her irregular earnings on the university fees. She never earned a penny for her future pension, nor for social or health benefits, and she started to be afraid that she would never become a pensioner, or even obtain any fulltime job as in next few years, after which time she would be too old to be accepted. (Desperak 2013, p. 125).

This experience draws Desperak's (2013) attention to questions regarding the female precariat. In order to examine gender issue she organized an anti-discriminatory experiment together with the students. Seven pairs of students of different sexes took part. They prepared "twin" CVs that were identical regarding education, qualifications and experience. The main difference between candidates was only their sex (Desperak 2013). The CVs were sent to companies. The results of this experiment surprised the researcher, because,

> ...all both male and female students experienced similar barriers – they didn't get any answers CV (communication skills, goal-orientation, and dedication to the

---

[1]The understanding of the precariat in the Polish language refers to "trash-contracts" and to "self-employment. (Desperak 2013).

job). Candidates who confirmed their will were sent to the street to sell products or services (expensive toothbrushes or frequent user cards) and promised to be paid after they sold an specific amount of them. The direct sale task was not a job, as the 'employees' didn't get any contract, usually they didn't get any money even if they succeeded and sold some products. (Desperak 2013, p. 127)

Another reaction of employers was to "'test' the candidates in call centers, and offering them 'trainings' which meant working for free in many cases. Call center jobs were the only real ones the candidates were offered, and in one case a candidate was accepted" (Desperak 2013, p. 127)

Before starting the experiment, Desperak (2013) assumed, that women would face more discrimination than men. The result was again surprising:

women got more offers. But the offers either considered jobs considered as typically female ones, as a street seller or call-center operator, or they were offered trainings or unpaid work instead of a job, as described above. Female candidates were preferred as either more talented in communication skills or as more likely to accept obviously deceiving 'offers,' in fact the male candidates more often disapproved invaluable offers. (Desperak 2013, p. 127).

Her conclusion is that women probably "are more needed by precarious labor market, on the other –by accepting its unfair rules they worsened their own position and legitimized labor market inequality, just as the grateful slave theory, mentioned above, explicates" (Desperak 2013, p. 127; also Standing 2014c). In the general terms, unemployment and underemployment of young-people is one of the main political and social concerns (Means 2014; Standing 2014c; OECD 2016). The statistical data about unemployment and underemployment of young people shows very clearly how serious this problem is in reality (see: ILO 2016):

Another group that could be considered the precariat are migrant workers. The example of the precariat consisting of rural migrants is found in the People's Republic of China:

As David McNally points out in his analysis of the Global Slump, fully three quarters of manufacturing workers in the country lack basic security of residence, access to social services and education. Given that China's workforce is currently larger than that of the OECD countries combined, this is no minor development. Within the developed capitalist societies, migration controls comprise part of a wider repertoire of racialised barriers, forms of segregation, ghettoization, 'workfare' and 'prisonfare', which according to Bourdieu's some time colleague Loïc Wacquant, is the truly novel feature of contemporary precarity (Seymour 2012, para. 14).

The Social and Political Implications of the Precariat ... 97

It is not very surprising that the phenomena of the precariat is much greater in emerging economies than in the OECD countries. In general job quality in emerging economies is significantly lower in every dimension in comparison to OECD countries (OECD 2016, p. 6). This concerns low-skilled workers. This group takes the high risk of falling into extreme low pay and it is a secondary significant source of insecurity. The OECD report points out that

> Youth and low-skilled workers are the worst off in terms of job quality in emerging economies, as in OECD countries. These two groups cumulate poor outcomes along the three dimensions of job quality together with low employment rates. Job quality is also substantially lower for workers with informal jobs compared to those in formal employment). Moreover, informality is hard to escape and starting a career with an informal job may have negative consequences for future labour market prospects (OECD 2016, p. 6).

To sum up: First of all the precariat consists of many different categories, which could be divided into two main groups: 1) "aristocracy" and 2) "subproletariat". To the first group we can count: those who possess high cultural and educational capital, such as cultural workers, academics and the Japanese 'freeters' (Standing 2011; Bodnar 2006 quoted Näsströma and Kalm 2015). The second group consists of all those, who possess low cultural and educational capital, or occupied work places that are highly uncertain/insecure, low waged, unhealthy, without any social protection. Undocumented migrants could be considered the Role Model Worker for the "subproletariat" (Ahmad 2008).

4   Social Europe and the Precariat

The future of improving the situation of the labour force (including the Precariat) in the EU seems to depend on the further realization of the project: Social Europe. Two German influential foundations: Friedrich Ebert Stiftung and Hans Böckler Stiftung published Report: Social Europe 2019 that contains the voices of leading experts and decision-makers, the voices of a deep concern. The political and social frames of the project: Social Europe have changed: The main promise of remedy of this crisis is—outside of Spain and, partly Greece—being made by the populist radical right.

> This new authoritarianism is not just manifested in anti-system leaders like Marine Le Pen of the Front National but in the nationalistic 'illiberal democracy' trumpeted by office-holders like Viktor Orban in Hungary, Recep Tayyip Erdoğan in Turkey and of course Vladimir Putin in Russia. (Wilson 2015, p. 59)

We could add Jaroslaw Kaczynski in Poland, AdF Party in Germany or PEGIDA –Movements. There is any doubt that the populist radical right enjoy a growing popularity among the populace (Foti 2009; Baranowski 2015).

The social projects of the populist radical right strengthens the impression that the State and not the European Community is much more able to respond to social problems: unemployment, precarity or poverty. To what degree can such regulations at the European level stem from the populist xenophobes, the regulations that "involves key measures to place a precarious labour market on a more secure foundation, notably a Europe wide minimum wage, the extension of the already-agreed youth guarantee to adults and the outlawing (as in the Netherlands) of zero-hours contracts?" (Wilson 2015, p. 60). Similar social program is—for instance—in process in Poland, sold as a great achievement of the government and the ruling party, that takes place independently from Brussels. Could we make the precariat responsible for growing social support for authoritarian and xenophobic solutions? Standing points out that "a particular concern is to reveal to native workers that they are not threatened by migrant workers. Both are victims of neoliberalism, and this fact should form the basis for collective action rather than feed xenophobia" (Standing 2011, p. 20).

The declared independence of a populist state policy from the European Community seems to result in the growing alienation of the citizens toward the European Community and weakens their support for it. Therefore the primary concern seems to be the integrity of the EC as a whole. The integrity of the EU could be questioned with the argument of the overstretching and possible decline the number of members. The potential candidate, who might leave the EC, is after Great Britain, France in the case the victory Presidency election by Marine Le Pen. Nobody could be absolutely sure, whether for instance Poland would not follow these countries states in the future? Assuming that one of the topics in this debate should be the situation of the Precariat and suggestions of possible improvements to its situation, it is a great surprise that the term "the precariat" does not appear in the official language of the EU. Even the question of the precariat is not *expressis verbis* mentioned in the Report. What we did find is the term: precarious part-time employment on the page; 13. Why is this issue ignored and why is it not worth receiving special attention? What does this mean? Is the precariat really "the dangerous class" or it is "the forgotten class" by politics, by trade unions or by civil society? What implications should be taken from the perspective of the precariat itself? If we consider the assessment of the perspectives of Social Europe in the next five years what can we expect in regarding the Precariat. What obstacles or threats for "Social Europe" are forecast by the experts? Schweighofer (2015) outlines a quite pessimistic scenarios in his contribution: It's

Now Or Never: More Social, Less Europe 2015! Indeed, Schweighofer (2015) starts his assessment with such astonishing words:

> The Union safeguards the interests of the employers and the mandarins in Brussels and 27 other capitals. Basically, this kind of integration is not in the interest of workers, trade unions, consumers et cetera. In the current state of affairs, more Europe means less social cohesion. Therefore, disintegration [....] could be in the interest of workers, at least to some extent (Schweighofer 2015, p. 5)

Does this mean that a large part of society, represented by trade unions is rather hostile to the EC? If we look at the present situation in Poland, we have to confirm that the coalition between the ruling party (Law and Justice) and the Trade Union "Solidarity" has indeed been based on the strong belief that the interests of workers could be better preserved domestically, independent from the EU state policy. Also, the situation of the precariat is a subject of the new domestic regulation, independently from the EC-regulation. The regulation of so called "trash contracts" did introduce two important changes that might improve the job security or quality: 1) the obligatory social security contribution and 2) minimum wage. The other feature of the precariat—short term contracts will be restricted, they have to be concluded in 3 years and after this period they must be changed into stable work relations. I am not going here to discuss the question, what the real background for this regulation is or how far we have to do with instrumental or populistic or value-driven (restoration of social justice) intentions. Independent from the answers, we can give, the fact is that the precariat is mostly a domestic issue. This impression seems to confirm this statement:

> Just take a quick look at meetings of the Social Question Working Party or the Employment Committee of the EPSCO council, a rather disillusioning experience. Europe does not give the feeling of community, solidarity, (social) security – all deep rooted emotions that the nation states and the regions do deliver, at least as far as globalisation allows and politicians stand up for them (Schweighofer 2015, p. 5).

The future prospects for the EC countries that might have a serious impact on the labour market in the coming five years, concern such issues: secular stagnation[2] that will have negative impact on the employment rate. It means:

---

[2]Secular stagnation is a condition of negligible or no economic growth in a market-based economy. When per capita income stays at relatively high levels, the percentage of savings is likely to begin exceeding the percentage of longer-term investments in, for example, infrastructure and education, that are necessary to sustain future economic growth.

Unemployment will rise in countries with lower rates (like Germany, the Netherlands and Austria) and will become structural in nature in the periphery (Greece, Spain, Portugal). Therefore, the social situation in the Euro area will get far worse, maybe in some kind of dramatic way for some countries. (Schweighofer 2015, p. 6)

Young people are the main concern of the EC as well every member state (Schweighofer 2015; Roth 2015). The EU has begun The European Youth Guarantee that could be understood as an instrument for combating the unemployment and underemployment of this social category. Schweighofer (2015) formulates a very critical reservations addressed to this program. He emphasises that although young people need primarily good-quality jobs, such job are not available in countries such as Spain, Portugal or Greece. Firstly, this was the main reason why a country like Spain argued against the Youth Guarantee in the Council negotiations. He adds:

Secondly, €6 billion in two years is not enough – we would rather need €21 billion, as the ILO says, or even more. Thirdly, almost two years after the EPSCO council made the decision on the guarantee (in February 2013), only a small amount of money has been used for programmes so far. There are two main reasons for this failure: over bureaucratic procedures in Brussels on the one hand and a lack of resources for even co-financing such small sums as 10–20% of the total on the other. All in all, in the eyes of the young unemployed, this "Youth Guarantee" must be a great disaster! (Schweighofer 2015, p. 7)

The ongoing practice and the failure of such program as the Youth Guarantee are rationales for Schweighofer's recommendation:

All structural policies in the area of education, labour markets and labour law, technology and innovation and the like are national competences (Schweighofer 2015, p. 7).

The absence of such investments (and consequently of economic growth) leads to declining levels of per capita income (and consequently of per capita savings). With the reduced percentage savings rate converging with the reduced investment rate, economic growth comes to a standstill – ie, it stagnates. In a free economy, consumers anticipating secular stagnation, might transfer their savings to more attractive-looking foreign countries. This would lead to a devaluation of their domestic currency, which would potentially boost their exports, assuming that the country did have goods or services that could be exported (Source: http://lexicon.ft.com/Term?term=secular-stagnation, last accessed: 28. November 2018).

Another contributor, Lindner (2015) points to missing the goals of the Europe 2020 strategy regarding inclusion:

> While employment has recently slightly increased in the EU's 28 member states, it still is 2% below its level of 2008 – with even bigger employment losses in the crisis countries. Most of new employment is precarious part-time employment and more and more people withdraw from the labour market altogether since they do not see any future for themselves. (2015, p. 5)

He accuses the Commission of reacting to the classic demand side crisis in a false or improper manner:

> the Commission tries to increase the labour supply by cutting back on workers' rights, decreasing employment protection, de-centralising collective bargaining and encouraging atypical and precarious employment. All those laws are implemented – often with dubious legal backing – to cut wages and prices and make Europe 'more competitive'. Never mind that this strategy backfires even in purely economic terms: decreasing incomes and prices leads to an increase in real debts, thus more defaults, lower demand and more unemployment (Lindner 2015, p. 15 f.).

From the view of the precariat the question of labour conditions is very crucial. Such regulation presents European Labour Conditions that fix the minimum standards for European Labour Conditions taking into account all new forms of labour (e.g. teleworkers, part-time workers) including the following:

- 'A guaranteed wage floor'
- basic social security services
- equal training opportunities (Diamantopoulou 2015, p. 31 f.).

Last but not least, among various suggestions for improvement addressed to the European
Community we can find providing basic income security for all:

> Providing basic income security for all in need, pursuing policies of full employment and keeping inequality within a reasonable range require regulations and institutions for quality public services, universal welfare state provisions, comprehensive collective bargaining coverage, public investment and sufficiently progressive taxation. (Hoffer 2015, p. 23)

Unconditional Basic Income appears for Standing and many others experts, or political and social movements as a response to the needs of the precariat, indeed to Post-Fordism society in general. By the way, in The Precariat Charter Standing enumerates 29 demands (Articles) important for changing conditions of the precariat (Standing 2014c, p. 151 ff.). It is worth to mention, that UBI is one of many aims of redistribution, the others are: uncertainty, time, space (the commons), education, financial knowledge and an equitable share of financial capital. (Standing 2014a, p. 8 f.). Standing (2014a) asserts that one of the crucial characteristic of the precariat is a failure of control over time "and its members must be on stand-by, flit between activities, wait for labour, do more work in case they are needed, because they never know the optimal way of allocating time. This is why the precariat can be said to suffer from an epidemic of the precariatised mind, unable to focus, undirected towards feasible goals. The precariat needs to have policies to enable it to gain control of its own time. We need a politics of time" (2014a, p. 9, similar Hardt and Negri 2005 quoted by Szlinder 2014). There is no doubt that UBI could be an effective solution to win control of time.

5 Unconditional Basic Income and the Precariat

As mentioned above Standing (Standing 2013a) belongs to the group of convinced supporters of Unconditional Basic Income (van Parijs 1995; McKay 2001; Offe 2005; Vanderborght and Van Parijs 2005; Vanderborght and van Parijs 2010; van der Veen 2010; Sałustowicz 2012; Szlinder 2014) In an interview he was asked: *You support the idea of the Universal Basic Income. Some economists say that it is—simply—economically irrational. Is it possible to put this idea into practice, or is it a utopia?* His response was:

> It is not only possible to implement a universal, unconditional basic income. It is essential to do so, if we want to escape from the awful prospect of having millions more join an increasingly insecure precariat. We have implemented a basic income in rural areas in a part of India, and in a conference in Delhi last week we showed how it could replace expensive subsidies that go mainly to the Salariat and the Indian plutocracy. Where we have implemented it, the basic income has transformed the lives of Indian villagers. If it can be operationalised in India, of course could be operationalised in every part of Europe. (Standing 2013b, p. 50)

We could ask the question, whether the social and political forces, which are able to implement UBI in Europe or in some European countries exist. Vandeborght and van Parijs (2010) give a short overview of the social and political forces that may play an eminent role in the debate on unconditional basic income. They mention the following actors or forces: trade unions, the unemployed and the precariat, political organisation (Green Parties, Left-liberal Parties, Social-democrat Parties, Left- Radical Parties). I would like to take a look at the role of the unemploymend and the precariat, which they can—according to both authors play role in the introduction of UBI. According to both authors the unemploymend and the precariat, who stay out of trade union movements, are a natural base of the supporters of unconditional basic income. At first glance, these social groups seem unfortunately to be badly equipped to organize a mass movement. In reality there are many examples of collective action carried out by both groups in order to demand or to support the UBI initiatives. Vandeborght and van Parijs (2010) mention associations of the unemploymend in the UK (1973), Netherlands (1987), Germany (2004) that were or are engaged in the networks of support for UBI. A special position seems to be held by the organisations in France: Syndicat des chomeurs (Trade union of the unemployment) and Mouvement national des homeurs et des précaires (Vanderborght and van Parijs 2010; Bescherer 2010). For Standing (Standing 2014a) the precariat represents truly transformative, dangerous lass:

> The precariat must become a class-for-itself – or enough of it must achieve sufficient commonality – in order to have the strength to abolish itself, through success. This makes it a truly transformative, dangerous class. Other classes in the current neo-liberal dystopia are utilitarian, wanting to perpetuate themselves and obtain more from existing structures. They are conservative, or reactionary, in that they are opposed to structural change. Only the precariat is positioned to be truly transformative, building on a struggle for what Hannah Arendt called 'the right to have rights'. (Standing 2014a, p. 8)

According to Standing (2014a) the precariat could be in a position to act autonomously in demanding an introduction of UBI. In fact, we probably have to expect stage to stage development. There are—according to Vandeborght and Van Parijs (2010)—already some solutions that can be considered transitive to UBI: negative tax, partial basic income, participation income and others. Participation income is defined as common and individualistic but independent from participation on social useful activities—this includes payroll work, freelance work or serving family or associations (Vanderborght and van Parijs 2010, p. 349). Regarding Polish case, it is an interesting question, whether the Program 500 plus could mean the first step to UBI in Poland. Can we say: we have crossed the Rubicon? This Program is not unconditional and is not individualistic and is not addressed to everybody (common) but to very large number of people (families with children). It is additional income for families. Some possible effects of this program could be similar to UBI—positive and negative as well. As a positive impact of the Program 500 plus could be counted:

1. A stimulation of consumption and of economic growth—this is a hope of the Polish government that 17 billion Polish Zloty of this program will encourage the growth of Gross Domestic Product. This could also have a positive impact on labour market;
2. It could help some families to improve their quality of life.
3. It could moderate the salary expectations especially of women. It might help to avoid dirty, hard, dangerous or boring and underpaid work.
4. It could contribute to spending more time on such activities as: childcare, sporting activities, community management, preparing food at home, repairing mechanical breakdowns, self- development, public education and thousands of other useful practices.

These allegedly positive effects will be strongly dependent on the individual level of family income. The families with relatively high income and with two or three children will probably take advantage. Those families with more than three children have very often very low living standards, or belong to the poor therefore we could not expect all these advantages as in case of former families. One of the crucial weakness of this program is the limitation of payment to the second and further children. The payment for the first child is possible under the condition of having of low income per head—800 zl per persons and 1200 zł in case, when one child is handicapped. In fact, the payment for the first child is exceptional because family income is defined very broadly and consists of many income resources (income from home or flat rent, from agriculture farms, even family allowances) and not only wages. The relatively low level of this additional income makes it possible to be financed from the state budget. The open question is, how far this program will encourage domestic demand and contribute to growth of GDP? What part of the profit coming from family expenditures will remain in the country and devoted to enlarge economic activities? And last but not least: the question of new taxes—who will be burdened with them? To tell the truth, the main rationale of the program 500 plus should be—from the government's view—demographic. From this perspective, this program is one of the instruments of so-called bio- politics. It means when this program achieves its main goal (desired population growth) it could be abolished. The opposition parties, which today are represented in the Parliament, seem more and less to agree with this program, because they are afraid to lose the support of the voters, but do not suggest any more radical proposals. Indeed, the results of polls show clear that overwhelming majority of the voters PIS and Kukiz 15 (95%) and more than 60% the voters of PO and Nowoczesna support the Program 500 plus. (CBOS 2016) Only Platforma Obywatelska is suggested to include also additional

The Social and Political Implications of the Precariat ... 105

income for first child as unconditional, but other parties did not make and any substantial proposal. Only the new left party "Together" (Razem) seems to be closer to the precariat and the question of UBI should be on their agenda. At the moment UBI is a subject of academic discourse, and keeps academic guys busy with dreams of a new, better society.

References

Ahmad, A.N. (2008). Dead men working: time and space in London's ('illegal') migrant economy´, Work, employment and society 22(2), 301–317.

Baranowski, M. (2015). Oblicza socjoekonomicznych nierówności - procesy prekaryzacji pracy. In Wołk, A. & Anny Potasińska, A. (Eds.), Nierówności społeczne we współczesnym świecie. Warszawa: Wydawnictwo Uniwersytetu Kardynała Stefana Wyszyńskiego, 145–156.

Bescherer, P. (2010). Alchimistes des Widerstands? Lumpen, Pauper und Prekäre im Spiegel antikapitalistischer Kritik. In K. Becker & L. Gertenbach & H. Laux & T. Reitz (Eds.), Grenzverschiebungen des Kapitalismus Umkämpfte Räume und Orte des Widerstand (253–279). Frankfurt: Campus.

Bodnar, C. (2006). Taking it to the Streets: French Cultural Worker Resistance and the Creation of a Precariat Movement. Canadian Journal of Communication 31(3), 675–694.

Buttler, J. (2013). Exercising freedom (Interview), Revolutions, Global Trends and Regional Issues 1. URL: http://revjournal.org/iss/, pp. 32–41. Last accessed: 30 March 2016.

CBOS (2016). Program „Rodzina 500 plus" jako element systemu wspierania rodzin i dzietności, Komunikat z badań, nr. 26, Warszawa

Diamantopoulou, A. (2015). A Binding Social Agenda For The European Union, in: Ebert Stiftung and Hans Böckler Stiftung (ed): Social Europe 2019, Report, 31–33.

Ebert Stiftung & Hans Böckler Stiftung (Eds.). Report: Social Europe 2019, 31–34. URL: www.socialeurope. Last accessed: 30 March 2016.

De Peuter, G. (2014). Beyond the Model Worker: Surveying a Creative Precariat, Culture Unbound 6, 263–284.

Desperak, I. (2013). [UN]Grateful slave gender dimension of the " dangerous classs of precariat, Revolutions, Global Trends and Regional Issues 1, 122–131. URL: http://revjournal.org/iss/. Last accessed: 30 March 2016.

Friedrich Ebert Stiftung & Hans Böckler Stiftung (2015). Report: Social Europe 2019, Available: www.socialeurope. Last accessed: 30 March 2016.

Foti, A. (2009). The Precariat and Climate Justice in the Great Recession. URL: http://independent.academia.edu/AlexFoti. Last accessed: 23. November 2018.

Fumagalli, A. & Lucarelli, M. (2014). Dochód podstawowy a wydajność w kapitalizmie kognitywnym, Praktyka Teoretyczna 2(12), 79–104.

Hardt, M. & Negri, A. (2005). Imperium, Warszawa: Wydawnictwo W.A.B.

Hoffer, F. (2015). Why We Need Movement of Free People. In Friedrich Ebert Stiftung & Hans Böckler Stiftung (Eds.), Report: Social Europe 2019, pp. 23–25. URL: www.socialeurope. Last accessed: 30 March 2016.

ILO (2012). From Precarious Work to Decent Work: Outcome Document to the Workers. In Symposium on Policies and Regulations to combat Precarious Employment. Geneva

ILO (2016). World employment social outlook, Trends for youth. Geneva

Jasiewicz, E. (2013). In Flux: precarious labor and fragile hopes. Revolutions, Global Trends and Regional Issues 1, pp. 152–159. URL: http://revjournal.org/iss/. Last accessed: 30 March 2016.

Lindner, F. (2015). Why We Need A European Solidarity Union, In Friedrich Ebert Stiftung & Hans Böckler Stiftung (Eds.) Report: Social Europe 2019, pp. 15–17. URL: www. socialeurope. Last accessed: 30 March 2016.

McKay, A. (2001). Rethinking Work and Income Maintenance Policy: Promoting Gender Equality Through A Citizens' Basic Income, Feminist Economics vol. 7(1), 97–118.

Means, A. J. (2014). Generational Precarity, Education, and the Crisis of Capitalism: Conventional, Neo-Keynesian, and Marxian Perspectives, Critical Sociology, 1–17. https:// doi.org/10.1177/0896920514564088.

Näsströma, S., & Kalm, S. (2015). A democratic critique of precarity, Global Discourse, An Interdisciplinary Journal of Current Affairs and Applied Contemporary Thought 5, 556–573. https://doi.org/10.1080/23269995.2014.992119.

OECD (2016). How good is your job? Measuring and Assessing job quality. URL: http:// www.oecd.org/std/labour-stats/Job-quality-OECD.pdf. Last accessed: 5 November 2016.

Offe, C. (2005). Nachwort. In Y Vanderborght & P. van Parijs (Eds.), Ein Grundeinkommen für alle? Geschichte und Zukunft eines radikalen Vorschlags. (pp. 131.150). Frankfurt am Main: Campus.

Ratajczak, M. (2015). Wprowadzenie do teorii kapitalizmu kognitywnego: Kapitalizm kognitywny jako reżim akumulacji. Praktyka Teoretyczna vol. 1(15), 57–94.

Rose, A. (2009). Nice Work If You Can Get It: Life and Labor in Precarious Times, New York: NYU Press

Roth, M. (2015). Why We Need A European Solidarity Union, In Friedrich Ebert Stiftung & Hans Böckler Stiftung (Eds), Report: Social Europe 2019, pp. 18–19. URL: www. socialeurope. Last accessed: 30 March 2016.

Sałustowicz, P. (2012). Welfare policy in time of economic crises – Is the concept of « unconditional basic income » a right response to protect the people from market failure? In G. Thiele (Ed.), Gesellschaftlicher Wandel – wohin? Innovative Entwicklungen in den Sozialwissenschaften. Regional, international (pp. 141–154). Frankfurt am Main: Peter Lang Verlag.

Schultheis, F. (2008). What's left? Von der Desorientierung zur selbstreflexiven Standortbestimmung linker Gesellschaftskritik. In R. Eickelpasch, & C. Rademacher & Ph. R. Lobato (Eds.), Metamorphosen des Kapitalismus – und seiner Kritik (pp. 21–28). Wiesbaden: VS Springer.

Schweighofer, J. (2015). It's Now Or Never: More Social, Less Europe in 2015! In Friedrich Ebert Stiftung and Hans Böckler Stiftung (Edd.), Report: Social Europe 2019, pp. 5–8. URL: www.socialeurope. Last accessed: 30 March 2016.

Seymour, R. (2012) We Are All Precarious – On the Concept of the 'Precariat' and its Misuses, First published: 10 February, 2012, https://www.google.pl/search?q=Van+der+Ve en%2C+R.+(2010)%3A+Basic+income+as+unconditional+subsistence%3A+desirabili ty+and+obstacles%2C+Introductory+lecture%2C+&ieutf-8&oe=utf-8&client=firefox-

b&gfe_rd=cr&ei=dZ3JWJDjJqTs8weokYHIBQ, http://www.newleftproject.org/index. php/site/article_comments/we_are_all_precarious_on_the_concept_of_the_precariat_ and_its_misuses. Last accessed: 5 April 2016.

Standing, G. (2011). The Precariat: The New Dangerious Class. London: Bloomsbury.

Standing, G. (2014a). The Precariat and Class Struggle´. In Revista Crítica de Ciências Sociais 103, 9–24.

Standing, G. (2014b). Prekariat, Nowa niebezpieczna klasa (The Precariat: The New Dangerious Class). Warszawa: Wydawnictwo Naukowe PWN.

Standing, G. (2014c). The Precariat Charter: From Denizens to Citizens London: Bloomsbury.

Standing, G (2013a). Tertiary Time: The Precariat's Dilemma. Public Culture 25(1), 5–23. https://doi.org/10.1215/08992363-1890432.

Standing, G. (2013b). Defining the precariat A class in the making, pp. 1–7, URL: www.eurozine.com. Last accessed: 5 April 2016.

Szarfenberg, R. (2016). ´Prekarność, prekaryjność, prekariat – krótkie wprowadzenie´, unpublished, URL: http://rszarf.ips.uw.edu.pl/pdf/prekariat3.5.pdf. Last accessed: 5 April 2016.

Szlinder, M. (2014). Powszechny dochód podstawowy – w stronę równości, Filo–Sofija 24(1), 247–257.

Vallas, S. P. (1999). Rethinking Post-Fordism: The Meaning of Workplace Flexibility, Sociological Theory 17(1), 68–101

Vanderborght, Y., & Van Parijs, Ph. (2005). Ein Grundeinkommen für alle? Geschichte und Zukunft eines radikalen Vorschlags. Frankfurt am Main: Campus.

Vanderborght, Y., & Van Parijs, Ph. (2010). Das bedingugslose Grundeimkommen, Ein Blick auf seine politische Realisierbarkeit, In M. Franzman (Ed.) Bedingungsloses Grundeinkommen als Antwort auf die Krise der Arbeitsgesellschaft, (pp. 329–359). Weilerswist: Velbrück Wissenschaft.

Van der Veen, R. (2010). Basic income as unconditional subsistence: desirability and obstacles, Introductory lecture. In 13th BIEN International Conference, Faculty of Economics and Public Administration, São Paulo, 30 June 2010. URL: https://www.google.pl/ search?q=Van+der+Veen%2C+R.+(2010)%3A+Basic+income+as+unconditional+ subsistence%3A+desirability+and+obstacles%2C+Introductory+lecture%2C+&ie= utf-8&oe=utf-8&client=firefox-b&gfe_rd=cr&ei=dZ3JWJDjJqTs8weokYHIBQ. Last accessed: 2 April 2016.

Van Parijs, Ph. (1995). Real Freedom for All. What (if anything) can justify capitalism? Oxford: Clarendon Press.

Wilson, R. (2015). Social Europe Needs A Positive Vision, In Friedrich Ebert Stiftung & Hans Böckler Stiftung (Eds.), Report: Social Europe 2019, pp. 59–61 URL: www.socialeurope. Last accessed: 30 March 2016.

Wright, E.O. (2016). Is the Precariat a Class?, Global Labour Journal, 7(2), 123–135.

Warsaw: Precarious Spaces, Precarious Memories

Piotr Skurowski

Abstract

Once almost totally obliterated, and on many occasions dramatically reinvented and reshaped, Warsaw can obviously be seen as a precarious urban space *par excellence* The uncertainties about its spatial order and civic symbolism have always been closely tied to the changing historical and ideological narratives, shaping not only the urban landscape, but along with it the remembrance of the past. This article takes a look at some of Warsaw's iconic spaces, tracing the fluctuations in their shape and symbolism stemming from the discontinuities of the city's history as well as from the narrative turns in the dominant ideology, be it domestic (national) or imposed by the external context (colonization, the Soviet model of socialism, more recently global capitalism).

Keywords

Precarious spaces · Historical memory · Uncertainty · Urban symbolism · Nationalism · Warsaw

Precarity seems to be firmly inscribed into the (post)modern condition, leading to the growing use of the term in a variety of contexts. This has been noted, for example, by Tadeusz Rachwał, reflecting on "the appearance, relatively quite

---

P. Skurowski (✉)
SWPS University of Humanities and Social Sciences, Warsaw, Poland
e-mail: pskurows@swps.edu.pl

© Springer Fachmedien Wiesbaden GmbH, part of Springer Nature 2020   109
T. Rachwał et al. (eds.), *Precarious Places*, Prekarisierung
und soziale Entkopplung – transdisziplinäre Studien,
https://doi.org/10.1007/978-3-658-27311-8_7

recent, of the term *precarity* in various contemporary discourses on human condition and its discontents" (Rachwał 2017, p. 111). If anything, the term (along with "precariousness," an intersecting concept) seems ideally suited to grasp the unsettling nature of the quickly transforming modern city. The ever evolving, morphing, forms of today's cities are obviously a phenomenon that needs to be taken for granted. What follows from this, is a sense of precariousness of city spaces, often doomed to be drastically remodeled, or replaced by new ones. In the process, the collective memories and socially constructed meanings attached to urban spaces become elusive and even sometimes disappear, with new sets of spatial meanings and practices coming to replace them instead. One is tempted to look at Warsaw as a precarious urban space *par excellence*—in the sense of being long caught in between overwhelming forces, destroyed and rebuilt, controlled and neglected in turns, uncertain and anxious about its identity, divided over its past and future.

A quick look at the city's past reveals the full extent of the city's precarious identity: depending on particular moments in history (and applied point of view), the city could be perceived as "Eastern", "Western", Polish, Russian, Jewish, German, capitalist, socialist, capitalist again; provincial, and cosmopolitan. Once the capital of a major European power, later to become a provincial Russian city, then the capital of a reborn Poland craving the distinction of Eastern Europe's "Little Paris" (Brzostek 2015). The near obliteration of the city in World War Two cruelly exposed the precariousness of the "Paris of the East" delusion. Indeed, the very existence of the city in the future was put in question. All but annihilated during the war, the city was reborn from the ashes as a "socialist metropolis," to become capitalist again (although without much capital, for a start) and fulfill its old dream of becoming "officially" European, through Poland's membership in the EU (only to discover, along with some of its inhabitants, that the "European" identity doesn't fit too well, after all). A quite bewildering repertoire of ascribed associations and identity choices, to be deployed, and cultivated, by the successive generations of the city's inhabitants and rulers.

One of the first things that comes to mind while raising the example of Warsaw as a "precarious" place with a "precarious" memory of itself, is the almost total annihilation of the city in World War Two, which, in the view of many, made the project of rebuilding it impractical, and unrealistic: according to a postwar estimate by the City Architect Józef Sigalin, 84% of buildings on the left bank were destroyed beyond repair (Murawski 2015, p. 56). It is, of course, beyond the scope and intention of this article to trace the causes and the history of that tragedy, or the history of the reconstruction of the Polish capital. Instead, the goal of this article is to demonstrate the changing symbolic status of certain spaces of the city, seen as a self-contradicting, often incoherent narrative, marked by the

Warsaw: Precarious Spaces, Precarious Memories

precariousness of the cultural and ideological meanings acquired, and lost, over successive decades after 1945. In order to facilitate the daunting task of rebuilding the entire city the government passed the so-called Dekret Bieruta ("Bierut Law")[1] which nationalized all land in Warsaw within the prewar city limits. The law rested on a premise that without nationalization the rebuilding could not take place. By turning private into national property, the city and country authorities could not only carry on with the reconstruction without being restricted by the rights of the owners, but were also able to call upon the country at large to help rebuild its capital (Cały naród buduje swoją stolicę, "the whole nation is rebuilding its capital") was one of the most famous propaganda slogans from the postwar period. That single decision, more than any other, had a tremendous influence on the future of the city, and its effects are still a powerful factor today. Ironically, while the short-term effects were salutary (clearing the legal obstacles in the way of massive reconstruction), its long-range results turned out to be quite destructive, particularly after 1989, when a lot of renovation and construction projects were buried, or significantly delayed, by incessant litigation from prewar owners or their legal proxies. Overall, the precarious and shaky legal status of much of real property in Warsaw continues to be the city's most painful ailment, accounting for the impossibility of much-needed redevelopment of a "true" city center, which, in the view of many, is still missing. As a result of its difficult history, Warsaw is still a city grappling with its—sometimes shaky—identity. The ravages of the war did much to erase the city's history, and the successive decades of communist rule were an attempt to build a new narration—that of a socialist metropolis, deriving its new-found identity from a redefined and renegotiated past, but most importantly from the vision of its current and future splendor as the capital of a new, socialist Poland. That new identity undeniably rested on shaky foundations, as in common perception the country was turned after 1945 into a Soviet satellite. The rebuilding of Warsaw (ironically it was Joseph Stalin's personal decision to overcome the skeptical voices putting in doubt the sense of reinstating Warsaw as Poland's capital), once decided upon, was evidently serving the political goal of legitimizing the communist party rule in Poland and changing its precarious status of Moscow's puppets into that of good Polish patriots ("Odbudowa Warszawy się nie zakończyła"). The most glamorous part of the restoration project was the reconstruction of the Old Town, which during and immediately

---

[1]This is, of course, an informal name for the Oct. 26, 1945 law regulating the ownership and use of lands within the limits of the city of Warsaw, proclaimed by Krajowa Rada Narodowa (State National Council) which was presided over by Bolesław Bierut.

after the 1944 Warsaw Uprising was almost entirely razed to the ground—to the extent that today, the only "authentic" old part in it are the cellars, underground corridors and sewage canals, which have largely remained unscathed by the war. Thus, the ontological status of the Old Town (Stare Miasto) as one that is "old" is rather precarious—one is tempted to think of it as a simulacrum, even though the term is usually applied to late capitalism and its (re)constructions. It certainly is "better than real," not only because this famous post-war reconstruction (its technical excellence and painstaking recreation of smallest details put it on the UNESCO list of architectural treasures) was meant to be as much as possible faithful to the eighteenth-century form of the city (paintings of Bellotto Canaletto of late-eighteenth-century Warsaw were used by the rebuilders for that purpose), but also because the reborn Stare Miasto was now in a far better condition than before its destruction in WWII (Brzostek 2015, Kindle loc. 3718). It lost the shabbiness that marked some of its badly maintained old buildings, and acquired the glamour of a place that was now the "showcase" of the unparalleled energy and effectiveness of the new socialist government, seeking legitimacy in demonstrating its great preoccupation with the restoration of Poland's national treasures, along with restoring pride in the national past. Apart from that, the painstaking reconstruction project seemed to provide an ideal escapist opportunity for the architects who were averse to the new social-realist dogma imposed on their profession from the above. They could instead dedicate themselves to "improving history" by providing the reconstructed buildings with better access to light, correcting the buildings' frontage alignment, adding grass lawns, and—because of the lack of documentation—often exercise their self-imposed right to architectural *licentia poetica* (Fudala and Skalimowski 2016, p. 222).[2] The pre-war Warsaw probably could not, and ultimately wasn't, rebuilt in its entirety, and the choices made by the reconstruction authorities were motivated by a number of factors. One can hardly resist the sense of irony inherent in the special status awarded to the Old Town by the new communist government. Yet apart from the obvious historical significance about the place that used to be the capital of the Polish Commonwealth before its dismantling by the neighboring powers in the late eighteenth century, the Old Town raised relatively few associations with the capitalist Poland. But the Royal Castle, which before the Second World War was the seat

---

[2]Reflecting today on the restoration of the Old Town, one is tempted to look at it from the perspective of Christine Boyer (1994), describing the now-classic preservation project in South Sea Seaport (NYC) in terms of a spectacle, with its "staged landscapes", "city tableaux" and "necessary illusions" pointing to the artificiality of reproducing an imagined past (pp. 421–476).

of Poland's president (a decidedly negative association, from the viewpoint of Poland's new rulers), was left not rebuilt until the Party's decision to reconstruct it in 1971—in large measure a political move, aimed at increasing the popularity of the Party's new First Secretary Edward Gierek and establishing his patriotic credentials. This is no place to summarize the history of that restoration project which indeed was born as soon as the war was over, but the fact that it took it so long to materialize seems to be strongly tied to its symbolic associations with the prewar rule (parallel to the still not rebuilt Saxon Palace, where many prewar ceremonies of state were routinely taking place). It is said that Gierek's predecessor, Władysław Gomułka, used his influence to block the reconstruction of the Castle because it symbolized to him the medieval oppression of peasants ("Odbudowa Warszawy się nie zakończyła"). As a result, the rebuilt Old Town was long left "bowdlerized" by being deprived of its major architectural and symbolic element: an interesting commentary on how reconstructions are, in fact, constructions, serving new ideological purposes through the practice of partial erasure, or deletion, of markers that could serve the contrary purpose. In contrast with the titanic effort to rebuild the Old Town, the fate of the largely destroyed central parts of prewar Warsaw, or at least the bulk of what constituted the central portions of the city, was doomed after 1945.

The most poignant case, of course, was that of the wartime Ghetto, leveled to the ground in the wake of its liquidation in 1943 and of what was in fact (if not in the Polish collective memory) Warsaw's first uprising. Indeed, the fate of the Warsaw Ghetto, more than any other place, demonstrates the precariousness of social and urban spaces in view of overwhelming destructive forces, in this case the relentless Nazi plan to carry out the Holocaust. One look at the surviving photos from January 1945 (made after the liberation of Warsaw by the Soviet army) of the place that used to be the Ghetto explains that nothing escaped the all-but-total destruction (with very few exceptions, including that of a Catholic church, evidently left undestroyed because of its religious symbolism). What remained was a sea of rubble, with virtually all the inhabitants of that area exterminated. It is beyond the scope of this article to go over the postwar history of building a new city on the ashes of the dead. Yet, a few points need to be made since one cannot talk about Warsaw without keeping in mind the fact that before the war it was world's second largest (after New York) Jewish city, the Jewish population altogether accounting to about one-fourth of the city's residents (during the war, for a time, Warsaw's Jewish population further increased because of the enforced relocation of many Jews from the surrounding areas). While the reconstruction of the quarters of the city that were predominantly Jewish before the war was plainly impossible in view of their total destruction, along with the all-but-total annihilation of their inhabitants, the now-vacant spaces were soon going to be converted into big-scale socialist housing projects totally unreminiscent of the prewar city topography and look (a similar process was underway throughout the city at large, even though the separation of the present from the past was nowhere so complete). Despite some efforts to the contrary (the monument to the heroes of the Ghetto; the preservation of some prewar street names and naming new streets after Jewish scientists or heroes: Mordechaj Anielewicz Street, Ludwik Zamenhof Street etc.; and the more recent preservation efforts to restore selected buildings and remnants of the Ghetto wall), the memories of the Ghetto, and of the Jewish Warsaw, have largely faded away, with the recently completed POLIN Museum of the History of Polish Jews playing a major role in a belated revival of interest in Warsaw's Jews. Most of the spaces that were once inhabited by the bustling Jewish community, their remnants razed down and developed after the war according to the canons of the socialist modernist architecture (with the ashes of the thousands of bodies, mixed with unremoved rubble, providing the foundations for the new developments) provide an uncanny urban parallel to Claude Lanzmann's phrase "non-lieux de mémoire" (coined in contrast to Pierre Norra's phrase "lieux de mémoire," places dedicated to the cultivation of national memory, surrounded with a symbolic aura)—the now-anonymous, nondescript, mostly deserted rural spaces left over from the Holocaust, defined by Dominic LaCapra as "traumatic sites that challenge or undermine the work of memory" (LaCapra 1997, p. 240), and described by Roma Sendyka as places that "are inconvenient to the surrounding community ... because the community that has been ascribed to a given localization doesn't feel like, or even refuses to, invest its memory in it; it prefers to forget, to not remember" (Sendyka 2013, p. 281, own translation).

It would be unfair to deny the recent efforts to validate and to integrate the history of Warsaw' Jews into the mainstream narrative of wartime memory, flawed as that narrative often gets (in fact there's been a number of divergent narratives, including the "official" Communist narrative, the unofficial "counter-narratives" celebrating the bravery of the Home Army, and the post-1989 cult of the 1944 Warsaw Uprising increasingly resonating through popular culture; what they had in common, though, was their mostly laconic reference to the Holocaust and to the role played in it by the ethnic Poles). Apart from the priceless role played in this rewriting of memory by the many activities and exhibits sponsored by the POLIN Museum, one should make note of the contribution of artists and various activists inserting the memory of the Jews into the present (the Footbridge of Memory installation designed by Tomasz de Tusch-Lec; the "I miss you, Jew" arts-social project originated by Rafał Betlejewski; most importantly perhaps,

Warsaw: Precarious Spaces, Precarious Memories

the long and distinguished history of Teatr Żydowski, a unique Yiddish repertory theatre, as well as a number of other activities and initiatives). This is no place, of course, to describe the long and arduous process of reclaiming the history of Jewish presence as a vital part of Warsaw's history, of reviving the precarious memories that have long been blocked, repressed and written over. However, I want to finish this fragment by pointing to the slow but significant shift in the public memory concerning the history of Warsaw during World War Two, in the form of celebrations of the anniversary of the Warsaw Ghetto Uprising. While the outbreak of the Warsaw Ghetto uprising (April 19, 1943) has been honored after 1945 with annual ceremonies featuring high-ranking Polish government officials, it is only in recent years that the weight of that anniversary has sunk deeper with the Polish public. This is witnessed by the increasingly noticeable wearing of the yellow daffodils stuck in the lapel in commemoration of the Ghetto uprising as well as by other signs of memory: the seventy-fifth anniversary of the Uprising, in 2018, was also honored, like the anniversaries of the Warsaw Uprising of August 1, 1944, with the citywide blaring of alarm sirens and the ringing of the city's church bells. Time will show if these new forms become domesticated in Warsaw's public memory.

The precarious place of Jewish history in the city memory reflects, of course, a parallel pattern in the national memory at large, where for a long time the recognition of the strong Jewish presence in Polish history was long denied in many mainstream narratives of Polish national identity. Warsaw's identity problems with its Jewish past have been, undeniably, part of a larger picture, stemming from the longstanding doubts and dilemmas reflected in the city's auto-narrations, as well as in its image seen from an outside perspective. Which brings us to the story of the central, "elegant" parts of Warsaw from before the war, and the way in which they (or rather, their remains) were redeveloped after 1945. Rebuilding the largely destroyed center of the capital, together with its elegant and often imposing buildings was a tall order for the government and the city authorities, given the lack of adequate resources and the mostly poor physical conditions of the surviving buildings. There was, inevitably, the political angle to the ongoing restoration work, as far as the prospect of rebuilding the city's main commercial streets: Marszałkowska and Aleje Jerozolimskie, which before the war were the showcases for Poland's vibrant capitalist economy. The status of the remains of the most "bourgeois" part of prewar Warsaw was thus precarious from the start; indeed, it was either entirely condemned or developed in a way that made it look dramatically different from its prewar shape. The debate on how much could be saved and rebuilt, but wasn't because of the political prejudices of the city's authorities (including the Biuro Odbudowy Stolicy, or City Reconstruction Office) has been launched with a new force after 1989, i.e. since it became possible to openly criticize and question the decisions underwritten by the Communist Party (Bojarski 2015). Yet, as demonstrated by Fudala, Skalimowski and others, the accusations that the City Reconstruction Office condemned or gave up many salvageable buildings for narrowly ideological reasons are largely unsubstantiated (Fudala 2016).

The fact remains that the bulk of today's city center consists of buildings erected from scratch after the Second World War, most of them completed during the People's Republic. The most outstanding of those realizations were the ones erected in the late 1940s and 50s, usually described as the Stalinist period in Warsaw architecture. It is in the Stalinist period that the topography of central Warsaw was reinscribed by the construction of the Palace of Culture (1955), the landmark that totally dominated the surrounding ruins of the ghetto and the existing buildings in the immediate area, imposing a new spatial-symbolic order on the city center. The Palace of Culture (named after Stalin in commemoration of the Soviet leader who died two years before the completion of the construction) was officially a gift from the Soviet Union to the "brotherly" Polish nation, whose out-of-scale visual impact was obviously meant to send a clear message that Poland was now in the orbit of a new empire. Dwarfing the surrounding city the Palace symbolized what at that point seemed a certainty: socialist Poland, together with its all-powerful Soviet patron, were there to stay, in contrast with the decaying remnants of the old order. The site for the future Palace complex (containing Plac Defilad–Warsaw's equivalent of the Red Square, a colossal, empty public space around the building, designed for the purpose of staging there state parades) was cleared from the still remaining prewar buildings, thus totally obliterating the still existing prewar street pattern. "After the Palace," the center of Warsaw could never again be made to look like before the war—its construction doomed any future plans of bringing back the old look and the old spatial order to the city. The Palace was a new, authoritarian, hegemonic presence, imposing a highly hierarchical and centralized spatial (as well as political and symbolic) order upon the city; a clearly phallic symbol of raw power, reducing to insignificance the (still) existing, precarious spaces of "bourgeois" Warsaw, and a key element in the socialist city planners' scheme to bring about a holistic, all-inclusive social and architectural environment realizing their utopian dreams of a new society. Christine Boyer's description of the Modernist architects philosophy as one marked by the "desire to totalize: master and dominate the city space, or to experience the city in a coherent and integrated manner" (Boyer 1994, p. 18) seems to fit the mental frame of the planners and architects grouped in the Warsaw Reconstruction Office (Biuro Odbudowy Stolicy), whose professional outlooks were formed by the prewar architectural Modernist avant-garde (Murawski 2015, p. 67; Fudala 2016, p. 27 ff.; Popiołek 2016, pp. 40 ff.).[3]

Needless to say, the Palace was but the most conspicuous sign of the new times having arrived: the vast rhetorical repertoire of the Soviet-imposed hegemonic model of socialism contained a lot of other tropes used to erase the memories of the past and establish new identities and reference points for the city and its inhabitants. The new order symbolized by the Palace and other high-profile architectural undertakings seemed to be further anchored in other practices, like renaming the city streets and erecting new monuments; the new street signs and monuments, honoring the socialist heroes from Marx, Engels and Lenin (the use of Stalin's name was soon going to be dropped—it even disappeared from the façade of the Palace) to Róża Luxemburg and Feliks Dzierżyński—the Polish "contributions" to the cause of worldwide communist revolution. Symptomatically, Woodrow Wilson Square was renamed as Paris Commune Square, and the Bank Square as Dzierżyński Square. There's no need here to go on listing the many architectural, topographical and linguistic changes effected under the communist rule; the main reason of providing the above examples was to demonstrate how, after 1989, what was once perceived as solid and irremovable, quickly turned out to be liquid. The famous phrasing from The Communist Manifesto, "what is solid melts into the air," originally referring to the dissolution of the bourgeoisie-controlled world, seems to perfectly (and ironically) apply to the meltdown of the socialist order as reflected in the spatial and symbolic order of the Polish capital. Among the first "to go" were the street signs and monuments. In a famous episode from 1989 Feliks Dzierżyński's statue was pulled down, and the name of the square hitherto hosting the monument (Feliks Dzierżynski Square) went back to Bank Square (Plac Bankowy). Yet the process of renaming the streets and removing monuments still continues, both in Warsaw and other cities; it has even gathered speed after the recent electoral victory of the Law and Justice party.[4]

The precariousness, or liquidity of once ostensibly "solid" markers of communist presence was exposed in a variety of ways, leading to the renaming of

---

[3]On the cultural semiotics of the Palace of Culture, see the excellent article by Magdalena J. Zaborowska (2001).

[4]One recent characteristic attempt to obliterate another symbol of the Communist past was the June 2018 decision of the Warsaw City Council to remove the Monument of Gratitude to the Soviet Soldiers; one of the main arguments raised in favor of the decision was one that stated that the monument "stirs up aggressive behavior."

streets, changing the function of such emblematic buildings as the central headquarters of the communist party (into the seat of Warsaw Stock Exchange; the symbolism of that change is plain enough) and, increasingly, demolition of the aging buildings and facilities that were once the pride of socialist Poland. Understandably, the status of the Palace of Culture ("Stalin's gift"—"small but tasteful," in Antoni Słonimski's ironic comment) was called into question right after Poland shook off its ties to the Soviet Union in 1989, which led to a long-lasting—and still unresolved—battle over the Palace's future. Suddenly, what had long seemed to be the most "solid" part of post-war Warsaw, turned out to be one of the city's most precarious places, standing in danger of being completely erased, as a symbol of a colonized past. While the radical solution to the "Palace problem"—getting entirely rid of it—did not ultimately prevail,[5] other strategies were proposed to lessen the spatial dominance of the Stalinist landmark. One such plan (prepared by the architect Jerzy Skrzypczak) called for surrounding the Palace with a ring of five colossal skyscrapers, to hide it from view. Another plan submitted by the architects Biełyszew and Skopiński (winner of the 1992 contest for the best plan to redevelop the Palace area) provided for the "corso", or a "crown" of skyscrapers to be built around the Palace (Murawski 2015, pp. 186 ff.). None of those plans has yet been put into effect (part of the reason being the precarious ownership status of a number of lots comprising the Parades Square, resulting from the 1945 Bierut Law), yet the Palace's visual hegemony has been already partly obliterated by the construction of a number of tall buildings in its immediate area, constituting Warsaw's new skyline. The Palace has also visibly aged (it recently celebrated its sixtieth birthday) and is beginning to show symptoms of decay, revealing its long-hidden vulnerability hidden under the marble façade. Yet so far it managed to avoid the apocalyptic scenario prophesied in the popular political comedy *Rozmowy kontrolowane* (*Controlled Conversations*, 1991), where in the final scene the pulling down of a flush toilet string sets in motion a domino-effect catastrophe with the whole Palace falling apart. In fact, the Palace has shown a high degree of resilience; it still stands, taking on new functions, displaying an uncanny ability to adapt itself to the changing times.[6] Having survived

---

[5]The call for tearing down the Palace was repeated like mantra by a number of prominent public figures, including the renowned architect Czesław Bielecki and the Foreign Minister Radosław Sikorski. Among the most curious schemes to „cover up" the dominating presence of the Palace was the plan to mask the building with ivy.

[6]The most conspicuous physical change undergone by the Palace after 1989 was the addition of a big tower clock, adding a "Western" touch to the Stalinist relic by inviting comparisons with London's Big Ben, or with a German-style Rathaus.

the main wave of iconoclasm in the immediately post-1989 period, it has truly become a "free-floating signifier," waiting to be colonized by new imaginaries and symbolic orders. After 1989, the Palace and the surrounding Parades Square became quickly commercialized; the Parades Square in particular became synonymous with the birth of small-time capitalism, as it was getting filled with the famous "jaws", or collapsible vendor stalls, the hatching place for a generation of Poland's new entrepreneurs. Today, the "jaws" have disappeared, but the Palace and the surrounding square perform a multiplicity of functions, depending on time and occasion. Chameleon-like, the Palace changes colors after dark (thanks to an advanced lighting system) to suit a particular occasion and send a political message: to give support to Ukrainian freedom-fighters, express solidarity with terrorist attack victims in Paris and Berlin, etc. The Parades Square in particular functions as Lefebvre's "space of representation," acting as a gathering place for different political marches and demonstrations or the venue for outdoor popular concerts, producing different "lived moments" on each individual occasion while providing a sense of continuity to those who can still remember the big spectacles of the communist era that were staged around in and around the Palace.[7]

The "second life" of the Palace of Culture coincides with the growth of a movement to preserve the highlights of socialist architecture against the persistent calls for their deletion and removal. Indeed, in recent years an important part of the public debate in Warsaw has been focused on that issue, with the right-wing nationalists often strongly urging the removal of the "unwanted" relics of the socialist past and, on the other side, many urbanists and architects calling for their preservation on account of their uniqueness and authenticity.[8] That the voices of the preservationists have often carried the day (saving some outstanding examples of socialist architecture) is probably owing to the fact that so many of the newly constructed buildings in downtown Warsaw seem to lack in authenticity, and would easily

---

[7]A useful review of Lefebvre's concept of the space of representation can be found, among others, in Marco Cenzatti 2008, pp. 80 f.

[8]For a sample of an emotional, nostalgic response to the Palace as a place symbolizing one's youth, see for example Chutnik (2017). Some other conspicuous constructions of the Socialist period did not get their second life, most notoriously perhaps the tenth-Anniversary of the People's Republic Stadium, the site of not only some major sports events but also major political events sponsored but the United Workers' Party, the main organ of the Communist rule. The Socialist-era colossus and symbol was razed down in 2009, to be replaced by a new facility, The National Stadium, which became one of the symbols of the new order.

qualify as "non-places", with little or no character of their own.[9] Thus it may be really worthwhile to preserve those still existing environments where the separation of space from place has not yet occurred. All this is not to say that most buildings constructed in the socialist era (which was long enough to produce a number of styles) were genuine and authentic—probably only a small number were, thus for a long time to come Warsaw, where still a vast majority of buildings date back to the socialist era, will remain a city full of unappealing and monotonous, more or less slowly decaying apartment blocks ("blokowiska") and old theindustrial sites from the bygone era—the city's ultimate precarious spaces, waiting for their turn to be condemned to the wrecking ball, while already "condemned" by history. Ironically, the status of some of the post-1989 constructions is likewise uncertain. Down went, for example, one of the first symbols of the new era of consumption, the City Center shopping mall, completed in 1991, to make room for a postmodern skyscraper designed by Daniel Liebeskind (2009–2017). Another short-lived post-1989 construction, the Ilmet Office Tower with a big iconic Mercedes-Benz logo and a conspicuous element in Warsaw's new skyline—completed in 1997—is soon to be torn down and replaced by a far taller skyscraper. It is true, of course, that the above dynamics of destruction, restoration and replacement, mixed with a degree of astonishing resilience, have marked the life of many other cities (even in the destruction suffered during the Second World War Warsaw is not entirely exceptional among the European cities: think of the destruction of such German cities as Hamburg, Dresden and Cologne, with the now-Polish cities of Gdańsk and Wrocław trailing not far behind in the amount of damage suffered). Yet, in comparison with so many others, the intensity of change experienced through most of the twentieth and the first two decades of this century, has shaped Warsaw's spaces into a unique mélange of authentic and inauthentic old (rebuilt from scratch), the not-so old (50s, 60s, 70s architecture) and the more recent, as well as into a fairly chaotic spatial and architectural pattern. Because of its past—and that past's remnants' precarious state of existence—the city's character consists in the multiplicity of its architectural styles

---

[9]As argued convincingly by Dariusz Czaja, Marc Auge's term "non-lieux," understood as places that are totally anonymous, characterless, and largely devoid of meaning, hardly in fact exist, as a site's meaning is always "under construction" by its users. Another explanation for the preservationist impulse may be pointedly suggested by Murawski who brings up Yael Navaro-Yashin's concept of "domesticated abject" (originally used in his discussion of the fate of Turkish property taken over by the Greeks in Cyprus) to account for the displays of nostalgia in the argumentation of the defenders of the Palace of Culture who oppose its liquidation (Murawski, 2011, pp. 9 f.).

and environments. In Warsaw, one might say after Christine Boyer, "different layers of historical time superimposed on each other or different architectural strata (touching but not necessarily informing each other) no longer generate a structural form to the city but (…) culminate in an experience of diversity." (Boyer 1994, p. 19). These words coming from Boyer's remarks on the "City of Collective Memory" which she contrasts with the totalizing visions of the modernist city planning, while evidently formulated with other cities in mind, seem to fit today's Warsaw particularly well. Yet, the collective memories Boyer was invoking in the context of the American and West European metropolises, have recently come back with a vengeance—in Warsaw, as in many other cities of the post-Soviet world. In the case of Warsaw, the diversity comes increasingly mixed with the passions aroused by the narrations of what actually happened to the city and the country after 1945.[10] In that regard, many of Warsaw's contested urban spaces serve as synecdoches of the state of the nation's historical memory, standing in the middle of the fierce battle over the meaning of the post-war national history. The precarious status of some of the city's buildings, monuments and street names symbolizing (in the eyes of the current state authorities) the Communist period in Poland's history is the hostage of that situation.

References

Augé, M. (1997). Non-places. Introduction to an Anthropology of Supermodernity. London: Verso.

Bojarski, A. (2015). Rozebrać Warszawę. Historie niektórych wyburzeń po roku 1945. Warsaw: KiW.

Boyer, M. C. (1994). *The City of Collective Memory*. Cambridge, Mass.: Mit Press.

Brzostek, B. (2015). Paryże innej Europy. Warszawa i Bukareszt, XIX i XX wiek. [Kindle version].

Cenzatti, M. (2008), Heterotopias of difference. In M. Dehaene & L. de Cauter (Eds.), *Heterotopia and the City: Public Space in a Postcivil Society* (pp. 75–85). New York: Routledge.

Chutnik, S. (2017). Kocham Pałac Kultury. Przy tej rakiecie czuję się kimś wyjątkowym. *Wyborcza.pl*. URL: http://warszawa.wyborcza.pl/warszawa/7,54420.2 2598471,kocham-palac-kultury-o-swojej-warszawie-pisze-sylwia-chutnik.html. Last accessed: 4. November 2017.

---

[10]Probably the most insightful recent treatment of the dominant mythical narrations distorting, and disavowing the significance of cultural and social change undergone by Poland in WWII and during the Communist period, is Andrzej Leder's 2014 study *Prześniona rewolucja*.

Czaja, D. (2013). Nie-miejsca. Przybliżenia, rewizje. In D. Czaja (Ed.), *Inne przestrzenie, inne miejsca* (pp. 7–26). Wołowiec: Czarne.

Fudala, T. (2016). Odbudowa Warszawy i miastobójstwo 'małego Paryża.'Spór o odbudowę 70 lat później. In T. Fudala (Ed.), *Spór o odbudowę Warszawy. Od gruzów do reprywatyzacji* (pp. 11–35). Warsaw: Muzeum Sztuki Nowoczesnej w Warszawie.

Fudala, T., & Skalimowski, A. (2016). Odbudowa Starego Miasta. Spór o odbudowę 70 lat później. In T. Fudala (Ed.), *Spór o odbudowę Warszawy. Od gruzów do reprywatyzacji* (pp. 222–243). Warsaw: Muzeum Sztuki Nowoczesnej w Warszawie.

LaCapra, D. (1997). Lanzmann's 'Shoah': Here There Is No Why. *Critical Inquiry*, 23/2 (Winter 1997), 231–269.

Leder, A. (2014). *Prześniona rewolucja. Ćwiczenie z logiki historycznej*. Warsaw: Wydawnictwo Krytyki Politycznej.

Majewski, J. S. (2017). Pałac Kultury do zburzenia? W Warszawie mamy długą tradycję barbarzyńskich rozbiórek. *Wyborcza.pl*. URL: http://warszawa.wyborcza.pl/wars zawa/7,54420,22689905,palac-kultury-do-zburzenia-w-warszawie-mamy-dluga-trady-cje. html. Last accessed: 02. December 2018.

Murawski, M. (2011). Inappropriate object: Warsaw and the Stalin-era Palace of Culture after the Smolensk disaster. *Anthropology Today* 27(4), 5–10.

Murawski, M. (2015). Kompleks Pałacu. Życie społeczne stalinowskiego wieżowca w kapitalistycznej Warszawie. Warsaw: Muzeum Warszawy.

Odbudowa Warszawy się nie zakończyła. Tomasz Ustrzykowski's interview with Tomasz Markiewicz (2015). *Wyborcza.pl*. URL: http://warszawa.wyborcza.pl/ warszawa/1,3486 2,18641792,odbudowa-warszawy-sie-nie-zakonczyla-miasto-to-nie-tylko-budynki.html. Last accessed: 12 December 2018.

Popiołek, Małgorzata (2016). 'Miastu–grunty, mieszkańcowi–dom'. Historia powstania dekretu Bieruta na tle europejskiej myśli urbanistycznej. In T. Fudala (Ed.), *Spór o odbudowę Warszawy. Od gruzów do reprywatyzacji* (pp. 37–58). Warsaw: Muzeum Sztuki Nowoczesnej w Warszawie.

Rachwał, T. (2017). Precarity and Loss. On Certain and Uncertain Properties of Life and Work. Wiesbaden: VS Springer.

Sendyka, Roma (2013). Pryzma—zrozumieć nie-miejsce pamięci. In D. Czaja (Ed.), *Inne przestrzenie, inne miejsca* (pp. 270–285). Wołowiec: Czarne.

Sikorski nagle podczas debaty: w miejscu Pałacu Kultury powinien powstać (2012). *Gazeta.pl*. URL: http://wiadomosci.gazeta.pl/wiadomosci/1,114873,10957240,Sikor ski_nag le_ podczas_debaty.html. Last accessed: 12 December 2018.

Zaborowska, Magdalena J. (2001). The Height of (Architectural) Seduction: Reading the "Changes" through Stalin's Palace in Warsaw, Poland. *Journal of Architectural Education* 54, 205–217.

On the Uses of Precarity. Knowledge, Innovation and Academic Labour in Precarious Times

Jan Sowa

Abstract

The first part the article offers a critical examination of the three alleged properties of precariat as analyzed by Guy Standing in his seminal book *The Precariat: The New Dangerous Class*: its newness, its class character and its dangerous nature. Recognizing the value of Standing's contribution the author argues that precariat possess none of these properties; it is rather just another consequence of primitive accumulation. As such, the urge to precarize is inscribed in the very logic of capitalist accumulation and can be found on every stage of its historical development, both in the past and in the present. The alleged class character of precariat is also called into question both on theoretical and political grounds. As it is demonstrated, precarization is happening to many social classes, however with different consequences on different levels of social hierarchy: those bestowed with some forms of capital (either material and symbolic) can actually benefit from what is called the flexible mode of accumulation). Finally, the article points to rather docile and passive character of precariat that does not seem to be dangerous for the capitalist *status-quo*. Dangers stemming from its existence are rather associated with the capture of precariat by right-wing extremism. In the second part the article focuses on the precarity of academic labour pointing to its negative impact on both teaching and research.

J. Sowa (✉)
Academy of Fine Arts, Warsaw, Poland
e-mail: sowa3141592@gmail.com

© Springer Fachmedien Wiesbaden GmbH, part of Springer Nature 2020
T. Rachwał et al. (eds.), *Precarious Places*, Prekarisierung
und soziale Entkopplung – transdisziplinäre Studien,
https://doi.org/10.1007/978-3-658-27311-8_8

Keywords

Precariat · Primitive accumulation · Social classes · Post-operaismo · Academic labour · Cognitive labour · Cognitive capitalism · Postcolonialism · Peripheries · Welfare state

The very term "precarity" as well as a broader notion of precarization it implies have made a remarkable advance in the realm of public discourse in the last decade. Coined as political notions in a fruitful exchange between Italian and French philosophers and activists in 1970ties they had long remained marginal and confined to radical progressive circles. Felix Guattari in his Brazilian lectures from early 1980s published in the volume *Molecular Revolution in Brazil* mentions "precarity" as a new, interesting concept describing a problematic social and existential condition of contemporary proletariat (Guattari and Rolnik 2007), however it was only with the Euro May Day of 2001 and initiatives such as the Italian San Precario of early 2000s that the notion of precariousness enters the main stage of public debate.

The seminal book *The Precariat: The New Dangerous Class* published by Guy Standing in 2011 has played a key role in shaping recent discussion around the problem of precarization and as such it has had an immense political importance. In what follows saluting both the merits of Standing's book and his intentions I'd like to polemically address some of his thesis and especially the three properties of precariat he affirms in the very title of the book: its novelty, its dangerous character and its class nature

1 The Unbearable Endurance of Primitive Accumulation

Is there something new about precarization? The term is quite recent as is a broader interest in the problem, however the phenomenon itself seems hardly novel. It falls, I believe, in the realm of classical Marxist analysis of primitive accumulation and its social consequences. Precarization historically operated via two means constitutive for the development of capitalism: separation of producers from means of production and enclosures of the commons. Combined they shattered a relative material equilibrium that lower classes enjoyed in the late Middle Ages and thus putting them in a never ending uncertainty of how and to whom they could have been selling the only resource they had left—their labour power. It is crucial and needs to be underlined that capitalism could have come to existence only with a huge effort of artificially creating the necessity for waged labour. Rendering people's existence uncertain and precarious via that double dispossession was instrumental in achieving this goal. Take the well-known enclosures. They were far from anecdotal or circumferential events in the history of capitalism. In the Seventieth century alone around ¼ of all common lands in England was enclosed. It happened with massive and devastating social consequences: the number of propertyless and homeless people forced to begging had risen by 1200% (yes, 12 times!) in that period, although the general population of England expanded only by 25% in the same period (Linebough and Rediker 2000). An newsworthy development that shutters the ideological illusion of capitalism as a system based on property and ownership: empirically speaking its rise produced much more dispossessed than owners. Along with a series of brutal legal measures aimed at eradicating vagabonds, beggars and other "lazy scum" enacted in late Middle Ages and early modern times (Lis and Soly 1981) enclosures were an early episode of precarization inscribed in capitalist economy from it's very beginning and playing the crucial role in establishing capitalist social relations.

There is another key element we need to add to this picture in order to better understand the ubiquitous and perennial character of precarization within the capitalist economy. We tend to automatically categorize primitive accumulation as a purely historical event, a phenomenon of the past. It is mainly due to the adjective "primitive" that evokes something pertaining to an overcome stage of history. That is however not the case with the Marxist notion of "primitive accumulation". It needs to be considered as a systemic factor characteristic of the capitalist mode of production as such and not pertaining only to the early phase of capitalist development. Primitive accumulation is never over. It is primitive in the sense of being a deep, structural (pre)condition and not as a matter of the past. Thus, when we look at the history of capitalism from its beginnings until today, we'll always find primitive accumulation at work with all its social consequences at each and every stage. It is very well documented in the *Capital's* chapter devoted to the working day (Marx 2010) as well as other historical analysis. Ulrich Beck is absolutely right when he claims that "unemployment and underemployment—or, to use the nicer-sounding modern terms, varied, fuzzy, precarious forms of work and income—were historically the rule." (Beck 2000, p. 21).

The ubiquitous and permanent character of primitive accumulation is sometimes difficult to grasp due to the fact that capitalism seems to exists in two distinct temporalities: in a linear, progressive temporality where it occupies a place between feudalism and a possible future of post-scarcity and post-work societies (or a brutal neo-barbarism; both developments are possible, I'll get back to this point at the end of the text) as well as in a circular, immutable temporality of constant (re)production of its own condition of possibility that boils down to various forms of dispossession and precarization.

The same holds true when we approach capitalism not in temporal but in spatial terms. Broadly speaking, precarious conditions typical for primitive accumulation have constituted a never changing social reality of the peripheries, while a more stable forms of employment have emerged and spread only in the core countries (and even that was a historical anomaly as I'll demonstrate later). A brilliant analysis provided by Mike Davis in his book *Late Victorian Holocausts* documents the reality of primitive, peripheral accumulation (David 2001). Postcolonial critique from Fanon's *Wretched of the Earth* to Spivak's *Critique of Post-colonial Reason* has painted in details the picture of precarious existence—both material and symbolic—of the colonized. There is some change, even progress, however it remains weak and inadequate. In today's' Brazil 60% of workers are not covered by a regular job contract, but remain employed in various precarious ways on the basis of part/limited time contracts or in a completely illegal way. So Standing's claim that what is new in precarization is the fact that there is no security offered in exchange for subordination (Standing 2011, p. 8) can hardly be defended outside of a very presentist approach centered on the recent reality of the core societies. In the very frame of Standing's conceptual system that links citizenship with a set of civic, cultural, social, economic and political rights, the colonial subjects can hardly be called differently than denizens in their own countries.

Yet, we instinctively feel that there is something true in Standing's diagnosis: precarization we are witnessing seems to be something new and different from predicaments of the past. This feeling is due to the fact that "we" usually means relatively well situated individuals from highly developed Northern/Western/core societies. In the center of capitalist system contemporary precarization follows a historically unique and exceptional period of twentieth century welfare states. It is only now with a deepening economic crisis of austerity and under-employment (especially among the young) that we can grasp a singular and specific character of redistribution that neoliberalism has brought to an end.

The welfare state developed in twentieth century due to a somehow contingent coincidence of several social and political factors that can be assembled in two groups: firstly, the struggle of the oppressed. Despite the liberal narrative of a welfare state just emerging as a stage of development of bourgeois societies—and a kind of gift of the enlightened upper classes to the lower ones—it had come into being as a result of decades of struggles. These confrontations had taken various forms. Antonio Negri demonstrated beyond a reasonable doubt that the October Revolution played a decisive role in shaping John Maynard Keynes' conviction that redistributive reforms of capitalism are the only alternative to a social revolution that would have otherwise massively disrupted the Western bourgeois societies (Negri 1994). Here is a significant example: many economic historian prize Henry Ford for the introduction of something that may look like the first example of a living wage. However, the truth is that Ford implemented his famous 5$-per-week wage not because of any humanitarian reasons, but as a remedy for a very high workers turnout that disorganized his plants. In 1913, he had a workforce of around 14,000 workers, but had to hire more than 52,000 men to maintain it throughout that year (Worstall 2012). Quitting jobs and refusing to work is also a strategy of resistance and as these data show it was widely used by workers at Ford's factories. The story illustrates how workers' struggle was the source behind redistribution of welfare.

There was another factor at play: a fundamental shuttering of the world order by two major wars and the October revolution in the first half of twentieth century. It resulted in a disruption of many earlier economic arrangements and gave labour an upper hand in shaping the relations at the workplace. This disruption created a condition of possibility for the so called three "glorious decades" after the world war 2: from mid 1940ties till mid 1970ties. In that period capitalist societies seemed do defy Marx' prognosis of ever increasing inequalities and created an illusion that capitalist economy is able to create welfare for all (again: the assumption possible only if you keep the peripheries off the picture). It only lasted 30 years. When the forces of capital reorganized and the Soviet Union's failure became undeniable in early 1980ties the situation started going back to what we know from earlier periods of history: growing inequalities, deteriorating working conditions, growing exploitation, and diminishing wages (the lowest 20% of the US society is now not better off than it was in the 1950ties despite almost 300% US GDP growth in the meantime; Pew Research center 2016). Welfare state seems to be just a curious anomaly within capitalist modernity, yet it is the background against which the progress of precarization is cast in our direct experience.

To credit Standing with an important insight I'll gladly agree there is an element of relative novelty in the situation: contrary to its earlier logic precarization is getting more and more on the ones we are used to treating as the main winners of capitalist modernization: the middle class. Actually, that is the main reason behind the spectacular growth of public interest in precarity: nobody cared as long as it had been happening to "savages" from the other side of the planet or to lower classes who might very well live on a different continent for all that an average bourgeois cares. But when it started denting into the middle class, when our dear children face at best an unstable and insecure employment despite literally hundreds of thousands of dollars invested in their education—well, that's the moment we start to collectively worry.

2   Diagonal Cut

This brings us to the second term used in the title of Standing's book—class. In a way it is a futile academic exercise to sort out the dilemma whether the precariat may or may not be called a class. It does not seem to influence neither the diagnosis of perils of precarization nor practical strategies of confronting it in political struggles. However, there is something interesting and revealing that stems from this exercise, so let's waste a moment on doing it.

There may be two ways of approaching the notion of class. The theoretical one in conformity with a taxonomic logic of scientific categorization focuses on a set of particular conditions that a group needs to fulfill in order to be called a class. In this spirit one might quite easily take the description of the precariat provided by Standing in his various books and try to map it on at least the most important sociological concepts of class. I'm not going to conduct it in details here as it is rather a matter for a class or a seminar. However even at the first glimpse it does not seem possible to describe the precariat as a class in terms · of classical or contemporary class theory, be it the one put forward by, let's say, Marx, Weber, Bourdieu or Wright. The precariat seems too diverse as a group in its relation to means of production, its life chances, its accumulation of different types of capital or its ability to command various kinds of resources to be called a class in any senseful way. It is surely a category, possibly a group, but not a class.

There is also another problem: a class is an element of classification that needs to be at least hierarchical or (also) antagonistic to make any systemic and structural sense. Otherwise even the stratification approach typical for American sociology does not make sense, not talking about any class-based categorizations. In one of his *Precariat Charter* Standing attempts a more detailed description of precariat as a class and even a brief examination of this attempt reveals the problem at hand.

For a class-system approach to make any sense, there needs to be a relative advantage that belonging to an upper class bestows upon its members as compared with lower classes. Construction put forward by Standing gives paradoxical results in that respect: for example the salariat seems to be better off than the elite as the former gets a higher score in every category of rights apart from economic, where it lags behind; however, this disadvantage seems to be offset by the fact that it dominates more in political terms, while proficians are worse off than both the proletariat ("core" in Standing's terms) and the salariat. In general, the order presented top-down in the table is different than the one inferred from the sum of rights; the latter would rather yield a following classification (from the highest to

On the Uses of Precarity … 129

the lowest "class"): salariat, elite, core, proficians, precariat, lumpen-precariat. It is a telling and symptomatic order as a fetishization of "classical", full time employment is often an unfortunate—even if understandable—byproduct of struggles against precarization. I'll go back to this point later on (Fig. 1).

There's is also another approach to the problem of class, a political one: along with very practical thinking of Karl Marx a class is defined not via any set of objective traits it may possess, but by its political articulation in the struggles it undertakes (see Tronti 2008). So, for instance, proletariat is a class not because of its systemic lack of ownership and control over means of production, but by the fact that it actively confronts the propertied classes in the struggle over the shape of social world. Is the precariat a class in this sense? Unfortunately, it is not. It may be very well true that precarization is one of the leading factors of political mobilization and the precariat takes a crucial role in concrete political mobilizations as it was epitomized by Occupy and Indignados movements. However, there are three problems in jumping from this assertion to the conclusion that the precariat is a class: firstly, these struggles mobilize a tiny fraction of precariat,

Class \ Rights	Civil	Political	Cultural	Social	Economic
Plutocracy, elite	●	●	•	○	●
Proficians	●	•	•	•	●
Salariat	●	●	●	●	●
Core	•	●	●	●	•
Precariat	•	◉	•	◉	✕
Lumpen-precariat	✕	✕	✕	✕	✕

Note: • weak ● quite strong ● strong ◉ doubtful, under attack ✕ absent ○ not needed

Fig. 1 Matrix of strength of right by class. (Source: G. Standing, A Precariat Charter. From Denizens to Citizens, London 2014., p. 402.)

nothing that could be compared to massive, international workers mobilizations in nineteenth and twentieth century, secondly, there are important actors in these mobilization that come from different "classes" in Standing's categorization (from salariat, core and proficians—like academics—and even, paradoxically, individuals close to the elite—just think about the critique of contemporary capitalism articulated by Joseph Stiglitz or George Soros) and, thirdly, there is a part of the precariat that actually enjoys precarity and considers it to be an opportunity and not a predicament.

The latter seems to be the smallest problem—after all there have always been proletarians who did not mind waged labour. However, I believe precisely this circumstance could provide a valuable starting point for a different conceptualization of precariat and precarization. The key and defining—also politically— trait of precarization is the fact that it cuts diagonally across the spectrum of class positions, producing different effects on different individuals based on their class positions. Standing is right to define the condition of precariat in multiple dimensions (various rights), however it is worth noticing that the only dimension where his classification yields a hierarchy consistent with his own notion of set of rights as defining the social position is the dimension of economic rights—there is a clear and monotonic (in mathematical sense) descent as you go down the class structure (unlike all other dimensions, where it happens that a "lower" "class" scores better than a "higher" one). It corresponds with a more general and widely accepted, I suppose, thesis that the precarization originates in the space of labour relations and has got most to do with changing conditions of employment. But it is precisely in this area that we encounter the biggest paradox: a less strictly defined and more flexible working conditions seem to benefit some groups of workers—especially in the so called creative industries—and they are preferred to stable working hours and top-down command typical for traditional employment even if they provoke a bigger instability and unpredictability. Of course, stability remains desirable, however not worth paying the price of working 8 h every day under a supervision of a boss in alienating conditions. That is, for example, the case with artistic labour—its autonomy and autotelic character is an advantage that counter-balances lack of stability. The example of artistic labour reveals further interesting class aspects and consequences of precarization: it seems to be more and more a domain of higher social classes—in order to practice art one needs to have some resources that allow them to stabilize their existence in the face of unstable income. Preferably, a flat as a key resource. A help from family or a passive income in the form of a rent is also helpful (Kozłowski et al. 2015).

To sum up this part, I believe it is more fruitful to look at precarization as factor that does not create a separate class, but rather operates within the existing class structure modulating the effects of loosening labour relations. The latter may be beneficial for the members of higher classes and decremental for individuals who are worse off. The key factor is the level of accumulation of different forms of capital (Bourdieu 1986) and the ability to successfully convert one form of capital into another (for example, getting new job assignments thanks to networking—a practice that illustrates conversion of social capital into material one). Abandoning the strict and rigid labour relation of classical employment as such is an ambivalent development and may lead to positive consequences if it is interpreted and treated in a correct way (capitals allowing). It is an argument made particularly explicit within Italian (post)operaismo (Conti, A., et al. 2007), one of very few intellectual and activist traditions, where the original Marxist critique of labour has not been replaced by the critique from the standpoint of labour. I'm sure Guy Standing is aware of this fact, given his research and activism around the idea—and practice!—of unconditional guaranteed income (sometimes called "basic income"). It is unfortunate that his theoretical framework leads to fetishization of the salariat as I mentioned above. This is the main reason I have decided to deal here with this issue.

3   Precarity of Politics and Politics of Precarity

Political redefinition of class in terms of actual struggles it undertakes and not sociometric qualities it may possess brings us to the third term employed in the title of Standing's book: precariat's allegedly dangerous character. Those two issues are intimately intertwined: not being a class precariat is not a political subject and as such has got only a limited power to influence socio-political reality. Of course, even individual acts of resistance may bear political fruits, however without a collective agency precariat remains more an object than a subject of politics.

Let me briefly note on the margin that this lack of collective agency and weak articulation of precariat's struggles is a somehow puzzling development. Compering contemporary social and political realities with anything we know from the history of nineteenth and twentieth century workers' movements, one must come to a conclusion that material possibilities of constructing a planet-wide common front of struggles have never been so big and punishment for disobeying the system has never been so light. There were times with no low-cost airlines—or no airlines at all for that matter—and no grant system to support the multitude of NGOes when working classes of Europe and beyond bravely organized into a world-encompassing international that effectively threatened the capitalist order.

These were also the times of severe punishments for any disobedience—it went far beyond mobbing or firing the most active union organizers as it is the case today. Arbitrary imprisonment for indefinite period of time, beating, torturing, mutilations, burning activists' houses and kidnapping their family members—all that and much more was part of a daily anti-activist routine all the way until the first decades of the twentieth century (Ealham 2005; Linebough and Rediker 2000). Despite that the working class movement was radically revolutionary—and not just reformist like it is today—all the way until 1960ties. The fact that October revolution managed to shake up the imagination of John Maynard Keynes and other political figures of the time to such a point as to provoke a major and deep reform of the logic of capitalist accumulation in the inter-war period stands in a stark contrast with lack of any important reforms after the 2008 debt crisis. Political mobilizations that followed the latter—Occupy, Indignados, new parties such as Syriza or Podemos—however inspiring an important had no effect whatsoever on the mainstream politics and surely nothing to compare with the conquests made by the revolutionary struggles of nineteenth and twentieth century.

This important phenomenon demands a separate investigation. However, a conclusion to be drawn from it is that ideological tools of control based on constructing a hegemonic symbolic order instead of exercising a direct physical domination have proven to be extremely efficient in controlling dissent. Combined with new techniques of separation and alienation in the form of electronic communication—and especially the so called social media that are, as a matter of fact, fundamentally anti-social as they actively destroy the fabric of engaged and direct social interactions—these tools shape the modern subject that is not only unwilling to engage in demanding and uncomfortable radical political action, but unable to act beyond the realm of an interpassive online "activism".

This fundamental weakness of the precariat that renders it not dangerous but docile and easy to control reveals an important feature of precarization. Along the lines of naturalization—the ideological master-trick of neoliberalism—precarity is sometimes presented in the liberal mainstream as an undesired but unavoidable outcome of technological and organization progress. It may be painted in negative light and condemned for diminishing life chances of younger generation, it is however treated like a natural phenomenon, something like a flood or a drought: regrettable, but "just happening". Contrary to this interpretation a systematic empirical, critical examination reveals that the precariat is an outcome of deliberate construction, a result of purposefully constructed socio-political strategy of austerity and intimidation. One may call it a perverse labour management tool allowing for maximum extraction of surplus-value. The latter goal is achieved by

On the Uses of Precarity … 133

the means of bringing down the price of precarious labour power and weakening the workers' ability to self-organize.

We have thus closed the loop and come back to the issue that opened this brief polemics with Standing's conceptualization of precariat as a new and dangerous class: primitive accumulation. Precarity is precisely one of the ways in which we experience the force of primitive accumulation invariably inscribed in the very fabric of capitalism on every stage of its development—in the past as well as present.

4 Precarious Academia

There was a moment in the good old 1990ties when it seemed that all the perils of neoliberal globalization are going to be reserved for the lower classes, while the middle and the upper ones were going to rip only the benefits. After all liberalization of trade, delocalization of production and tertiarization of services affected mostly the lower classes whose jobs were disappearing on the other side of the planet and who had to compete with peripheral workforce ready to work for much less than its counterpart in the core countries. That is no longer the case. Precarization is now used as a cost-optimizing technique in the areas of economy that directly affect the middle-class—even the upper-middle—of highly skilled cognitive workers such as lawyers, physicians and, of course, academics. With a bigger part of academic work being done by part-time staff members or even not formally employed PhD candidates, academia looks more and more like a neoliberal factory always in need for more cost-optimization and boosting of output. This unfortunate development has been the subject of various investigations and is a widely known problem. It has also been politically addressed by researchers and activists such as, for example, the Italian Uninomade collective and Edu-factory network (Edu-factory Collective 2009; Roggero 2011). I do not want to repeat what has already been said but rather add to this bulk of diagnosis a small element from my home country, Poland.

In 2015 a group of researchers and activists associated with an informal organization called New Opening of University (pol. *Nowe Otwarcie Universytetu*, shorter: NOU) conducted a wide research focused on working conditions of young academic stuff in Poland (academics who have just done their PhDs and got their first academic positions). One needs to add that Poland, being an ultra-neoliberal country where most free market mechanisms have much more freedom that it is the case in the West, is currently in the midst of neoliberal reforms of its university system started by the government of Donald Tusk 6 years ago. Higher education has still remained free, but market-like mechanisms were introduced to boost competition among academic workers and to make them more productive in terms of getting research grants and publishing in high ranking academic journals. A ubiquitous benchmarking has been introduced to evaluate academic labour and a grant-based competitive system of resources allocation has replaced a more stable and predictable structural funding. At the same time employment stability has been reduced and a tenure was reserved for the absolute elite of full professorship possessing the official title of professor awarded by the country's President (it may sound ridiculous, however one needs to remember that Poland is a society deeply buried in its feudal past and actively hostile to modernity, so along these lines full professors are appointed by the President of the country). The distinction is more than just a curious feudal residuum: it serves a very modern purpose of creating hierarchies within the academic field and splitting academic labourers into a core and peripheral group. A strategy often employed in the field of cognitive labour (Newfield 2010). The result is a mix of the worst aspects of Anglo-saxon liberal system with its famous "publish or perish" logic and a more bureaucratic continental solutions where administrative control over academic labour is compensated with a relatively stronger employment and a bigger funding stability. In Poland we have the worst of two worlds: viscous competition and lack of stability within a bureaucratic and feudal empire of professorship.

The academics-cum-activists from NOU paint a bleak picture of academia as a space of precarization. Inadequate income creates a pressing need for supplementary activities. The latter are sometimes linked with the academic field, but there are also numerous cases of young researchers taking any part-time jobs to complement their meager salaries. A peril well known to students around the world. Polish young academics fit quite well in a neoliberal phenomenon of "working poor": people who remain on the verge of poverty line—or below—despite having a full-time job (Brady et al. 2010).

There's a series of practical, social and psychological consequences of precarization within the field of Polish academia. One of the most reported problem is linked with time management: as the very title of the NOU's report states, after fulfilling all duties of teaching, fund-rising, writing and getting additional income to supplement their small salaries, young polish academics have virtually "no time left for doing research". Their free time and labour time are completely mixed up—there is only a minimal distinction between the one and the other. They often feel anxiety provoked by fundamental uncertainty over not only their professional, but also material survival. Small resources does not allow them for mobility and they feel they are confined to few possibilities they have in their direct surrounding. Alienation is a recurring theme: they feel alienated from their peers by ubiquitous competition (for positions, grants, publications, conferences etc.) and from the very process of their labour by weak employment conditions and emphasis on benchmarkable performance instead of knowledge production. All this results in a kind of cynical detachment: they do not see academic labour as linked in any way with their identity, but only with a contingent and unsatisfying role they play. (Kowzan 2016). Young academic workers in Poland truly deserve the title of academic denizens.

5 Sorcerer's Nemesis

One might argue that even if all of the above is true, it is hardly problematic in any objective sense as it only infringes upon the ideal image of society that a Marxist may have and does not provoke any bad consequence beyond that. We know the (neo)liberal argument: the entire history of mankind and of life on Earth has been an endless stream of competition, struggle and elimination of the weak. A human being with all her astonishing capacities is, after all, a product of an equally dreadful and amazing process of natural selection. Well, actually the problem is much deeper than this. Neoliberal precarization of academic labour may be beneficial for some—like huge publishing conglomerates earning millions from publicly financed and privately run circulation of academic texts or high-tech industry blessed with a stream of skilled, motivated and educated cognitive workers—society as whole is not in a wining position. The disruption created by precarization interferes with the very process of knowledge production making academia more profitable financially for some but less fruitful in terms of actually generating relevant and valuable knowledge for all.

The core of the problem lies in motivational structures precarization entails. They basically operate mostly with the proverbial stick and relay on stress (anxiety and fear) as motivating factor: we need to apply for grants and write articles, because otherwise our very job positions would be gone and we'll be left with no means of material and symbolic reproduction. Now, cognitive academic labour is to an important extend a kind of labour like any other and the stick may somehow work in motivating academics to perform better. However, the essentially creative character of this endeavor makes it unique and different from, let's say driving a track or working in a call center (it is not supposed to be an evaluation, but just a pure description). High levels of stress and anxiety are strongly degrading factors for creative thinking (even if they may be stimulating in small doses). Being afraid to lose the job or to fail in competition with others does not make one more creative, but precisely the contrary: it makes them less willing to take risks and innovate and more focused on acting within the safe limits of tested procedures.

Creativity thrives on surplus—look at California!—and thus austerity is its major enemy.

There is also another problem, a more structural and general one reaching far beyond the academic field as such: lowering the costs of labour encourages economic development towards labour intensive solutions as opposed to the ones based on innovation and technological progress (rising the proportion of absolute surplus value to the relative one in Marx' terms). Although the hegemony of liberal mainstream has taught us to automatically link innovation with capitalism, the truth is capitalists innovate not because it is in their nature, but because there is a material reason for it: namely profit. If the profit can be secured easier and with less investments by increasing the labour component of the production process than by innovating, the entrepreneur would always go for the former and not for the latter. A reduction of labour costs is one of the main advantages of innovation for the capitalists and thus if the labour is cheap, innovations stagnate as it has been demonstrated by peripheral organization of production that focuses on labour-intensive economic activities that bring relatively little profit.

It is a deeply ironic development: contemporary capitalism thrives on technological innovations, however its innermost logic presents the biggest danger for production of scientific knowledge that provides the basis for these innovations. That is, unfortunately, typical for capitalist modernity. Precarization is just another trick in the vast arsenal of bourgeoisie that, as it was affirmed by Marx and Engels more than 150 years ago, "cannot exist without constantly revolutionizing the instruments of production, and thereby the relations of production, and with them the whole relations of society. [...] Constant revolutionizing of production, uninterrupted disturbance of all social conditions, everlasting uncertainty and agitation distinguish the bourgeois epoch from all earlier ones. All fixed, fast-frozen relations, with their train of ancient and venerable prejudices and opinions, are swept away, all new-formed ones become antiquated before they can ossify. All that is solid melts into air." (Marx and Engels 2010, p. 487) This creative/destructive process is blind and has got no rationality beyond a direct logic of capital accumulation and as such it turns against the capitalist system itself. "Modern bourgeois society—Marx and Engels remark—with its relations of production, of exchange and of property, a society that has conjured up such gigantic means of production and of exchange, is like the sorcerer, who is no longer able to control the powers of the nether world whom he has called up by his spells."(ibid, p. 489) That's precisely what the precarization is: sorcerer's nemesis, the force brought to life by his spells shaking up the very foundations of his own castle.

One might think it is a reassuring vision: if we only wait long enough, capitalism is going to crumble under the load of its own internal contradictions.

It is actually difficult to be further from the truth. Technically it may be correct: capitalism is its own biggest enemy and is continually destroying the very conditions of its own survival (nowadays we see it even on the most basic biological level). However, there is no guarantee of progress attached to this destruction. We surely are in a decisive moment, a point of bifurcation as Immanuel Wallerstein (1998) likes to point it out. What is certain is that the liberal *status quo* of the post-war period supported by the gains of the welfare state cannot continue anymore (see for example Žižek 2015). Its material and geopolitical conditions of possibility are destroyed by quick advances of free-market globalization and technological progress that made mechanisms of welfare state devised to control the force of capital obsolete. What is going to emerge from this rubble is far from certain. It may very well be a new dark age or a new kind of authoritarian rule. It's precisely here that the precarization may turn out to be an utterly dangerous, destabilizing force. The political developments of the years 2015–2016 demonstrated to what extend the precariat is prone to being captured by chauvinistic and nationalistic right. We are faced again with a dilemma known from the past: socialism or barbarism. Which one of them is going to win depends largely on how well we deal with the perils of precarization and what kind of use we make of it.

References

Beck, U. (2000). *Brave New World of Work*. Cambridge: Polity Press.

Davis, M. (2001). Late Victorian Holocausts. El Niño Famines and the Making of the Third World. London: Routledge.

Bourdieu, P. (1986). The Forms of Capital. In J. G. Richardson (Ed.), Handbook of Theory and Research for the Sociology of Education. Westport: Greenwood.

Brady, D., Fullerton, A. S., &, Moren Cross, J. (2010). *More Than Just Nickels and Dimes: A Cross-National Analysis of Working Poverty in Affluent Democracies*. *Social Problems* 57(4). URL: https://www.ncbi.nlm.nih.gov/pubmed/20976971. Last accessed: 12. November 2018.

Conti, A., et al. (2007). The Anamorphosis of Living Labour, „Ephemera", V 7(1) 2007.

Ealham, C. (2005). Class, Culture and Conflict in Barcelona 1898–1937, London: Routledge.

Edu-factory Collective (2009). Toward A Global Autonomous University: Cognitive Labor, The Production Of Knowledge, And Exodus From The Education Factory, New York: Autonomedia.

Guattari, F., & Rolnik, R. (2007). *The Molecular Revolution in Brazil*. Boston; Mit Press.

Kozłowski, M., Sowa, J., & Szreder (2015). The Art Factory. The Division of Labor and Distribution of Capitals in the Polish Field of Visual Art. Warsaw: Free/Slow University of Warsaw.

Kowzan, P., Zielińska, M., Kleina-Gwizdała, A., & Prusinowska, M. (2016). Nie zostaje mi czasu na pracę naukową". Warunki pracy osób ze stopniem doktora zatrudnionych na polskich uczelniach. Gdańsk: Nou.

Linebough, P, & Rediker, R. (2000). The Many-Headed Hydra. Sailors, Slaves, Commoners, and the Hidden History of the Revolutionary. Boston: Atlantic.

Marx, K. (2010). Capital. A Critique of Political Economy, V. 1, Ch. X, K. Marx, F. Engels, Collected Works, Vol. 35 (pp. 239–307). London: Lawrence & Wishart.

Marx, K., Engels, F. (2010). Collected Works, London: Lawrence & Wishart Electric Book.

Lis, S., & Soly, H. (1981). *Capitalism and Poverty in Preindustrial Europe*. London: Branch Line.

Negri, A. (1994). *Keynes and the Capitalist Theory of the State*. In M. Hardt & A. Negri (Eds), *Labor of Dionysus: A Critique of the State-form* (23–52). Minneapolis:The University of Minnesota.

Newfield, C. (2010). *The Structure and Silence of the Cognitariat*, „Eurozine". URL: http://www.eurozine.com/the-structure-and-silence-of-the-cognitariat/. Last accessed: 23. April 2018.

Pew Research Center (2016). *America's Shrinking Middle Class: A Close Look at Changes Within Metropolitan Areas*, 2016, http://www.pewsocialtrends.org/files/2016/05/Middle-Class-Metro-Areas-FINAL.pdf. Last accessed: 12 December 2018.

Roggero, G. (2011). The Production of Living Knowledge. The Crisis of the University and the Transformation of Labor in Europe and North America, trans. E. Brophy, Philadelphia: Temple University Press.

Standing, G. (2011). *The Precariat: The New Dangerous Class*. London: Bloomington.

Standing, G. (2014). *A Precariat Charter: From Denizens to Citizens*. London: Bloomsbury.

Tronti, M. (2008). *Classe*, Libera Universita' Metropolitana, *Lessico Marxiano. 12 concetti per pensare il presente*. URL: http://www.lumproject.org/pubblicazioni/lessico-marxiano-12-concetti-per-pensare-il-presente/. Last accessed: 12. November 2018.

Wallerstein, I (1998). Utopistics: Or Historical Choices of the Twenty-First Century, New York: The New Press.

Worstall, T. (2012). *The Story of Henry Ford's $5 a Day Wages: It's Not What You Think*, „Forbes", https://www.forbes.com/sites/timworstall/2012/03/04/the-story-of-henry-fords-5-a-day-wages-its-not-what-you-think/#47d61910766d. Last accessed: 12 December 2018.

Žižek, S. (2015). Trouble in Paradise: From the End of History to the End of Capitalism. London: Verso.

Start Ups, Social Networking and Self-Tracking—The Neoliberal Freedom of the Entrepreneurial Self in the Digital Age

David Kergel and Rolf Hepp

Abstract

The notion 'freedom' transformed from a leftist concept into a neoliberal interpellation within the digital age. To unfold this thesis, the discourse about start ups, online based social networking and the practice of digital self-tracking will be analyzed. Against the background of these analysis, it is possible to reconstruct the concept of freedom as manifestation of a neoliberal ‚new spirit of capitalism'in the digital age.

Keywords

Digitalization · Neoliberalism · Entrepreneurial self · Start-Up · New spirit of capitalism

1 Introduction

There are various definitions towards the notion of freedom. One possible definition is that freedom means the potential to act in self-determined, free from constraints ways. From this point of view, freedom always refers to social practices. In other words: The notion freedom has social implications. The individual is

D. Kergel (✉)
HAWK Hildesheim, Hildesheim, Germany
e-mail: davidkergel@gmail.com

R. Hepp
Soziologisches Institut der Freien Universität Berlin, Berlin, Germany
e-mail: kerghepp@gmx.de

© Springer Fachmedien Wiesbaden GmbH, part of Springer Nature 2020
T. Rachwał et al. (eds.), *Precarious Places*, Prekarisierung
und soziale Entkopplung – transdisziplinäre Studien,
https://doi.org/10.1007/978-3-658-27311-8_9

- free *from* social and economic constraints,
- free *from* imposed value systems and hierarchies.

A free individual is always a self-determined and self-responsible individual: Because of its freedom, the free individual is an individual which is free to think, to act and to choose.In the sense of a postmodern ethics (*cf.* Baumann 1995; Kergel 2017) such an individual freedom/freedom of the individual is restricted by the freedom of other individuals. From this point of view, a free society is a dialogical process, where the individuals are negotiating which each other on the basis of their individual freedom. On the basis of a tolerant an respectful interaction the individual construct and re-produce performatively a free society in the postmodern sense of this term.

In the course of the emancipation movements of the 1960s and 1970s the concept of the free individual is connected with new ways of a self-determined living. Freedom turns into a socio-cultural project. Thus the narration of the free emancipated individual is linked with an anti-capitalist attitude and criticism of the capitalism and its authoritarian and passive consuming culture (*cf.* Kergel 2018)

New ways of living emerged the places in which people lived in communes and had a self-organized way of living. One approach to a new socio-cultural kind of living is the so called shared economy. The concept of a shared-economy has been developed to enable a new economic approach beyond the exploitative relationships of capitalism. A.O. (money free) exchange of services via platforms were organized and founded alternative cultures: In the course of the 1960´s, 1970´s and 1980´s in Germany and, especially in Frankfurt and West-Berlin, the so called leftist alternative culture emerged (*cf.* Reichhardt 2014). This alternative culture has been defined by an artistic-anarchistic way of living. This lifestyle undermined symbolically the established hierarchies of the authoritarian society. Instead of following the authorial structure of an authoritarian capitalism, a new way of living emerged.

This new way of living had been orientated on values like creative self-unfolding and solidaristic anti-capitalistic value system. The attitude of this life-style in turn influenced the self-understanding discourses of capitalism and evoked the so called 'new spirit of capitalism'.

2 The New Spirit of Capitalism

With reference to the management-literature of the 1990s Boltanksi and Chiapello provide an discourse-analytical study on the change of the self-understandings discourses of capitalism. One main result of their study was the observation that capitalism developed a new spirit. This new spirit of capitalism absorbed the critique which was formulated in the course of the emancipation movements within the 1960s and 1970s.

Thus, for example, the qualities that are guarantees of success in this new spirit—autonomy, spontaneity, rhizomorphus capacity, multitasking (in contrast to the narrow specialization of the old division of labor), conviviality, openness to others and novelty, availability, creativity, visionary intuition, sensitivity to differences, listening to lived experienced and receptiveness to a whole range of experiences, being attracted to informality and the search for interpersonal contacts—these are taken directly from the repertoire of May 1968 (Boltanski and Chiapello 2007, p. 97).

The leftist, emancipative notion of freedom which combines alternative culture and anti-capitalistic critique was absorbed by a capitalistic self-understanding discourse. As a result the alternative anti-authoritarian counter culture/life style and the anti-capitalist critique were detached from each other. In the course of this transformation process a new spirit of capitalism emerged. This new spirit bases on the concept of an artistic-anarchistic individual: "It is not difficult to find an echo here of the denunciations of hierarchy and aspirations to autonomy that were insistently expressed at the end of the 1960s and in the 1970s" (Boltansky and Chiapello 2007, p. 97). This new spirit of capitalism is still vivid in the so-called Start-Up-aesthetics (*cf.* Kergel 2017) and the concept of the so called entrepreneurial self.

3 The Entrepreneurial Self

The entrepreneurial self can be considered as the cultural/discursive effect of the neoliberal restructuring of the Western welfare state. Neoliberal thinking has increasingly come to shape social policy in western countries such as the United States, Britain, and Germany.

Beginning in the Ronald Reagan-era United States, a roll-back of the welfare state also occurred in Britain with the Thatcherism of the 1980s, and spread to Germany in the early years of the new century (*cf.* Biebricher 2011). Basic assumption of neoliberal logic is the concept of a ‚free'/liberal market. According to this logic economic processes are rational based and orders themselves invisible for the individuals. Consequently any regulation should be avoided to not 'disturb'the rational dynamics of the market (*cf.* Hayek 1981). The rational structure of economic processes is thereby defined by efficiency and cost benefit.

For neoliberals, there is one form of rationality more powerful than any other: economic rationality. Efficiency and an `ethic´ of cost-benefit analyses are the dominant norms. All people are to act in ways that maximize their own personal benefits. Indeed, behind this position is an empirical claim that this how all rational actors act. Yet, rather than being a neutral description of the world of social motivation, this is actually a construction of the world around the valuative characteristics of an efficiently acquisitive class type. (Apple 2006, p. 60 f.)

The unfolding of neoliberal policy required an appropriate understanding of the new neoliberal state of society. An interpretation/narration were needed which gave the neoliberal re-structuring of society a meaning. Thus neoliberal narrations emerge and formulate discursive *topoi* of a neoliberal way of living. The sociologist Bröckling has analysed the construction of such neoliberal narratives in several works (e.g. 2003; 2005; 2015). Bröckling uses the metaphor of the entrepreneurial self as the societal interpellation/the normative societal requirement towards the individual (*cf.* Althusser 2012). These interpellations are directed at the individual to act as a neoliberal entrepreneur. The entrepreneurial self is thereby inextricably linked with the new spirit of capitalism. The new spirit of capitalism bases on the assumption of an free individual on a liberal market. The free individual as the entrepreneurial self is the precondition of the free market: The individual needs to be free to react appropriately towards the challenges and requirements of the market: "The neoliberal individual must be free of any particularist spatial ties that prevent him or her from competing effectively in the global marketplace" (Gökariksel and Mitchell 2005, p. 150). In other words: The entrepreneurial self performatively reproduces the neoliberal concept of freedom—an "ideal model for the future is the individual as self-provider and the entrepreneur of their own labour. The insight must be awakened; self-initiative and self-responsibility, i.e. the entrepreneurial in society, must be developed more strongly" (Bröckling 2015, p. xi).

The leftist ideals of the 1960s and 1970s were discursively transformed: The ideals of autonomy and freedom provided the discursive frame in which the new spirit of capitalism could unfold itself. The ideal image of the new spirit of capitalism is metonymically represented in the metaphor of the entrepreneurial self. The entrepreneurial self is as well characterized by freedom and autonomy. But instead to unfold within a economic solidarity, the neoliberal freedom unfolds in a permanent competition: The own entrepreneurial identity is always challenged in "sporting competition[s]" (Bröckling 2015, p. 77). Within the narration-logic of neoliberalism the entrepreneurial self turns into an object which can be compared and valued: The entrepreneurial self reflects itself as a product which can

Start Ups, Social Networking and Self-Tracking ... 143

be compared with other products. One interpellation is that "[e]veryone should become an entrepreneur [...] Success at this can only be measured against the competition and therefore only temporarily" (Bröckling 2015, p. 77).

This comparison is carried out according to neoliberal parameters like efficiency—"It is a context no one is excused from, but not everyone plays in the same league. No matter how unequal the chances of climbing the ladder really are, every play can, in theory, improve her position, as long as she is more alert, innovative, self-reliant and assertive than others" (Bröckling 2015, p. 49). This permanent, performative competition effects precarity as a stable instability (*cf.* Kergel and Heidkamp p. 2017). As an effect of this permanent competition, everyone is threatened by descent, in the worst case by abyssal descent, if the competition starts overtaking. Since everyone´s existence is at stake, there is not much room for playful levity and noble sportsmanship. As an ideal image, everyone is supposed to model their own self, on the flipside of the entrepreneurial self is the image of fear. What everyone is supposed to become is at the same time what menaces everyone (Bröckling 2015, p. 77).

Within the logic of the entrepreneurial self, the stable instability - which is the essential feature of precarity—is the effect of a permanent competition between neoliberal individuals. This competition and the threatened scenario of social descent, when losing competitiors, causes fear. With reference to Standing (2011) one can analyze this fear of the entrepreneurial self as an emotional state which is a typical for precarious conditions: "The precariatised mind is fed by fear and is motivated by fear" (Standing 2011, p. 20).

4 Start up as Digitalized Leftist Platform Models

One might ask, how the social-cultural transformation of neoliberalism is linked to the digital age. One interesting link is the temporal overlap and the unfolding of digitalization:

Neoliberal policy started to unfold within the Western sphere with the election of Ronald Reagan at the beginning of the 1980s.

According to Prensky (2001) everybody who was born since the 1980s and onwards can be considered as a digital native. These people are socialzed by digital media and the increasing unfolding and spreading of the internet and computer culture.

The internet in turn promises on a semiotic level a flexible unconventional space for economic adventures. It is the ideal space where flexibility and autonomy of the new spirit of capitalism can unfold. A symbol for this flexibility in the digital age are the so called start-ups. Start-ups represents mostly capacity, multitasking (in contrast to the narrow specialization of the old division of labor), conviviality, openness to others and novelty, availability, creativity, visionary intuition, sensitivity to differences, listening to lived experience and receptiveness to a whole range of experiences, being attracted to informality and the search for interpersonal contacts (Boltanski and Chiapello 2007, p. 98).

With this features Boltanski and Chiapello described the new spirit of neo-liberalism. But this features can also be read as characteristics of start-ups. Thus the new spirit of capitalism is discursively reproduced in the concept of start-ups. Start-ups like Airbnb and Uber have a discursively rebellious attitude towards established business models and seem to stand in the tradition of the emancipatory movements of the 1960s and 1970s: One main business model of Start-ups is to challenge/overcome established, authoritarian business models. These business models are mostly attacked with the platform model which has been developed within the alternative culture of the 1960s, 1970s and 1980s. As an example one can refer to AirBnB: Instead of booking an anonymous hotel room the users have the chance to of an experience, 'being attracted to informality' and make 'interpersonal contacts' while renting an apartment. By renting an apartment instead of a hotel room, the user saves money. AirBnB in turn have an economic profit, because they provided the platform. Finally, the owner of the rented apartment receives a little extra-money. In this constellation everyone act as an entrepreneurial self at the expense of established structures (in this case the hotel).

With reference to this example one can conclude that the neoliberal new spirit of capitalism and the entrepreneurial self are inscribed into the digital economy/ the economy of the digital age.

5 The Assignable Self in the SNS-Universe

There is also a more subjective dimension of the freedom of the entrepreneurial self within the digital age: The entrepreneurial self is defined by sportive competition. This competition is one essential feature of the social networking sites (*cf.* Kergel and Heidkamp 2017). The communication culture of social networking sites is defined by the self-narrations of the members, These self-narrations are structured according the main narration topoi of the entrepreneurial self. Via social networking sites like Facebook, Google+, Snapchat, Instagram users can connect to each other, and share information. Social media like social networking sites "became informal but all-embracing identity management tools, defining access to user-created content via social relationships" (Mitrou et al. 2014, p. 2; see also Boyd and Ellison 2008). The self-narration of the users on social networking sites is exposed to valuations. As an example one could refer to the Facebook thumb up: The Facebook thumb up can be analyzed as a performance benchmark for a successful self-narration. It is possible to measure the success of a self-narration by its social impact/the received thumps up. The Facebook thumb up represents a "digitized gesture signalling approval, approbation, agreement, praise or even on occasion a reminder to the receiver of the sender's existence" (Faucher 2013, p. 1). From this point of view, the individual get fixed the entrepreneurial self within the social networking universe (*cf.* Kergel 2018) becomes a social assignable self.

6 Self-Tracking

Within the last years, the mobile internet changed the way we use the internet. In 2015 more young people entered for the first time the internet via mobile devices instead of using a home pc. At the latest since then, the Internet accompanies us everywhere and provides the culture of self-tracking. That means that we use apps which record our activities/measure our lifestyle. The individual subjects itself to metric power of digital devices in terms to become more efficient and to optimize the own capabilities/competences. From this point of view, self-tracking can be considered as "an expression of neo-liberal entrepreneurialism, enabling self-maximization and promoting self-critique and responsibilisation through the presentation of `objective´ measures of performance" (Lupton 2013, p. 28).

Capitalist success and the success of the entrepreneurial self follow the same logic: A successful self-tracking chart has the same structure as a successful development of profits - the increase of gain/the increase of competence. Via the digital constructed data, one can narrate oneself as active individual which expands its competences and therewith its competitiveness. The individual uses his freedom for self-optimization via self-tracking: Self-Tracking "can make waiting, resting, and daily routines recognized and even valued: in terms of physiological recovery, ´useless´ activities gain a new kind of value by becoming physiological beneficial" (Ruckenstein 2014, p. 80).

7   Summary

The supposed freedom of the entrepreneurial self stems discursively from the emancipative movements of the 1960s and 1970s. In the course of the unfolding of the new spirit of capitalism this freedom—which is metonymically manifested in the characteristics of flexibility and autonomy—is adjusted to the logic of neoliberalism. In the digital age, the neoliberal freedom manifests itself on different levels: The Start-Up-Discourse mirrors the rebellious attitude against authoritarian capitalistic structures. The Social Networking Sites demand a neoliberal self-narration of a successful individual. The success is measured by its social impact. The emergence of the mobile internet paved the way for a total self-measurement via self-tracking devices like wearables. From this point of view the ephemeral structure of the internet (cf. Kergel 2018) enables a neoliberal flexibility and autonomy in the sense of an entrepreneurial self.

References

Apple, M., W. (2006). Educating the 'Right Way'. Markets, Standards, God, and Inequality. New York: Routledge.
Althusser, L. (2012). Ideology and Ideological State Apparatuses (Notes Towards an Investigation). In M. G. Durham & D. M. Kellner (eds.), *Media and Cultural Studies. Keyworks* (pp. 80–88). New Jersey: Wiley-Blackwell.
Baumann, Z. (1995). *Moderne und Ambivalenz*. Frankfurt am Main: Suhrkamp.
Biebricher, Z. (2011). *Neoliberalismus*. Hamburg: Junius.
Boltanski, L., & Chiapello, È. (2007). The New Spirit of Capitalism. London: Verso.
Boyd, D. M. & Ellison, N. B. (2008). Social Network Sites: Definition, History, and Scholarship. *Journal of Computer-Mediated Communication*, 13(1), 210–230.
Bröckling, U. (2003). You are not responsible for being down, but you are responsible for getting up. Über Empowerment. *Leviathan*, 31, 323–344.
Bröckling, U. (2005). Gendering the Enterprising Self. Subjectifcation Programs and Gender Differences in Guides to Success, Distinktion: *Scandinavian Journal for Social Theory*, 11, 7–25.
Bröckling, U. (2015). The Entrepreneurial Self. Fabricating a New Type of Subject. Thousand Oaks: Sage.
Faucher, K. X. (2013). Thumbstruck: The Semiotics of Liking via the "Phaticon," *Semiotic Review*, Issue 3. URL: http://www.semioticreview.com/pdf/open2013/faucher_semiotic-sofliking.pdf. Last accessed: 23 December 2016.
Gökariksel, B., & Mitchell, K. (2005). Veiling, secularism, and the neoliberal subject: national narratives and supranational desires in Turkey and France, Global Networks, 5 (2), 147–165.
Hayek, F. A. v. (1981). *Recht, Gesetzgebung und Freiheit, 3. Bd.* München: Moderne Industrie.

Kergel, D. (2017). The Postmodern Dialogue and the Ethics of digital based Learning. In D. Kergel, B. Heidkamp, T. Rachwal, S. Nowakowski, & P. Kjærsdam Telléus (Eds.) (2017), *Digital Turn. Teaching and Learning in a changing World* (pp. 47–66). Wiesbaden: VS Springer.

Kergel, D. (2018). Kulturen des Digitalen. Postmoderne Bildung, subversive Diversität und neoliberale Subjektivierung im Digitalen Zeitalter. Wiesbaden. VS Springer.

Kergel, D. & Heidkamp (2017). Media change – Precarity through or Precarity within the internet. In. D. Kergel & B. Heidkamp (Hrsg.), *Precarity within the Digital Age. Media Change and Social Insecurity* (pp. 9–30). Wiesbaden: VS Springer.

Lupton, D. (2013). Quantifying the body: Monitoring and Measuring Health in the Age of Health Technologies. In *Critical Public Health* 23(4), 393–403.

Mitrou, L., Kandias, M., Stavrou, V., & Gritzalis, D. (2014). Social Media Profiling: A Panopticon or omnipoticon tool? URL: https://www.infosec.aueb.gr/Publications/2014-SSN-Privacy%20Social%20Media.pdf. Last accessed: 23 December 2016.

Prensky, M. (2001). Digital Natives, Digital Immigrants. In On The Horizon, 9(5). URL: http://www.marcprensky.com/writing/Prensky%20-%20Digital%20Natives,%20Digital%20Immigrants%20-%20Part1.pdf. Last accessed: 22.01.2018.

Reichardt, S. (2014). Authentizität und Gemeinschaft. Linksalternatives Leben in den siebziger Jahren. Frankfurt am Main: Suhrkamp.

Standing, G (2011). *The Precariat: The New Dangerous Class*. London: Bloomsbury.

Revisiting Territories of Relegation: Class, Ethnicity and State in the Making of Advanced Marginality

Loïc Wacquant

Abstract

In the postindustrial city, relegation takes the form of real or imaginary consignment to distinctive sociospatial formations variously and vaguely referred to as "inner cities," "ghettos," "enclaves," "no-go areas," "problem districts," or simply "rough neighborhoods." How are we characterize and differentiate these spaces, what determines their trajectory (birth, growth, decay and death), whence comes the intense stigma attached to them, and what constellations of class, ethnicity and state do they both materialize and signify? These are the questions I pursued in my book Urban Outcasts (2008) through a methodical comparison of the trajectories of the black American ghetto and the European working-class peripheries in the era of neoliberal ascendancy. In this article, I revisit this cross-continental sociology of "advanced marginality" to tease out its broader lessons for our understanding of the tangled nexus of symbolic, social and physical space in the polarizing metropolis at century's threshold in particular, and for bringing the core principles of Bourdieu's sociology to bear on comparative urban studies in general.

Keywords

Urban relegation · Collective activity · Urban outcasts · Hyperghetto · Comparative sociology of urban inequality

L. Wacquant (✉)
University of California, Berkeley, USA
e-mail: loic@berkeley.edu

© Springer Fachmedien Wiesbaden GmbH, part of Springer Nature 2020
T. Rachwał et al. (eds.), *Precarious Places*, Prekarisierung
und soziale Entkopplung – transdisziplinäre Studien,
https://doi.org/10.1007/978-3-658-27311-8_10

1   Introduction

To relegate (from the late Middle English, *relegaten*, meaning to send away, to banish) is to assign an individual, population or category to an obscure or inferior position, condition, or location. In the postindustrial city, relegation takes the form of real or imaginary consignment to distinctive sociospatial formations variously and vaguely referred to as "inner cities," "ghettos," "enclaves," "no-go areas," "problem districts," or simply "rough neighborhoods." How are we characterize and differentiate these spaces, what determines their trajectory (birth, growth, decay and death), whence comes the intense symbolic taint attached to them at century's edge, and what constellations of class, ethnicity and state do they both materialize and signify? These are the questions I pursued in my book *Urban Outcasts* through a methodical comparison of the trajectories of the black American ghetto and the European working-class peripheries in the era of neoliberal ascendancy.[1] In this article, I revisit this cross-continental sociology of "advanced marginality" to tease out its broader lessons for our understanding of the tangled nexus of symbolic, social and physical space in the polarizing metropolis at century's threshold in particular, and for comparative urban studies in general.

To speak of *urban relegation*—rather than "territories of poverty" or "low-income community," for instance—is to insist that the proper object of inquiry is not the place itself and its residents but the multilevel structural processes whereby persons are selected, thrust, and maintained in marginal locations, as well as the social webs and cultural forms they subsequently develop therein. Relegation is a *collective activity*, not an individual state; a *relation* (of economic, social, and symbolic power) between collectives, not a gradational attribute of persons. It reminds us that, to avoid falling into the false realism of the ordinary and scholarly common sense of the moment, the sociology of marginality must fasten not on vulnerable "groups" (which often exist merely on paper, if that) but on the *institutional mechanisms* that produce, reproduce, and transform the network of positions to which its supposed members are dispatched and attached. And it urges us to remain agnostic as to the particular social and spatial configuration assumed by the resulting district of dispossession. In particular, we cannot

---

[1] Loïc Wacquant, *Urban Outcasts: A Comparative Sociology of Advanced Marginality* (Cambridge, UK: Polity Press, 2008). For an account of the biographical, analytic, and civic underpinnings of this project, see idem, "The Body, the Ghetto and the Penal State," *Qualitative Sociology*, 32, no. 1 (March 2009): pp. 101–129, esp. pp. 106–110.

Revisiting Territories of Relegation ... 151

presume that the emerging social entity is a "community" (implying at minimum a shared surround and identity, horizontal social bonds, and common interests), even a community of fate, given the diversity of social trajectories that lead into and out of such areas.[2] We also should not presuppose that income level or material deprivation is the preeminent principle of vision and division, as persons with low income in any society are remarkably heterogenous (artists and the elderly, service workers and graduate students, the native homeless and paperless migrants, etc.) and form at best a statistical category.

Urban Outcasts is the summation of a decade of theoretical and empirical research tracking the causes, forms, and consequences of urban "polarization from below" in the United States and Western Europe after the close of the Fordist-Keynesian era, leading to a diagnosis of the predicament of the *postindustrial precariat* coalescing in the neighborhoods of relegation of advanced society. The book brings the core tenets of Bourdieu's sociology to bear on a wide array of field, survey, and historical data on inner Chicago and outer Paris to contrast the sudden implosion of the black American ghetto after the riots of the 1960s with the slow decomposition of the working-class districts of the French urban periphery in the age of deindustrialization. It puts forth three main theses and sketches an analytic framework for renewing the comparative study of urban marginality that I spotlight to help us elucidate the relations of poverty, territory, and power in the postindustrial city.

2 From Ghetto to Hyperghetto, or the Political Roots of Black Marginality

The study opens by parsing the reconfiguration of race, class, and space in the American metropolis because the foreboding figure of the dark ghetto has become epicentral to the social and scientific imaginary of urban transformation at century's turn.[3] On American shores, the abrupt and unforeseen involution of

---

[2]A historical recapitulation of the loaded meanings and persistent ambiguities of the notion of "community" in US history is Thomas Bender, *Community and Social Change in America* (New Brunswick: Rutgers University Press, 1978).

[3]The mutual contamination and common intermingling of scholarly and ordinary visions of urban life is stressed by Peter Hall, *Cities of Tomorrow: An Intellectual History of Urban Planning and Design in the Twentieth Century* (Oxford: Basil Blackwell, 1988), and Setha Low, "The Anthropology of Cities: Imagining and Theorizing the City," *Annual Review of Anthropology* 25 (1996): pp. 383–409.

the "inner city"—a geographic euphemism obfuscating the reality of the ghetto as instrument of ethnoracial entrapment imposed uniquely upon blacks—was the target of a fresh plank of policy worry and scholarly controversy. Across Western Europe, vague images of "the ghetto" as a pathological space of segregation, dereliction, and deviance imported from America (with rekindled intensity after the Los Angeles riots of Spring 1992) suffused as well as obscured journalistic, political and intellectual debates on immigration and inequality in the dualizing city.

The first thesis, accordingly, charts the *historic transition from ghetto to hyperghetto* in the United States and stresses the pivotal role of state structure and policy in the (re)production of racialized marginality. Revoking the trope of "disorganization" inherited from the Chicago school of the 1930s and rejecting the tale of the "underclass" (in its structural, behavioral and neo-ecological variants) which had come to dominate research on race and poverty by the 1980s, *Urban Outcasts* shows that the black American ghetto collapsed after the peaking of the civil rights movement to spawn a novel organizational constellation: the hyperghetto. To be more precise, the "Black Metropolis," lodged at the heart of the white city but cloistered from it, which both ensnared and enjoined African-American urbanites in a reserved perimeter and a web of shared institutions built by and for blacks between 1915 and 1965,[4] collapsed to give way to a *dual sociospatial formation*.

This decentered formation, stretching across the city, is composed of the *hyperghetto* proper (**HyGh**), that is, the vestiges of the historic ghetto now encasing the precarized fractions of the black working class in a barren territory of dread and dissolution devoid of economic function and doubly segregated by race and class, on the one hand, and of the burgeoning *black middle-class districts* (**BMCD**) that grew mostly via public employment in satellite areas left vacant by the mass exodus of whites to the suburbs, on the other. Whereas space unified African Americans into a compact if stratified community from World War I to the revolts of the 1960s, now it fractures them along class lines patrolled by state agencies of social control increasingly staffed by middle-class blacks charged with overseeing their unruly lower-class brethen.[5] The encapsulating dualism of

---

[4]This parallel "black city within the white" is depicted by St. Clair Drake and Horace Cayton in their classic study, *Black Metropolis: A Study of Negro Life in a Northern City* (Chicago: University of Chicago Press, [1945] 1993).

[5]This spatial and social differentiation, leading to contest and confrontation over the norms and fate of the "neighborhood," is skillfully documented in the work of the preeminent sociologist of black America of her generation, Mary Pattillo, *Black Picket Fences: Privilege and Peril Among the Black Middle Class* (Chicago: University of Chicago Press,

the Fordist half-century inscribed in symbolic, social and physical space, summed up by the equation White:Black :: City:Ghetto has thus been superseded by a more complex and tension-ridden structure **White:Black :: City::BMCD:HyGh** following a fractal logic according to which the residents of the hyperghetto find themselves doubly dominated and marginalized.

Breaking with the stateless cast of mainstream US sociology of race and poverty, *Urban Outcasts* then finds that hyperghettoization is economically under-determined and politically overdetermined. The most distinctive cause of the extraordinary social intensity and spatial concentration of black dispossession in the hyperghetto is not the "disappearance of work" (as argued by William Julius Wilson) or the stubborn persistence of "hypersegregation" (as proposed by Douglas Massey), although these two forces are evidently at play.[6] It is government *policies of urban abandonment* pursued across the gamut of employment, welfare, education, housing, and health at multiple scales, federal, state, and local, and the correlative breakdown of public institutions in the urban core that has accompanied the downfall of the communal ghetto. This means that the conundrum of class and race (as denegated ethnicity) in the American metropolis cannot be resolved without bringing into our analytic purview the shape and operation of the state, construed as a stratification and classification agency that decisively shapes the life options and strategies of the urban poor.

3   The "Convergence Thesis" Specified and Refuted

The second part—and central thesis—of *Urban Outcasts* takes the reader across the Atlantic to disentangle the same spatial nexus of class, ethnicity, and state in postindustrial Europe. Puncturing the panic discourse of "ghettoization" that has swept across the continent over the past two decades, crashing Nordic countries

---

2000), and *Black on the Block: The Politics of Race and Class in the City* (Chicago: University of Chicago Press, 2007).

[6]William Julius Wilson, *When Works Disappears: The World of the New Urban Poor* (New York: Knopf, 1996), and Douglas Massey and Nancy Denton, *American Apartheid: Segregation and the Making of the Underclass* (Cambridge, MA: Harvard University Press, 1993).

head on in the 2000s,[7] it demonstrates that zones of urban deprivation in France and neighboring countries are not ghettos *à l'américaine*. Despite surface similarities in social morphology (population makeup, age mix, family composition, relative unemployment and poverty levels) and representations (the sense of indignity, confinement, and blemish felt by their residents) due to their common position at the bottom of the material and symbolic hierarchy of places that make up the metropolis, the remnants of the black American ghetto and European working-class peripheries are separated by enduring differences of structure, function, and scale as well as by the divergent political treatments they receive.

To sum them up: repulsion into the black ghetto is determined by ethnicity (E), inflected by class (C) with the emergence of the hyperghetto in the 1970s, and intensified by the state (S) throughout the century, according to the algebraic formula $[(E > C) \times S]$. By contrast, relegation in the urban periphery of Western Europe is driven by class position, inflected by ethnonational membership, and mitigated by state structures and policies, as summed up by the formula $[(C > E) \div S]$. It is not spawning "immigrant cities within the city," endowed with their own extended division of labor and duplicative institutions, based on ethnic compulsion applied uniformly across class levels. It is not, in other words, converging with the black American ghetto of mid-twentieth century characterized by its joint function of social ostracization and economic exploitation of a dishonored population.

To lump variegated spaces of dispossession in the city under the label of "ghetto" bespeaks, and in turn perpetuates, three mistakes that the book dispels. The first consists in invoking the term as a mere rhetorical device intended to shock public conscience by activating the lay imaginary of urban badlands.[8] But a ghetto is not a "bad neighborhood," a zone of social disintegration defined (singly or in combination) by segregation, deprivation, dilapidated housing, failing institutions, and the prevalence of vice and violence. It is a *spatial implement of ethnoracial closure and control* resulting from the reciprocal assignation

---

[7]This is evidenced by the confused announcement by prime minister Lökke Rasmussen of a 2010 government plan to "confront the parallel societies of Denmark" by targeting 29 officially designated "ghettos," defined by the confounding combination of immigration, joblessness, and crime (see *Ghettoen tilbage til samfundet—et opgør med parallelsamfund i Danmark*, Copenhagen, Regeringen, Oktober 2010, esp. pp. 1–7 and 37–39).

[8]The protean cultural production of the city underbelly or underworld as the "accursed share" of urban society is dissected by Dominique Kalifa in *Les Bas-fonds. Histoire d'un imaginaire* (Paris: Seuil, 2013).

of a stigmatized category to a reserved territory that paradoxically offers the tainted population a structural harbor fostering self-organization and collective protection against brute domination.[9] The second mistake consists in conflating the communal ghetto with the hyperghetto: impoverishment, economic informalization, institutional desertification, and the depacification of everyday life are not features of the ghetto but, on the contrary, *symptoms of its disrepair and dismemberment.*

The third error misreads the evolution of traditional working-class territories in the European city. In their phase of postindustrial decline, these defamed districts have grown more heterogenous ethnically while postcolonial migrants have become more dispersed (even as nodes of high density have emerged to fixate media attention and political worry);[10] their organizational ecology has become more sparse, not more dense; their boundaries are porous and routinely crossed by residents who climb up the class structure; and they have failed to generate a collective identity for their inhabitants–notwithstanding the fantastical fear, coursing through Europe, that Islam would supply a shared language to unify urban outcasts of foreign origins and fuel a process of "inverted assimilation."[11] In each of these five dimensions, neighborhoods of relegation in the European metropolis are consistently *moving away from the pattern of the ghetto* as device for sociospatial enclosure: they are, if one insists on retaining that spatial idiom, *anti-ghettos.*

To assert that lower-class districts harboring high densities of bleak public housing, vulnerable households, and postcolonial migrants are not ghettos is not to deny the role of ethnic identity—or assignation—in the patterning of inequality in contemporary Europe. *Urban Outcasts* is forthright in stressing the "banali-

---

[9]For elaborations, see Loïc Wacquant, "A Janus-Faced Institution of Ethnoracial Closure: A Sociological Specification of the Ghetto," in Ray Hutchison and Bruce Haynes (eds.), *The Ghetto: Contemporary Global Issues and Controversies* (Boulder, CO: Westview, 2011), pp. 1–31; also idem, "Ghettos and Anti-Ghettos: An Anatomy of the New Urban Poverty," *Thesis Eleven* 94 (August 2008): pp. 113–118.

[10]Jean-Louis Pan Ké Shon and Loïc Wacquant, "Le grand hiatus: tableau raisonné de la ségrégation ethnique en Europe," paper presented at the Journée INED on "La ségrégation socio-ethnique: dynamiques et conséquences," Institut national d'études démographiques, Paris, 13 June 2012. On the Danish case, see Andersen H. Skifter, "Spatial Assimilation in Denmark: Why do Immigrants Move to and from Multi-ethnic Neighbourhoods?," *Housing Studies* 25, no. 3 (June 2010): pp. 281–300.

[11]Raphaël Liogier, Le Mythe de l'islamisation. Essai sur une obsession collective (Paris: Seuil, 2012).

zation of venomous expressions of xenophobic enmity" and the "cruel reality of durable exclusion from and abiding discrimination on the labor market" based on national origins; it fully acknowledges that "ethnicity has become more a more salient marker in French social life" (pp. 195–196) as in much of the continent. But *cognitive salience is not social causation.* The sharp appreciation of the ethnic currency in the political and journalistic fields does not mean that its weight has grown *pari passu* as a determinant of position and trajectory in the social and urban structure, nor that it now routinely skews ordinary interactions and everyday experience.[12] Moreover, ethnic rifts, when they do surge and stamp social relations, do not assume everywhere the same material form.

To maintain that ghettoization is *not* at work in the pauperized and stigmatized districts of the European city is simply to recognize that the modalities of ethnoracial classification and stratification, including their inscription in space, differ on the two sides of the Atlantic, in keeping with long-standing differences in state, citizenship, and urbanism between Western Europe and the United States. In the urban periphery of the Old World, resurging or emerging divisions based on symbolic markers activated by migration do not produce "ethnic communities" in the Weberian sense of segmented collectives, ecologically separate and culturally unified, liable to act as such on the political stage,[13] as the inflexible hypodescent-based cleavage called race has for African Americans—and only for them in the sweep of history in the country. Ethnicity is defined by shifting and woolly criteria that operate inconsistently across institutional domains and levels of the class structure, such that it does not produce a coordinated alignment of boundaries in symbolic, social and physical space liable to foster a dynamic of ghettoization.[14]

---

[12]Collapsing these three levels conflates collective conscience with social morphology, elite discourse and everyday action, and mechanically leads to overestimating both the novelty and the potency of ethnicity as determinant of life chances, as does Jean-Loup Amselle, *L'Ethnicisation de la France* (Fécamp: Nouvelles Éditions Lignes, 2011).

[13]A stimulative reinterpretation of this characterization is Michael Banton, "Max Weber on 'Ethnic Communities': A Critique," *Nations and Nationalism* 13, no. 1 (2007), pp. 19–35.

[14]For a model study breaking down ethnicity across social forms and scales, see Rogers Brubaker, Margit Feischmidt, Jon Fox and Liana Grancea, *Nationalist Politics and Everyday Ethnicity in a Transylvanian Town* (Princeton: Princeton University Press, 2008); a germane argument from an analytic angle is Andreas Wimmer, *Ethnic Boundary Making: Institutions, Power, Networks* (New York: Oxford University Press, 2013).

4   The "Emergence Thesis" Formulated and Validated

Refuting the thesis of transatlantic convergence on the pattern of the black American ghetto leads to articulating the thesis of the *emergence of a new regime of urban marginality*, distinct from that which prevailed during the century of industrial growth and consolidation running roughly from 1880 to 1980. The third part of *Urban Outcasts* develops an ideal-typical characterization of this ascending form of "advanced marginality"—thus called because it is not residual, cyclical, or transitional, but rooted in the deep structure of financialized capitalism—that has supplanted both the dark ghetto in the United States and traditional workers' territories in Western Europe.[15] A cross-sectional cut reveals six synchronic features (Chap. 8) while a longitudinal perspective ferrets out four propitiating dynamics (Chap. 9), including the polarization of the occupational structure and the reengineering of the state to foster commodification. Here I want to spotlight two of those features, the one material and the other symbolic, to emphasize the novelty of advanced marginality.

The paramount material attribute of the emerging regime of marginality in the city is that it is *fed by the fragmentation of wage labour,* that is, the diffusion of unstable, part-time, short-term, low-pay and dead-end employment at the bottom of the occupational structure—a master trend that has accelerated and solidified across advanced nations over the past two decades.[16] Whereas the life course and household strategies of the working class for much of the twentieth century were anchored in steady industrial employment set by the formula 40-50-60 (40 h a week for 50 weeks of the year until age 60, in rough international averages), today the unskilled fractions of the deregulated service proletariat face a simul-

---

[15]Curiously, this thesis has gone virtually unnoticed in the extended symposia devoted to *Urban Outcasts* by the journals *City* (December 2007 and April 2008), *International Journal of Urban and Regional Research* (September 2009), *Revue française de sociologie* (December 2009), *Pensar* (Winter 2009), and *Urban Geography* (February 2010), which have moreover concentrated either on the diagnosis of the black ghetto or on the evolution of the French/European periphery at the cost of scotomizing the book's comparative agenda.

[16]Cingolani, P. (2011), La Précarité. Paris: Puf. Kalleberg, A. (2011). Good Jobs, Bad Jobs: The Rise of Polarized and Precarious Employment Systems in the United States, 1970s–2000s. New York: Sage. Pelizzari, A. (2009). Dynamiken der Prekarisierung. Atypische Erwerbsverhältnisse und milieuspezifische Unsicherheitsbewältigung UVK (Konstanz: Verlag, 2009).

taneous dearth of jobs and plethora of work tenures that splinter and destabilize them. Their temporal horizon is shortened as their social horizon is occluded by the twin obstacles of endemic unemployment and rampant precarity, translating into the conjoint festering of hardship and proliferation of the "working poor."[17]

This double economic penalty is particularly prevalent in lower-class neighborhoods gutted out by deindustrialization. One illustration: in France between 1992 and 2007, the number of wage earners in insecure jobs (short-term contracts, temporary slots, government-sponsored posts and traineeships) increased from 1,7 million to 2,8 million to reach 12,4% of the active workforce against the backdrop of a national unemployment rate oscillating between 7 and 10 percent; for those ages 15 to 24 that proportion jumped from 17 to 49%.[18] But, in the 571 officially designated "sensitive urban zones" (ZUS) targeted by France's urban policy, the combined share of unemployed and precariously employed youths zoomed from 40% in 1990 to above 60% after 2000. Far from protecting from poverty as it expands, fragmented wage labor is a vector of *objective* social insecurity among the postindustrial proletariat as well as *subjective* social insecurity among the inferior strata of the middle class—whose members fear social downfall and proving unable to transmit their status to their children due to intensified school competition and the loosening of the links between credentials, employment, and income. On this count, *Urban Outcasts* is an invitation to *relink class structure and urban structure* from the ground up and a warning that an exclusive focus on the spatial dimension of poverty (as fostered, for instance, by studies of "neighborhood effects")[19] partakes of the obfuscation of the new social question of the early twenty-first century: namely, the spread and normalization of social

---

[17]For a varied panorama, David K. Shipler, *The Working Poor: Invisible in America* (New York: Knopf, 2004); Denis Clerc, *La France des travailleurs pauvres* (Paris: Grasset, 2004); and Hans-Jürgen Andress and Henning Lohmann (eds.), *The Working Poor in Europe: Employment, Poverty, and Globalization* (Cheltenham, UK: Elgar Publishing, 2008). The Danish case is examined by Finn K. Hansen, *Fattigdom i EU-landene—og dansk fattigdom i europærisk perspektiv* (Copenhaguen: CASA, 2010). Revealingly, the US-inspired category of the "working poor" was introduced into French official statistics in 1996, in European Union statistics in 2003, and in German government reports in 2009.

[18]Louis Maurin and Patrick Savidan, *L'État des inégalités en France 2009. Données et analyses* (Paris: Belin, 2008).

[19]The built-in blindness of such research to macrostructural economic and political forces is stressed by Tom Slater, "Your Life Chances Affect Where You Live: A Critique of the 'Cottage Industry' of Neighbourhood Effects Research," *International Journal of Urban and Regional Research* 37.2 (2013): pp. 367–387.

insecurity at the bottom of the class ladder and its ramifying impact on the life strategies and territories of the urban precariat.

But the inexorable propagation of "McJobs"—*petits boulots* in France, *Billig-Jobs* in Germany, "zero-hour contracts" in the United Kingdom, *lavoretti* in Italy, *biscate* in Portugal, etc.—is not the only force impinging on the precariat. A second, properly symbolic vector acts to entrench the social instability and redouble the cultural liminality of its constituents: *territorial stigmatization*. Mating Bourdieu's theory of symbolic power with Goffman's analysis of the management of spoiled identities,[20] I forged this notion to capture how the blemish of place affixed on zones of urban decline at century's turn affects the sense of self and the conduct of their residents, the actions of private concerns and public bureaucracies, and the policies of the state toward dispossessed populations and districts in advanced society. First, I document that territorial taint is indeed a distinctive, novel and generalized phenomenon, correlative of the dissolution of the black American ghetto and of the European working-class periphery of the Fordist-Keynesian period, that has become superimposed on the stigmata traditionally associated with poverty, lowly ethnic origins, and visible deviance. Since the publication of the book, proliferating studies have documented the rise, tenacity and ramifying reverberations of spatial stigma in cities spread across three continents.[21]

Next, I show that the denigration of place wields causal effects in the dynamics of marginality via cognitive mechanisms operating at multiple levels. Inside districts of relegation, it incites residents to engage in coping strategies of mutual distancing, lateral denigration, retreat into the private sphere and neighborhood flight that converge to foster diffidence and disidentification, distend local social ties, and thus curtail their capacity for proximate social control and collective action. Around them, spatial disgrace warps the perception and behavior of operators in the civic arena and the economy (as when firms discriminate based on

---

[20]Pierre Bourdieu, *Language and Symbolic Power* (Cambridge: Polity Press, 1990), and Erving Goffman, *Stigma: Notes on the Management of Spoiled Identity* (Englewood Cliffs, NJ: Prentice-Hall, 1964).

[21]See the articles and the wide-ranging bibliography gathered by Tom Slater, Virgílio Pereira and Loïc Wacquant (eds.), Special issue on "Territorial Stigmatization in Action," *Environment & Planning D*, Summer 2013. An extension to Denmark is Sune Qvotrup Jensen and Ann-Dorte Christensen, "Territorial Stigmatization and Local Belonging," *City* 16, no. 1–2 (February 2012): pp. 74–92; see also Ove Sernhede, "Territorial stigmatisering: unges uformelle læring og skolen i det postindustrielle samfund," *Social Kritik*, 118 (2009): pp. 5–23.

location for investment and address of residence for hiring),[22] as well as the delivery of core public services such as welfare, health, and policing (law-enforcement officers feel warranted to treat inhabitants of lowly districts in discourteous and brutal manner). In the higher reaches of social space, territorial stigma colors the output of specialists in cultural production such as journalists and academics; and it contaminates the views of state elites, and through them the gamut of public policies that determine marginality upstream and distribute its burdens downstream. To label a depressed cluster of public housing a *"cité-ghetto,"* a "sink estate," or a *"ghetto-område"* fated by its very makeup to devolve into an urban purgatory closes off alternative diagnoses and facilitates the implementation of policies of removal, dispersal, or punitive containment.[23]

Lastly, I propose that territorial stigmatization actively contributes to *class dissolution* in the lower regions of social and physical space. The sulfurous representations that surround and suffuse declining districts of dispossession in the dual metropolis reinforce the objective fragmentation of the postindustrial proletariat stemming from the combined press of employment precarity, the shift from categorical welfare to contractual workfare, and the universalization of secondary schooling as path to access even unskilled jobs. Spatial stigma robs their residents of the ability to claim a place and fashion an idiom of their own; it saddles them with a noxious identity, imposed from the outside, which adds to their symbolic pulverization and electoral devalorization in a political field recentered around the educated middle class. So much to say that the precariat is *not* a "new dangerous class," as proposed by Guy Standing,[24] but a miscarried collective that can never come into its own precisely because it is deprived not just of the means of stable living but also of the means of producing its own representation. Lacking a shared language and social compass, riven by fissiparity, its members do not flock to support far-rightist parties so much as disperse and drop out of the voting game altogether as from other forms of civic participation.

---

[22]In April 2011, the High Council for Fighting Discrimination and for Equality (HALDE) recommended to the French government that residential location be added to the 18 criteria on the basis of which national labor law sanctions discrimination, in recognition of the prevalence of "address discrimination."

[23]For a demonstration covering the 29 areas officially designated as *"ghetto- område"*—which conveniently obscures the fact that they are simply *"forsømt"* (dilapidated)—in Denmark, see Troels Schultz Larsen, "Med Wacquant i det ghettopolitiske felt," *Dansk Sociologi* 22, no. 1 (Spring 2011): pp. 47–67.

[24]Guy Standing, *The Precariat: The New Dangerous Class* (London: Bloomsbury, 2011).

5 A Bourdieusian Framework for the Comparative Sociology of Urban Inequality

Urban Outcasts sketches a historical model of the ascending regime of poverty in the city at century's turn. It forges notions—ghetto, hyperghetto, anti-ghetto, territorial stigmatization, advanced marginality, precariat—geared to developing a comparative sociology of relegation capable of eschewing the uncontrolled projection across borders of the singular experience of a single national society tacitly elevated to the rank of analytic benchmark. It does so by applying to urban questions five principles undergirding Pierre Bourdieu's approach to the construction of the sociological object. These principles are worth spotlighting by way of closing since this is a facet of the book that has been overlooked even by its more sympathetic critics.[25]

The first principle derives directly from "historical epistemology," the philosophy of science developed by Gaston Bachelard and Georges Canguilhem, and adapted by Bourdieu for social inquiry: clearly demarcate folk from analytic notions, retrace the travails of existing concepts in order to cast your own, and engage the latter in the endless task of rational rectification through empirical confrontation.[26] Such is the impulse behind the elaboration of an institutionalist conception of the ghetto as Janus-like contraption for ethnoracial enclosure, commenced in this book and completed in its sequel, *The Two Faces of the Ghetto,* which further differentiates the ghetto from the ethnic cluster and the derelict district; compares it with its functional analogues of the reservation, the camp, and the prison; and stresses the paradoxical profits of ghettoization as a modality of structural integration for the subordinate population.[27] Second comes the relational or topological mode of reasoning, deployed here to disentangle the mutual connections and conversions between symbolic space (the grid of mental categories

---

[25]For a signal exception, see Kristian Delica, "Sociologisk refleksivitet og feltanalytisk anvendelse af etnografi: om Loïc Wacquants blik på urban marginalisering," *Dansk Sociologi* 22, no. 1 (Spring 2011): pp. 47–67. These principles are explicated and exemplified in Pierre Bourdieu and Loïc Wacquant, *An Invitation to Reflexive Sociology* (Chicago: University of Chicago Press, 1992).

[26]Pierre Bourdieu, Jean-Claude Chamboredon and Jean-Claude Passeron, *The Craft of Sociology: Epistemological Preliminaries* (New York and Berlin: Walter de Gruyter [1968] 1991), and Donald Broady, *Sociologi och epistemologi. Om Pierre Bourdieus sociologi och den historiska epistemologin* (Stockholm: HLS Förlag, 1991).

[27]Loïc Wacquant, *The Two Faces of the Ghetto* (New York: Oxford University Press, 2014).

that orient agents in their cognitive and conative construction of the world), social space (the distribution of socially effective resources or capitals), and physical space (the built environment resulting from rival efforts to appropriate material and ideal goods in and through space).

The third principle expresses Bourdieu's radically historicist and agonistic vision of action, structure and knowledge: capture urban forms as the products, terrains, and stakes of struggles waged over multiple temporalities, ranging from the *longue durée* of secular constellations to the mid-level tempos of policy cycles to the short-term phenomenological horizon of persons at ground level. In this perspective, America's Black Belt and France's Red Belt, like districts of relegation in other societies, emerge as historical animals with a birth, maturity, and death determined by the balance of forces vying over the meshing of class, honor, and space in the city. Similarly, the hyperghetto of the US metropolis and the anti-ghettos of Western Europe are not eternal entities springing from some systemic logic but time-stamped configurations whose conditions of genesis, development, and eventual decay are sustained or undermined by distinct configurations of state and citizenship. The fourth tenet recommends the use of ethnography as an instrument of rupture and theoretical construction, rather than simple means for producing an experience-near picture of ordinary cultural categories and social relations. It implies a fusion of theory and method in empirical research that overturns the conventional division of intellectual labor in urban inquiry marked by the routine divorce of microscopic observation and macroscopic conceptualization.[28]

Last but not least, we must heed the constitutive power of symbolic structures and track their double effects, on the objective webs of positions that make up institutions, on the one side, and on the incarnate systems of dispositions that compose the habitus of agents, on the other. As illustrated by territorial stigmatization, this principle is especially apposite for the analysis of the fate of deprived and disparaged populations, such as today's urban precariat, that have no control over their representation and whose very being is therefore moulded by the

---

[28]The peculiar genre of research unthinkingly labelled "urban ethnography" in the English-speaking academy is blissfully atheoretical, as if one could carry out embedded observation of anything without an orienting analytic model, while grand theories of urban transformation show little concern for how structural forces imprint (or not) patterns of action and meaning in everyday life. One of the aims of *Urban Outcasts* is to bridge that chasm and to draw out the manifold empirical and conceptual benefits arising from continual communication between field observation, institutional comparison, and macroscopic theory.

Revisiting Territories of Relegation ...

categorization—in the literal sense of *public accusation*—of outsiders, chief among them professionals in authoritative discourse such as politicians, journalists, and social scientists. So much to say that the sociologist of marginality must punctiliously abide by the imperative of epistemic reflexivity and exert constant vigilance over the myriad operations whereby she produces her object, lest she gets drawn into the classification struggles over districts of urban perdition that she has for mission to objectivize.

These five principles propel the comparative dissection of the triadic nexus of class (trans)formation, graduations of honor, and state policy in the nether regions of metropolitan space across the Atlantic presented in this book. They can also fruitfully guide a triple extension of the sociology of urban relegation in the era of social insecurity across continents, theoretical borders, and institutions. Geographically, they can steer the adaptation of the schema of advanced marginality via sociohistorical transposition and conceptual amendment to encompass other countries of the capitalist core as well as rising nations of the Second world where disparities in the metropolis are both booming and shape-shifting rapidly.[29] Theoretically, taking Bourdieu's distinctive concepts and propositions into city trenches offers a formidable springboard to both challenge and energize urban sociology *in globo*.[30] It does not just add a new set of powerful and flexible notions (habitus, field, capital, doxa, symbolic power) to the panoply of established perspectives: it points to the possibility of reconceptualizing the urban as the domain of accumulation, differentiation and contestation of manifold forms of capital, which effectively makes the city a central ground and prize of historical struggles.

On the institutional front, the consolidation of a new regime of urban marginality begs for a focused analysis of the policy moves whereby governments

---

[29]An amplification across the Channel is offered by Will Atkinson, Steven Roberts and Michael Savage (eds.), *Class Inequality in Austerity Britain: Power, Difference and Suffering* (Basingstoke: Palgrave Macmillan, 2012); partial adaptations to South Africa, Brazil, and China, respectively, are Martin J. Murray, *City of Extremes: The Spatial Politics of Johannesburg* (Durham: Duke University Press Books, 2011); Janice Perlman, *Favela: Four Decades of Living on the Edge in Rio de Janeiro* (New York: Oxford University Press, 2010); and Fulong Wu and Christopher Webster (eds.), *Marginalization in Urban China: Comparative Perspectives* (New York: Palgrave Macmillan, 2010). See also the diverse works of the scholars affiliated with the interdisciplinary network at www.advancedurbanmarginality.com.

[30]Cf. the varied contributions to the special issue on "Bringing Bourdieu to Town," *International Journal of Urban and Regional Research*, Spring 2014, in press.

purport to curb, contain, or reduce the very poverty that they have paradoxically spawned through economic "deregulation" (as re-regulation in favor of firms), welfare retraction and revamping, and urban retrenchment. It calls, in other words, for *linking changing forms of urban marginality with emerging modalities of state-crafting*. This is done in my book *Punishing the Poor*, which enrolls Bourdieu's concept of bureaucratic field to diagram the invention of a punitive mode of regulation of poverty knitting restrictive "workfare" and expansive "prisonfare" into a single organizational and cultural mesh flung over the problem territories and categories of the dualizing metropolis.[31] The wards of urban dereliction wherein the precarized and stigmatized fractions of the postindustrial working class concentrate turn out to be the prime targets and testing ground upon which the neoliberal Leviathan is being manufactured and run in. Their study is therefore of pressing interest, not just to scholars of the metropolis, but also to theorists of state power and to citizens mobilized to advance social justice in the twenty-first century city.

---

[31]Loïc Wacquant, *Punishing the Poor: The Neoliberal Government of Social Insecurity* (Durham and London: Duke University Press, 2009), and "Crafting the Neoliberal State: Workfare, Prisonfare and Social Insecurity," *Sociological Forum* 25, no. 2 (June 2012): pp. 197–220. For an analysis of the international diffusion of the penalization of poverty as a core component of neoliberal policy transfer, see Loïc Wacquant, *Prisons of Poverty* (Minneapolis: University of Minnesota Press, 2009).

Printed in Great Britain
by Amazon